John Freeman

of Norfolk County, Virginia

His Descendants in North Carolina and Virginia

And Other Colonial North Carolina Freeman Families

Merrill Hill Mosher

HERITAGE BOOKS
2006

HERITAGE BOOKS

AN IMPRINT OF HERITAGE BOOKS, INC.

Books, CDs, and more—Worldwide

For our listing of thousands of titles see our website
at
www.HeritageBooks.com

Published 2006 by
HERITAGE BOOKS, INC.
Publishing Division
65 East Main Street
Westminster, Maryland 21157-5026

Copyright © 1994 Merrill Hill Mosher

International Standard Book Number: 978-0-7884-0109-2

TABLE OF CONTENTS

iv

APPENDIX

ILLUSTRATIONS

ACKNOWLEDGEMENTS

With greatest thanks to my friend and colleague Lona Price Downing, C.G., for her help in editing and for the preparation of the index; to Harriette Riggs of Raleigh and the Staff at the North Carolina Archives without whose help the military data could not have been included; and to Anna Kirk Faulkner (1871-1927), my grandmother, who started the Freeman research in 1920 and whose correspondence files have been invaluable.

JOHN FREEMAN OF NORFOLK COUNTY, VIRGINIA

HIS DESCENDANTS IN VIRGINIA AND NORTH CAROLINA

The surname Freeman is quite common in North Carolina. Not only does it include a very large family which first moved from Virginia to Chowan Precinct of Albemarle County in 1718, but also numerous other families of the name which arrived at other times during the Colonial Period.

Much of the genealogical work previously done on North Carolina Freeman families has depended on secondary sources and tradition; and, as is usual when primary sources are not extensively used, much misinformation has worked its way into the literature. It is my hope, to develop a sound, documented genealogical base of the first five generations of the subject family by depending heavily on primary sources, to correct previous errors. In a few cases, material on the sixth generation came to light. It is included where available. Coverage of that generation is not extensive.

Other pre 1800 Freeman families in North Carolina are covered in brief summaries in a separate section. It is the author's hope that future North Carolina Freeman research will be made easier by presentation of this material and that future researchers will attempt to use primary evidence in their efforts to connect with these families.

This work could not have been completed without the help of the people of North Carolina who have made such wonderful efforts to preserve their history by providing for the deposit of records at the North Carolina State Archives, and by providing funds for a professional and helpful Archives Staff.

No research effort is perfect and without doubt some errors and many omissions are present in this work. The author would greatly appreciate receiving documentation of any errors or omissions in this volume, in hopes that corrections can be included in future publications.

Merrill Hill Mosher, C.G.
(Mrs. Donald Mosher)
9855 Cape Arago Hwy
Coos Bay, OR 97420

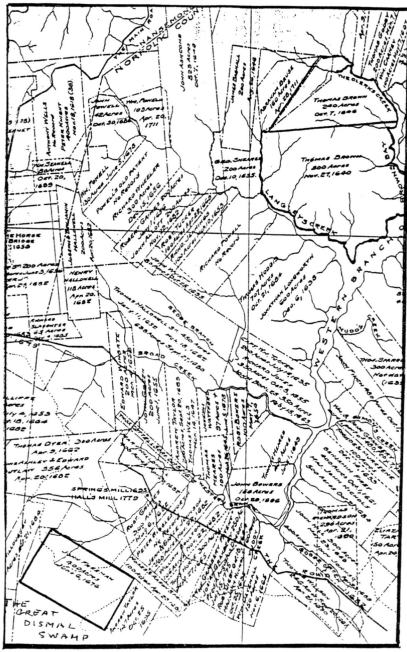

Map of Freeman and Brown Patents, Western Branch of Elizabeth River, Norfolk Co., VA. Virginia Historical Society, ViHMap F232 N2 1964. Printed with permission of copyright holder, Virginia Granbery Walter.

JOHN FREEMAN
of
NORFOLK COUNTY, VIRGINIA,
AND HIS DESCENDANTS

ORIGINS

The Freeman[1] family of Chowan and Bertie Counties in North Carolina has long been the subject of genealogical interest. Some research was undertaken in the 1920's.[2] In December of 1960 a chart, purporting to give the lines of descent of the family, was accessioned to the North Carolina Department of Archives and History. It gives the earliest known generation as brothers John Freeman who died in 1732 and William Freeman who died in 1736, both in Chowan precinct, North Carolina, and attributes to them a sister, Elizabeth Freeman, who married on 26 March 1669 in Perquimans County to Robert Harmon. As will be shown, the chart makes numerous demonstrable errors, misidentifying a number of Freeman family connections.[3]

Other publications have omitted the "sister" Elizabeth who appears to have been a generation older than her purported brothers, and have correctly added John Freeman of Lower Norfolk County, Virginia, as father of John and William of Chowan but claiming *Mayflower* ancestry for the family, through Major John Freeman who married Mercy Prence, daughter of Thomas and Patience (Brewster) Prence and granddaughter of Elder William Brewster.[4] Other versions claim that Major John Freeman came to Massachusetts in 1635, married Mercy

---

[1]The surname Freeman is variously spelled Freman, ffreeman, ffreman. The spelling Freeman will used throughout this report except in quotations where the spelling will reflect that in the original record.

[2]Letters from Robert A. Freeman, Dobson, NC to Mrs W. S. Faulkner, Alameda, CA. 22 Feb 1922; 14 Sep. 1925. Originals in possession of the author.

[3]Freeman Chart, accessioned to the NC Dept of Archives & History in December 1960. Handwritten. Copy in possession of the author. Referred to by Library staff to the author as "the paper bag chart."

[4]David H. Reese, "Freeman Ancestors." *Rees Genealogy,* Vol. 13 (Jan-Feb 1980). Address in 1980 112 E. North Ridge Drive, Ashville, NC 28804.

Brewster, and moved to Norfolk County, Virginia.[5]   No documentation is given to support either of these erroneous claims.   Other publications, most recently Jeanette Holland Austin's *The Georgians* and the LDS *Ancestral File*, misidentify numerous generations.[6]

It is the purpose of this research effort to present only that material for which evidence can be found in primary sources or which can be reasonably deduced therefrom.   Fortunately, Lower Norfolk County, Virginia,[7] has not suffered the massive record destruction of neighboring Nansemond and other Virginia counties, and, with the exception of Hertford County, the North Carolina records of the areas where descendants of this Freeman family resided have largely survived.

Origin of the tradition of a New England connection may stem from early researchers who found reference to a grandson William Freeman in the will of Major John Freeman of Eastham, Massachusetts, and erroneously assumed that the William who died in 1736 in Chowan County, North Carolina, was he.   A John Freeman first appears in Lower Norfolk, Virginia, records in 1673 when he was cited with others for "...being delinquent in nott clearing the high ways...."[8]   Evidently he had already been a

---

[5]Hester Bartlett Jackson, ed. *The Heritage of Surry County, North Carolina*, Vol I, (Winston Salem, NC: Surry Co. Geneal. Assn. in Cooperation with Hunter Pub. Co., 1983): 188-190.

[6]Jeanette Holland Austin, *The Georgians: Genealogies of Pioneer Settlers*, (Baltimore: Genealogical Publishing Co., Inc., 1984):122-124; *Ancestral File 4.02*, (Church of Latter Day Saints, Includes submissions through 1 October 1990).

[7]Lyndon H. Hart III and J. Christian Kolbe, comp. *A Preliminary Guide to Pre-1904 Municipal Records in the Archives Branch, Virginia State Library and Archives*, (Richmond: VA State Library and Archives, no date):5,27,37.   New Norfolk County was established in 1636 from Elizabeth City County.   In 1637 New Norfolk was divided into Lower Norfolk and Upper Norfolk (renamed Nansemond in 1646).   In 1691 Norfolk County was formed from Lower Norfolk and became extinct in 1963 when it was consolidated with the City of South Norfolk to form the City of Chesapeake.   The independent cities of Norfolk and Portsmouth also cover much of the area of original Norfolk County.

[8]Lower Norfolk Bk E (pt 2):103a. 16 October 1673, Court order to persons to answer charge of being delinquent in "nott clearing the high ways." Hereafter abbreviated as L. Norfolk.

resident of the area for some time. As will be shown, this John Freeman, who patented land in 1676 in Lower Norfolk County, was father of John and William Freeman who moved to North Carolina and also of a son Thomas Freeman, unmentioned by previous researchers, who remained in Norfolk County. If the *Mayflower* tradition were correct, it would be necessary to show that a John Freeman with *Mayflower* connections, adult by 1673, disappeared from New England by that date. Some record should also be found which would identify such a Massachusetts emigrant as the Virginia patentee.

Research in Massachusetts records clearly shows that a John Freeman did marry Mercy Prence, daughter of Thomas Prence, fourth Governor of the Colony of New Plymouth and granddaughter of William Brewster of the Mayflower. However, that John Freeman remained in New England, leaving a long trail of records, first in Sandwich and then in Eastham, where he died on 28 October 1719. His will mentions several children and grandchildren, including a son John and grandson William.[9]

John Freeman, Junior, son of Major John and Mercy (Prence) Freeman, was born December 1651 and died 27 July 1721. His life and death, like that of his father are well documented in Massachusetts records.[10] Although there are several other Freeman families this early in New England, Major John Freeman and his son John are the only ones who are known to have *Mayflower* connections and who would have been old enough to be our subject of Lower Norfolk County, Virginia. Both remained in New England. Therefore, the tradition of a *Mayflower* descent must be discounted. While it is remotely possible that John of Virginia descends from another Freeman family of New England, no evidence has been found to indicate

---

[9]Letter, Elizabeth P. White, Editor of the *Mayflower Quarterly*, to the author, 16 Nov. 1985. "Enclosed is a printout of our research into John Freeman of Eastham, Massachusetts, whose wife was Mercy Prence, a descendant of Elder William Brewster of the *Mayflower*. As you can see, you are absolutely right in your conclusion that the John Freeman of Virginia is a quite different person from the John Freeman of Massachusetts....they were contemporaries, living in two separate parts of the eastern seaboard; "Frederick Freeman. comp., *Freeman Genealogy* (Boston: Franklin Press, Rand, Avery, & Co., 1875):28.29; Barnstable County, MA, Records 3:527, 529, 530, 597.

[10]Barnstable County, MA. Records 4:13. Will of John Freeman.

3

New England origins for John Freeman of Lower Norfolk County,
Virginia.

EARLY FREEMAN RESIDENTS OF NORFOLK COUNTY

Early Virginia records show numerous references to men
surnamed Freeman, none of whom show any connection to John
Freeman who first appeared in 1673 in Lower Norfolk County.[11]
Several Freemans, however, do appear fleetingly in early Lower
Norfolk records. Earliest was a Robert Freeman, deceased by
1638, whose estate, administrated in that year by Capt. William
Brocas, was owed a debt by Thomas Skills (Skeels) of
Lynnehaven.[12]

About 1653 Nicholas Freeman became a resident of Lower
Norfolk[13] and remained there until his death in 1670.[14] He was
a member of the small persecuted Quaker Meeting which included
several who would later be neighbors and associates of John

---

[11]Nell Marion Nugent, *Cavaliers & Pioneers, Abstracts of Virginia
Land Patents and Grants 1623-1666, Vol I.* (Baltimore: Genealogical Pub.
Co., 1963). Numerous of the surname are listed as headrights or patentees. Of
particular interest is the listing for a servant, John Freeman, transported by
William Croutch who received a 50 ac patent in 1637 in the Upper Co. of New
Norfolk (later Nansemond Co.) [*C&P* 1:75]. This transportee appears to have
been too old to be the John who appeared in 1673.

[12]New Norfolk, Bk A:fol. 8. The county was first created in 1636 from
Elizabeth City County as New Norfolk. In 1637 it was divided into Lower
Norfolk (changed to Norfolk County in 1696) and Upper Norfolk (renamed
Nansemond in 1646).

[13]L. Norfolk Co., VA. Bk C:51 Jno Chandler ordered to pay Nicholas
Freeman 620 lb tobo at next crop.

[14]L. Norfolk Co., VA. Bk E(pt. 2):fol. 54. 16 Nov 1670 Joseph Wilder and
Jno Wallis summoned to next court to give evidence concerning Nicholas
Freeman's Last will & testament; On 21 Sep 1671 (E(pt. 1):fol. 101. Thomas
Blanch was granted administration on the estate of Nicholas Freeman.
Apparently a will was either not found or not adequately proved.

Freeman, our subject.[15] He first appeared in court records in 1653 when Jno Chandler was ordered to pay him 620 lb of tobacco at the time of the next crop. Nicholas did not receive a patent but purchased 200 acres on a point in Broad Creek in 1662 from Edward Wilder which he sold to Arthur Mosely who later repatented the land.[16] No mention of spouse or issue is found in the county records. The time period and association with the Spring and Wallis families makes him an attractive candidate for father of John Freeman, but no evidence has been found of such a relationship and no known descendant of John Freeman bears the given name Nicholas.

In 1684 a David Freeman appeared in county records. He married Sarah the widow and executor of William White.[17] He died by 15 Sept 1690 when his widow Sarah petitioned for probate on his estate.[18] Although there is no deed or patent to him, he was apparently residing on the Southern Branch of Elizabeth River.[19] A Rachell ffreeman was owner of a Hogg illegally killed by Danll Deane in September 1692[20] and on 4 October 1694 she witnessed the will of John Gabon.[21] Her connection to Nicholas or David, if any, is unknown.

No connection has been found between John Freeman of the Western Branch of Elizabeth River and Robert, Nicholas or David Freeman.

---

[15]L. Norfolk Co., VA. Bk D:360. 20 Dec 1662, John Sidney, the sheriff, lists names of those who were at an unlawful gathering of Quakers; William Wade Hinshaw, *Encyclopedia of American Quaker Genealogy, Vol 6* (Ann Arbor: The Author, 1950) 11. The group included Robert Spring and wife whose descendant witnessed deeds of John Freeman.

[16]Nugent, *C&P I*:474. The repatent to Mosely gives the date of the Wilder patent as 6 Mar. 1662 but the Wilder Patent itself is dated 9 Mar. 1652 [*C&P I*:273].

[17]L. Norfolk Co., VA. OB 1675-1686:258. 17 Nov. 1684.

[18]L. Norfolk Co., VA. Bk 5 (pt 1):190.

[19]L. Norfolk Co., VA. Bk 5 (pt. 1):134.

[20]Norfolk Co., VA. Bk 5(pt 1):270.

[21]Norfolk Co., VA. 5(pt 2):fol. 215.

On 7 February 1749 Mr. William Freeman appeared in the Borough of Norfolk where he married Tabitha Wilson, daughter of Solomon Wilson.[22] In 1751 he was elected a Councilman and in 1774 he was appointed Clerk of the Market of the Borough.[23] This William had a daughter Mary, who married in Norfolk County in 1770 to Thomas Burke, and a daughter Frances, who married in 1769 to John McCariel.[24] William's will showed sons named John and Robert.[25] There was possibly a son William who died young.[26] Mr. William Freeman made several purchases of land in Bertie County, NC,[27] and about 1775 the family moved there. William died in Bertie County in 1782, leaving a very large estate.[28] His widow moved to Warren County, North Carolina where her will was probated in 1797.[29] Although this family followed the same migration pattern as our subject family, there appears to be no interaction or relationship between them. However, some researchers have confused this man with William[3] Freeman #6 (William [2], John[1] Freeman). A fuller discussion of this family appears in the section on "Other Early Freeman Families."

---

[22]Elizabeth B, Wingo, *Marriages of Norfolk County, Virginia 1706-1792,* Vol 1 (Norfolk:by the author, n.d.),25.

[23]Brent Tarter, ed. *The Order Book and Related Papers of the Common Hall of the Borough of Norfolk, Virginia, 1746-1798* (Richmond: Virginia State Library, 1979),80, 178.

[24]Wingo, *Marriages*:10, 44.

[25]Bertie Co., NC, WB C:33.

[26]Norfolk Co., VA. OB 22 Jul 1768:257. "William Freeman senr and William Freeman Jun: against Henry Rothery for fifty pound Tobacco Each for two days attendance each in his suit against Mathias Christian." Tithable lists show no other William Freeman and fail to show this man with a son William. Therefore if this William had such a son he must have died young.

[27]Bertie, DB I:114, 415.

[28]N.25. *Supra.*

[29]Warren Co, NC WB 9:156.

GENERATION 1

JOHN FREEMAN OF LOWER NORFOLK

1. **JOHN[1] FREEMAN** was probably born sometime before 1650 since he appeared to be adult by 1673, when he first appeared in Lower Norfolk County records.[30] On 17 December 1675, "A Certificate for 50 acres of Land is granted Jn° freeman for ye Importation of himself into yis [this] Country proved due by his oath."[31] On the same date the court ordered Freeman and Tho: Lovell to receive payment of witness fees from Edward Sholder for three days attendance as an evidence against William Defnall.[32] Six months later, in June 1676, Freeman received a patent of 400 acres for transportation of himself, Jane Williams, Jno Tutte, Cha Morgan, Mary Cutter, Rich. Reynolds, Edwd. Browne and Mary Hartly. This tract, lying in Lower Norfolk County, was near the head of the Western Branch of Elizabeth River formerly surveyed by William Defnall and Thomas Lovell, running to a white pine on the "Inchaunted ridge".[33] The location of the land was very near the boundary of Lower Norfolk with Nansemond County.

---

[30]N. 8, *supra*.

[31]L. Norfolk Co., VA. OB 1675-1686:11. This proof of importation is further evidence that John Freeman was probably born in England. Some researchers have overlooked the ample evidence that John is father of William #2 claiming that William was a son of a James Freeman, son of Bridges and Bridget (Fowler) Freeman of Chickahominy, but cite no primary evidence. No son James is shown in the research published on that line in *Adventurers of Purse and Person in Virginia, 1607-1624/5*, Revised and Edited by Virginia M. Meyer and John Frederick Dorman (Richmond: Order of First Families of Virginia, 1607-1624/5, 3rd ed. 1987): 294-296.

[32]L. Norfolk Co., VA. OB 1675-1786:12.

[33]Virginia Land Patent Bk 6:609, LDS film # 029323; Nell Marion Nugent, *Cavaliers & Pioneers, Vol II* (Richmond: VA State Library, 1977)176. A certificate for the headrights for Williams, Tutte, Morgan, and Cutter was recorded for Jane Rigglesworth in 1652 (L.Norf C:26) and to her (Jane Yates Rigglesworth Horne) in 1658 for Edward Browne and Mary Hartly (L. Norf. D:148). These headrights were never used until Freeman's patent. How Freeman acquires the headrights is unknown. Jane Yates m.(3) Tho. Lovell, witness with Freeman for Sholder v. Defnall. An extended search on Yates and Riggleworth families failed to produce evidence of a relationship to John or Hannah.

Freeman received no headright for importation of his wife and so was probably unmarried when he arrived. Sometime prior to 1683/4 John Freeman married. His spouse was named Hannah but extensive research in Lower Norfolk records has produced no evidence of her surname. The only evidence of her given name is found with her husband on two land transactions:

> ...**John ffreeman** of the Westerne branch of Elizabeth River in the County of Lower Norfolk planter for and In Consideration of the Sum of fowerteen Hundred pounds of Tobacco & Caske...sell unto Thomas fforgison of the same place miller a tract of Land Containing fifty acres more or less...part of a tract of fower hundred acres of Land whereon I the above said Jno ffreeman do now live...west side Poplar neck Runn...line of Jno ffreemans survey...19 Febry 1683/4.
>
> /s/ John "F" ffreeman & seale
Hannah "t" freeman & seale
>
> Signed Sealed and delivered in presence of
> Moses Spring   Acknowledged in Court June 1686
> Elizabeth + Spring
> John Knight[34]

> 1 October 1687 **John ffreeman** of the County of Lower Norfolk of the one part and John Whitehall of the same...the sd ffreeman by and with the consent of Hannah his wife...three thousand pounds of good sound merchantable tobacco in Caske already paid...That parcell of tract of Land...on Western branch of Lower Norfolk Adjoining on Robert Capps line...John ffreeman...Poplar Neck run to Thomas fforkestone line...one hundred & thirty acres.
>
> /s/ John "F" ffreman & seale
Hannah "t" ffreeman & seale
>
> Signed Sealed and Delivered in presence of us
> Moses Spring   Acknowledged in Court 15 Nov 1687
> Robert Spring[35]

The two land sales by John and Hannah total 180 acres, substantially reducing their known land holdings to 220 acres. However, the 1704 Rent Rolls show him as owner of only 190

---

[34]L. Norfolk Co., VA. Bk 4:228. This deed does not appear in the Norfolk Deed Index.

[35]L. Norfolk Co., VA. Bk 5(pt 2):45. Also recorded in Norf. Bk 7:5. The word Caske is spelled Casque in the latter recording.

acres,[36] leaving 30 acres of his original 400 acre patent unaccounted for at that date. After the death of John and Hannah Freeman their son William Freeman executed deeds of lease and release to his brothers.

> 2 & 3 October 1711 **William ffreman** of the county of Norfolk of the one part and **John ffreman** for and in consideration of the **brotherly love and affection** that he bears unto the said John ffreman...about 50 acres now in tenure and occupation of the said John ffreman bounded on the Land of Thomas Willoughtby and Thomas Wooden and is part of a patent of four hundred acres granted unto **my father John Freeman decd** dated the 6th day of June 1676. Wit: John Ferebee
>
> /s/ William "W" ffreman
> Mary X ffreman
>
> Acknowledged 18 Aprill 1712 by Wm ffreman and mary his wife being first privately examined hath acknowledge her right and relinquishmt of Dower....[37]

The same day a similar deed was also made by William to his brother **Thomas Freeman**. That deed, also for 50 acres, was for land bounded by that of William and of John Freeman. Thomas apparently was not resident on the land at date of the deed.[38] William himself retained 60 acres which he later sold. These deeds show a total of 160 acres, thirty acres shy of the amount shown on the rent roll. Thus there is a total of 60 acres of the original patent unaccounted for, which raises the possibility that part of John Freeman's land holding may have extended over the boundary in Nansemond County.

Hannah appears to be the mother of John Freeman's three known children, all males, who must have been born near the dates of the making of these deeds, since all were adult by October 1711 when William Freeman deeded land to his

---

[36] Annie Laurie Wright Smith, *The Quit Rents of Virginia* (n.p., 1957)34.

[37] Norfolk Co., VA. Bk 9(pt 1):179-180.

[38] Norfolk Co., VA. Bk 9(pt 1):180-181.

brothers.[39] John Freeman, Junior, the only one of the sons known to have female offspring, named a daughter Hannah and mentioned her first of the several daughters named in his will.[40]

From 1687 to 1710 Norfolk record books contain no reference to John Freeman except as an adjacent landowner. He witnessed no will or deed, nor did he appear as plaintiff or defendant in as suit or serve as a juror. Since his property was so close to the county line it is tempting to believe that some records pertaining to him might have been recorded in the destroyed record books of Upper Norfolk/Nansemond County.

A close association, perhaps a family relationship, existed between the Freemans and the family of William Wallis. On 15 May 1710 John went before the County Court stating that he had under his care several small orphans of William Wallis, deceased, and prayed the court take care of them. The court ordered him to appear with them at next court in order that they might be bound out.[41] On the same date he applied for and was granted administration on the estate of William Wallis, "said Wallis and his wife dying intestate."[42]

Just a year later on 18 May 1711 "Hannah Wallis an orphan girl of Wm Wallis...aged six years being sometime since bound out to Jno ffreman and his wife and they being both removed by Death...." was bound of her free will to Andrew Taylor.[43] In July of the same year William Freeman applied for and was granted administration on the estate of William Wallis.[44] John Wallis was bound to John Freeman, Jr, and on 17 May 1717 complained to the court against his master.[45] These references

---

[39]Norfolk Co., VA. Bk 9 (pt 1):179-182.

[40]Will of John Freeman, North Carolina Archives. Secretary of State Wills.

[41]Norfolk Co., VA. Bk 8:*f*. 148. Orphans Court.

[42]Norfolk Co., VA. Bk 8:*f*. 149.

[43]Norfolk Co., VA. Bk 9(pt 2):8.

[44]Norfolk Co., VA. Bk 9(pt 1):193 and 9(pt 1):15.

[45]Norfolk Co., VA. Bk 9(pt 2):178.

are tantalizing and lead to speculation as to the nature of the relationship between the families. It is interesting that the known Wallis children bear the given names John and Hannah. Were they grandchildren, niece and nephew, cousins? Unfortunately insufficient evidence exists to draw a conclusion.

These court records pertaining to the Wallis children place the date of death of John Freeman and his wife between 15 May 1710 when he was granted administration on William Wallis, and 18 May 1711 when the death of John Freeman and his wife caused his ward to be bound to Andrew Taylor. County records contain no will or probate record for John or Hannah.

Based on the assumption that John Freeman was of age when he first appeared in Norfolk County records, his birth must have taken place about 1650 or before. His place of birth is unknown but was probably in England. He arrived in Lower Norfolk County before 1673 having paid his own way. He married, probably in Norfolk County, sometime before February 1683/4 to Hannah (surname unknown). Evidence shows he was the father of at least three sons as follows:

Issue of John and Hannah (_?_) Freeman.

+   2   i.   William² Freeman, prob. b.c. 1680-85; d.
ante 13 Aug. 1736; m. before 2 Oct 1711,
Mary Cording.

+   3   ii.   John² Freeman, prob. b.c. 1680-90; d. ante,
6 May 1732, Chowan Pct, NC.; m(1)
_____, m(2) Mary _____.

+   4   iii.   Thomas² Freeman, prob. b.c. 1685-90;
d. post Jan. 1774; m(1) Sarah ____, m(2)
Sarah (neé Low) Wingate.

11

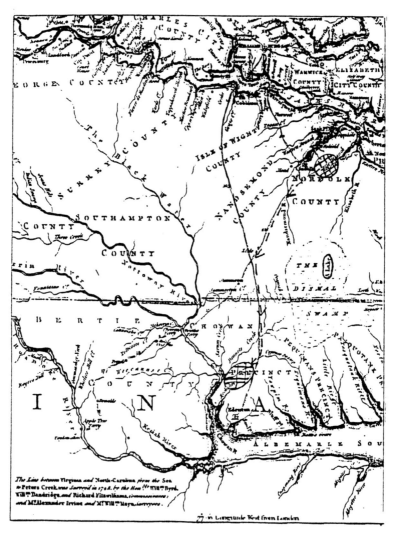

Route of travel for William Freeman family in
1718 from Western Branch of Elizabeth River,
Norfolk County, Virginia, to Catherine Creek,
Chowan Precinct, North Carolina.

GENERATION TWO

2. WILLIAM[2] FREEMAN (John[1] Freeman) wrote his will in 1736. At that time he had three sons who were old enough to maintain separate households and three minor sons. His marriage date must have been about 1705-08 to allow for birth of these older sons. If this estimate of his marriage date is correct, he must have been born by 1680-1685. The first mention of William in Norfolk County is found in 1711. In June of the same year he brought suit against Robert Cannada.[1] In July, following his father's death, he replaced his father as administrator of the estate of William Wallis.[2] And, as seen in the preceeding section, in October of 1711 William, apparently as heir at law of his father, with his wife Mary, made deeds of gift of a portion of his father's land to his brothers John Freeman, Jr., and Thomas Freeman.[3]

William's wife was Mary Cording, daughter of Thomas Cording and wife Elizabeth.[4] Evidence of Mary's identity is found in a court action brought on 14 October 1714:

> Upon the pet: of W[m] ffreeman and Mary his wife Daughter of Thomas Cording deced: it is ordered the Sherif Sum°: the Executrix of the said Cording to appear at next Court to answer the said pet[r]:[5]

A parallel action was brought by John Wright and Elizabeth his wife, also a daughter of Thomas Cording.[6]

---

[1]Norfolk Co., VA. Bk 9(2):13.

[2]Norfolk Co., VA. Bk 9(1):193 and 9(2):15.

[3]See discussion of land holdings in *Generation I, John Freeman of Lower Norfolk*. Norfolk Co., Bk 9(1):179-181.

[4]L. Norfolk Co., VA. Bk B:76, 142, 82; Bk D:312-313; Thomas Browne will. L. Norfolk Bk E: f. 12.

[5]Norfolk Co., VA. Bk 9(2):98.

[6]Norfolk Co., VA. Bk 9(2):98, 105, 110.

13

William Freeman and his growing family did not remain long in Norfolk. By 1718 he had joined the increasing stream of those moving south past Dismal Swamp to North Carolina. He settled in Chowan Precinct in Albemarle County, North Carolina, where on 10 July 1718 he purchased 250 acres for £80 sterling from Thomas Garrett, Sr. and his wife Bethia. The tract was located on Catherine Creek Swamp, a tributary of the Chowan River, near Cypress Branch adjacent to land of Walter Draughan and Michael Brinkley.[7] The following day William and Mary of Chowan Precinct sold 100 acres of the tract for £40 to Michael Ward.[8]

The Chowan River had been used as a temporary haven by Blackbeard, North Carolina's most famous pirate who was killed at Ocracoke Inlet just four months after William Freeman's purchase.[9]

In 1719 a deed was recorded in Norfolk County records which directly identifies William And Mary Freeman as those who previously resided in Norfolk.

17 March 1719 **William ffreeman of Chowan in NorCarolina** and with full consent of Mary his wife for 28£ actuall mony sold to William Perkins 60 acres joyning upon the land of ffrancis Hodges and also of Thomas ffreeman upon a Runn commonly called fforgissons Runn...part of a patent fformerly granted to **John ffreeman deced ffather of ye said Willm ffreeman**, Wit: John Yates, Mary Yates, Andrew Wallis.
/s/ W^m ffreeman
Mary ffreeman
Acknowledged 18 March 1719/20 by Wm ffreeman and Mary his wife.[10]

---

[7]Chowan Co., NC. DB B#1:607. Chowan Co. was first designated a precinct of Albemarle Co. and later became a county.

[8]*Ibid*:608.

[9]Hugh F. Rankin, *The Golden Age of Piracy* (New York, Holt, Rinehart, and Winston, 1969),118-123 and *The Pirates of North Carolina* (Raleigh: Dept of Cultural Resources, Div. of Archives and History, 1984),43-61.

[10]Norfolk Co., VA. *Court Orders, Wills, Appraisements*:15. (This deed does not appear in Norfolk County Deed Index on LDS Film #032821.

William added to his North Carolina holdings when he acquired 150 acres for £90 sterling on the south side of Catherine Creek Swamp called Poplar Neck by purchase in 1725 from Epaphroditus Brinkley.[11]

Three years later the people of the neighborhood must have been excited at the news of the arrival of the Virginia and North Carolina Commissioners appointed to survey the disputed dividing line between the two colonies. William Byrd II, Virginia Commissioner, left two journals describing the happenings surrounding the survey. On 19 March 1727/28, while camped on the western edge of Dismal Swamp awaiting the surveyors, he wrote:

> Some Borderers, too, had a great Mind to know where the Line wou'd come out, being for the Most part Apprehensive lest their Lands Should be taken into Virginia....There some good Women brought their children to be Baptiz'd....our chaplain Christen'd above an Hundred" of the children brought to the camp.[12]

Since the surveyor's camp was only a few miles from the Freemans' North Carolina homes it seems possible that some of the younger children of William Freeman or his brother John may have been among the group.

On 25 March, New Years Day of the Old Style calendar, and on the several days following, William Byrd made extensive observations which provide us with an unusual contemporary picture of the Chowan area and its people:

> The Road leading from thence to Edenton, being in distance about 27 Miles, lies upon a Ridge call'd Sandy Ridge, which is so wretchedly Poor that it will not bring Potatoes....Surely there is no place in the World where the Inhabitants live with less labour than in N. Carolina. It approaches neared to the Description of Lubberland than any other, by the great felicity of the Climate, the easiness of raising Provisions, and the Slothfulness of the People...

---

[11]Chowan Co., NC. DB C:468.

[12]William Byrd, *Histories of the Dividing Line betwist Virginia and North Carolina* (New York: Dover Publication, Inc., 1967):74. Dover Press states that material in the Byrd's diaries is is the public domain and requires no permission for reprint.

The Men, for their Parts, just like the Indians, impose all the Work upon the poor Women. They make their Wives rise out of their Beds early in the Morning, at the same time that they lye and Snore, till the Sun has run one third of his course, and disperst all the unwholesome Damps. Then, after Stretching and Yawning for half and Hour, they light their Pipes, and, under the Protection of a cloud of Smoak, venture out into the open Air; tho', if it happens to be never so little cold, they quickly return Shivering into the Chimney corner. When the weather is mild, they stand leaning with both their arms upon the cornfield fence, and gravely consider whether they had best go and take a Small Heat at the Hough: but generally find reasons to put it off till another time.

Thus they loiter away their lives, like Solomon's Sluggard with their Arms across, and at the Winding up of the Year Scarcely have Bread to Eat.

To speak the Truth tis a thorough Aversion to Labor that makes People file off to N Carolina, where Plenty and a Warm Sun confirm them in their Disposition to Laziness for their whole Lives....

Betwixt this and Edenton there are many thuckleberry Slashes which afford a convenient Harbour for Wolves and Foxes. The first of these wild Beasts is not so large and fierce as they are in other countries more Northerly....

Most of the Houses in this part of the country are Log-houses, covered with Pine or Cypress Shingles, 3 feet long, and one broad. They are hung upon Laths with Peggs, and their doors too turn upon Wooden Hinges, and have wooden Locks to Secure them, so that the Building is finisht without Nails of other Iron-work. They also set up their Pales without any Nails at all, and indeed more Securely than those that are nail'd....[13]

Despite Byrd's opinion, Edenton had been incorporated in 1722 as the first capital of the province of North Carolina. When Byrd arrived at the town he must have seen the Cupola House, built circa 1725, and now considered the finest surviving example of a Jacobean House south of Connecticut.[14]

---

[13]*Ibid*:90, 92, 94.

[14]*Guide Book: Historic Edenton and Chowan County*, (Edenton Woman's Club, 1984):30; Edenton-Chowan Chamber of Commerce, *Historic Edenton and Chowan County, North Carolina*, brochure.

In 1733, several years after the excitement of the survey had abated and with the inhabitants now sure of their North Carolina residency, William Freeman purchased a 640 acre tract located across the Chowan River in Bertie County from Henry Roads of Bertie.[15] William had prospered in his new home and on 7 February 1736, he wrote his will which was probated on 13 August 1737. The will was proved before Wm Smith, Esq, & Chief Judge of the Province and was ordered recorded but according to a deed from John Freeman, son of William, to his brother, Samuel, the will was subsequently lost.[16] It apparently was later located, since it is now on file with the State of North Carolina.[17]

The will conditioned each legacy on the change of condition of William's wife by death or marriage. To his son John he left the plantation where John lived and a negro woman; to his son William he left the land where William then lived and a negro man; to son Thomas he left the plantation where he was living in the Indian neck and a negro boy; to Son Richard he left the land whereon "I now Live" and a negro girl with the proviso that Richard not seek to deprive "my well beloved wife Mary of her right of Dowry"; To sons Aron and Samuel he left the plantation and land containing 640 acres lying in Bertie to be divided between them and to son Aron a negro girl and to Samuel the first negro child that shall be borne of any of the negro women or girls. His personal estate he left to Mary his wife and at her death to be divided between his six sons except that the three youngest sons, Richard, Aron and Samuel were each to receive a bed and the furniture belonging to it before the division.

Mary probably either died or remarried about 1740, since John Freeman as his father's executor deeded to each of his brothers the land left in their father's will contingent on Mary's death.[18]

---

[15]Bertie Co., NC. DB E:143. Reference to purchase of this land is made by William Freeman in his will written in 1736 but the deed, dated 22 Sept. 1733 is recorded as being from Henry Rhodes to _Thomas_ Freeman and was not proved until 13 Aug. 1737, the same date as the probate of William's will.

[16]Bertie Co., NC. DB G:65.

[17]North Carolina, Secretary of State Original Wills. LDS Film #1605224.

[18]Chowan Co., NC. DB A:70, 309, 312 Deeds Jno Freeman and Tabitha to brothers William Freeman and Richard.

Some researchers have suggested that William may have been married more than once, since three of his children appeared from the wording of the will to be minors. Evidence that Mary Cording was mother of at least the oldest five and probably all six sons is found in a deed from their oldest son John to his youngest brother Samuel. In the deed John states that he is heir at law of his second youngest brother Aaron, proving that the two were full brothers. Had John been a half brother he could not have inherited from Aaron.[19]

The family was active in the affairs of St. Paul's Parish. In July 1738, after the death of William Freeman, his widow, Mary, appears in the Vestry Minutes, paid eighteen pounds for Keeping Margrett Rodgerson 9 months. The next year several Vestry meetings were held at her house and she was paid for keeping John Foard, a poor man.[20] Later, two of her sons would become Vestrymen.

Issue of William and Mary (Cording) Freeman:

+	5	i.	John[3] Freeman, prob. b.c. 1710; will proved June 1777; m. Tabitha.[21]
+	6	ii.	William[3] Freeman, prob. b.c. 1712; will proved Aug. 1781; m. Christian (Outlaw?).
+	7	iii.	Thomas[3] Freeman, b.c. 1715; d. post 1763.
+	8	iv.	Richard[3] Freeman, b.c. 1715-20; Will proved July 1761; m. Ruth Hunter.

---

[19]Bertie Co., NC. DB G:65. See also Note 30, *infra*, for further discussion on Intestate Succession in North Carolina.

[20]Raymond Parker Fouts, *Vestry Minutes of St. Paul's Parish, Chowan County, North Carolina, 1701-1776* (Cocoa, FL: GenRec Books, 1983):60-62.

[21]Much earlier birth dates have been proposed by some for John Freeman and his brothers William and Thomas. However, since Mary Cording was not married at the time her father wrote his will 4 Oct. 1698, the birth of her first child could probably not have taken place at the earliest until 1700 but more probably was circa 1710.

9	v.	Aron[3] Freeman, b.c. 1720-22; d. ante 1747 (a minor). No issue.[22]
+ 10	vi.	Samuel[3] Freeman, b.c. 1725-6 ; d. 1796. m. Elizabeth (traditional surname Alexander).

BROWNE - CORDING EXCURSIS

Mary Cording, wife of William Freeman, was daughter of Thomas Cording, granddaughter of Richard Cording and his wife Ann Browne, great granddaughter of Lt. Col. Thomas Browne of Lower Norfolk County.

No man named Thomas Browne appears in the Muster of 1624/5. However, a number of listings appear in the early land patents using the name Thomas Browne as a headright.[23]

Thomas Browne first appeared in the records of Lower Norfolk County indebted to Henry Rudkins in 1640[24] and was probably a resident there much earlier since his land holdings included land on "Browne's Bay" on the Western Branch of Elizabeth River which is named in patents as early as 1635 and in 1640 with John Slaughter assigned 200 acres to John Radford.[25]

Thomas Browne had a brother John Browne who also resided in Lower Norfolk County on the East Branch of Elizabeth River. Thomas was agent in sale of this land on 15 April 1656.

On 6 June 1648, Mr. Thomas Browne was among those appointed as Commissioner for Lower Norfolk County. In August of that year he became a Vestryman for Elizabeth River Parish and was appointed High Sheriff of the county on 13 March 1649.[26] When

---

[22]Bertie Co., NC. DB G:65. William Freeman deeded a 640 acre tract jointly to sons Aaron and Samuel. Aaron died a minor. His oldest brother John was his heir at law and in that capacity deeded Aaron's portion to Samuel.

[23]Nell Marion Nugent, *Cavaliers and Pioneers; Abstracts of Virginia Land Patents and Grants, 1623-1666* (Baltimore: Genealogical Publishing Co., Inc., 1963):30,46,59,68,78,86,96,97.

[24]Lower Norfolk Records A:50.

[25]Nugent, *Cavaliers and Pioneers, 1623-1666*:21, 123.

[26]Lower Norfolk Co., VA. BK B:76, 82, 123.

the rebels under Oliver Cromwell came into power, Browne refused to serve under them. At the time of the Restoration the Governor and General Council in Virginia limited the size of the County Courts to eight members, those with the earliest appointments. A petition was presented to William Berkeley to restore Thomas Browne to his former position. The petition was granted and Thomas Browne served again as Commissioner and Sheriff.[27]

> The humble peticon of John Hill Showeth that whereas at ye last session of assembly it was marked that the Commrs of ye County Courts should bee reduced to ue number of eight in each county, & those to bee ye ones first in each Commission unless by some known defects or to never ..(illeg.).. made..(illeg.)pable. And whereas there is in the County of Lower Norf. one M^{r}Tho: Browne who being one of the commissioners in time of his Maties [Majesties] father of our blessed memory & of his Matie that now is before ye governm^t of the Country & then lost out for no other offense of defect byt because hee could not engage, nor would not serve under ye rebells And now not put in againe at ye regulacon only because not named, & so yor peticoner at that Instant not remembered & others left in not so much deserving in y^t they never served in that office in his Maties time but ownely placed there when ye rebells ruled and hee only of those y^t did faithfully serve his Matie & was next unto yor peticon^{er} then refusing to engage to do service under them left it out contrary to ye expectation of all y^t know him & as hee takes to his great disparagement --
> The peticoner humbly supplicateth ye^r Honor y^t ye s^d Mr Tho: Browne may bee restored to his former place to serve his Sacred Matie & your Honor as formerly hee hath done - and yor petitioner shall as hee is bound pray.
> The petition is granted and Mr Browne for no fault of defect excluded for the manifestation of his loyalty to his Matie bee restored to his place wch hee held in the Comission before ye red..(illeg.)
> 5 Jun 1661   William Berkeley

Browne died testate in 1666, leaving "unto my Eldest daughter ye wife of Ric: Cording to _hir_ I say and not to him" a cow, bed and

---

[27]L. Norfolk Co., VA Bk D:312-313. Petition of Mr. John Hill to William Berkeley, granted 5 June 1661.

bedding. He names sons Thomas, John, Henry, Christopher and William; daughters Ann Cording, Elizabeth Browne and Mary Browne.[28]

Richard Cording, chirurgion (surgeon), appeared in the Norfolk County records in November 1655.[29] Never receiving a patent, he bought no land in Lower Norfolk and appears in the records usually in conjunction with collection of fees for his services. In March 1669 he was sued by Jno Bowering for failing to perform a cure on his indentured servant Jno Bowering. Mr. Tho Browne "for his dauther Cordon her husband being absent gave Bowering his freedom."[30] He apparently went briefly to the Northern Neck appearing as a witness in Westmoreland County and later in as debtor in Lancaster County records.[31]

Richard Cording apparently died soon after his father-in-law, Thomas Browne, since no further record is found of him. In 1668 Anne Cording deeded to her son Thomas Cording two cowes and their increase.[32] She apparently married a second time by 26 March 1670 when, as Ann Southerland, she is named in the wills of her brothers, John Browne and Henry Browne.[33] Mr. Southerland does not appear in Lower Norfolk records but by the late 1600s and early 1700s several Southerlands are mentioned, some residents of Nansemond County, probably her sons.[34]

No record exists of other children of Richard and Ann (Browne) Cording, but in 1711 a Richard Cording was named as son-in-law of John Graham and in 1720 he witnessed the will of John Southerland. The probability is high that Ann had at least one Cording

---

[28]L. Norfolk Co., VA BK E:f.12.

[29]L. Norfolk Co., VA. Bk C:172.

[30]L. Norfolk Co., VA BK C:212, 230; D: 19, 32-33, 151, 156, 162, 168, 175, 186, 190, 227, 291, 298.

[31]Westmoreland Co., VA. Records 1660-62:f.34; Lancaster D&W 1661-1702:24-25.

[32]L. Norfolk Co., VA. DB E(pt.1):fol. 52.

[33]L. Norfolk Co., VA. DB E(pt.1):fol. 87a.

[34]Norfolk Co., VA. DB 6:fol. 162.

son other than Thomas and also several sons by her second marriage.[35]

3. JOHN² FREEMAN (John¹ Freeman) was probably born in Norfolk Co., Virginia, about 1685-90. The deed of 1711 to him from his brother indicates that John was already living on the tract of land he received and was, therefore, probably already of age at that time.[36] In 1714, John Freeman, "house carpenter," increased his holdings by purchase of 70 acres of land in Norfolk County from Richard Wooden, adjoining the land "left to him by his father John ffreman Deced."[37]

Norfolk records hold several references to him. In 1713 he witnessed the will of Edward Outlaw. In 1717 John Wallis, probably the orphan of William Wallis, brought suit against his master, John Freeman, who was ordered to appear in court. In 1719 an order was granted Sampson Powers against Jno Freeman for 1000 pounds of tobacco for concealing a tithable and in 1722 he witnessed the will of William Perkins who had purchased from William Freeman.[38]

John Freeman married at least twice as will be shown by a later discussion of deeds executed by his children after his death. No record exists of either marriage. The date of the first marriage can be estimated by the fact that his oldest son, John, was under eighteen at the time John made his will in 1729/30 and so must have been born after 1711. The will states that, if his widow remarried, this son, John, is to be considered adult at age eighteen. It is unknown whether she did, in fact, remarry; but the first business transacted by this eldest son John is a 1740 deed, at which date he must have been at least eighteen, thus born between 1711 and 1721. There is no record of the name of his first wife.

---

[35]Norfolk Co., VA. DB

[36]*N.3. Supra.*

[37]Norfolk Co., VA. Bk 9:315.

[38]Norfolk Co., VA. Bk 9(1):360, 9(2):187; Orders, Administrations, Wills (1):fol. 14; OAW(2):15-17.

In 1722, John, still described as a resident of the Parish of Elizabeth and County of Norfolk, bought from John Goodwin and Mary, his wife, 50 acres in North Carolina on the North side of Wareek Swamp at the mouth of Wallnutt Branch, joining Deep Branch that issueth out of Fox Branch, adjacent to Edward Wood. Two years later the evidence appears which positively identifies the John Freeman of Chowan Precinct, North Carolina, as the same man as John Freeman of Norfolk. On September 1724, John Freeman and Mary his wife **of Chowan**, sold to William Wallis and Elizabeth his wife 120 acres, their total holdings, **"in Norfolk County where sd John ffreeman did formerly dwell"** bounded by Thos. Hobgood Jr and Samson Powers, Thomas Taylor and Thomas ffreeman.[39] The Mary named as wife in this deed is probably the same Mary named in John's will since the last marriage produced four children.

John's will was written on 19 February 1729/30 and proved in 1732. It creates a note of confusion by making reference to Mary, his wife, as though she were the mother of all of his children. The eldest son, John, was to inherit "all my land and plantation where on I now live at the change of my wifes condition either by death or maridge also 6 puter plates, he allowing and paying to his brother James ffreeman twelve pound of the good pay of this Government at the time his brother Comes to the age of twenty one years...." James was also to receive a bed, six puter plates, a long gun and three iron weges. Mathew, the third son, but only son by the last wife was favored with two hundred and fifty acres of land on the south side of the Indian Creek. His wife Mary was given the use of all the rest of his personal estate during the time of her widowhood. At the change of her condition to be divided between "my foure children Hannah ED Elizabeth and Mathew..."[40]

The evidence that Mary was not the mother of all of the children is found in two 1746 Chowan County land transactions:

11 September 1746. John Smith and **Hannah Smith (Late Hannah Freeman)**, John Davison Jr., and **Edie Davison (Late**

---

[39]Norfolk Co., VA. DB F:116.

[40]North Carolina, Secretary of State Original Wills. The lack of commas between names of the daughters has led many to overlook "ED" as an abreviation of Edith.

Edic Freeman), Benjamin Hollyman & Elizabeth Hollyman
(Late Elizabeth Freeman), all of Bertie Co., for 30 £ Bills
paid by our kinsman & Brother John Freeman of Bertie
Co. afsd millwright. 250 acres on South side Indian Creek
in Chowan County. **Hannah, Edie, and Elizabeth being sole
Coheirs to our deceased only brother (of the whole blood)
Matthew Freeman youngest son and Legatee to our
deceased father John Freeman** late of Chowan of the afsd
Land.... Wit: John (S) Berry, Jeremiah Maul, John Davison.
/s/ John (X) Smith,
Hannah (H) Smith, John
(D) Davison, Edie (ED)
Davison, Benjamin (H)
Hollamon, Elizabeth
(X) Hollaman.[41]

John Freeman of Bertie County Millwright to Patrick Hicks
of Chowan Planter in consideration of Ninety five Pounds...All
my part of a tract in Chowan County...Indian Creek 300 acres.
Part of 400 acres conveyed by John Jordan to George White
and by him to **John Freeman** decd. **and by him bequeathed
unto (my brother) his son Matthew Freeman now deceased
intestate whereby the said 250 acres descended unto
Hannah Edie & Elizabeth sister of the whle blood unto
the sd Matthew. Fifty acres more or less undivided being
in the possession of my sd father in fee & not bequeathed
descends to me as heir at Law** to him and the sd Hannah,
Edie, and Elizabeth sisters afsd having by their deed joyned
with their respective husbands conveyed the sd 250 acres to
me...31 December 1746.
Wit: Joseph Harris, John Jordan Sr.
/s/ John Freeman[42]

The Colony of North Carolina followed English Common
Law in the case of an intestate estate. If a man died intestate and
without legitimate issue, his heir would have been his oldest brother
of the whole blood. If there were no brothers or only half brothers,
then full sisters would inherit equally. The deeds are very specific
in pointing out that Mathew died intestate and that the girls are sisters
of the "Whole Blood". The deeds also confirm the fact that John

---

[41]Chowan Co., NC. DB E:167.

[42]Chowan Co., NC. DB E:190.

24

was the eldest son and heir at law of his father, since he inherited the residuum of land not specifically bequeathed by his father. By the second deed above, John Freeman conveys the 250 acres deeded him by his half sisters, he also makes it clear that second 50 acres tract had been acquired by his father by purchase not inheritance. Had the tract been inherited, it might have been entailed by a previous will. Since neither John nor James inherited the land from Matthew, both must have been his half brothers. No conclusion can be drawn from these deeds as to whether John and James had the same mother, but it is clear that John Freeman was married at least twice.[43]

Issue of John Freeman as shown by his will:

By his first wife.

+   11   i.   John[3] Freeman, b. between 1711-1721; will prvd, Bertie Co. May 1785; m(1) Ann ____, (2)Elizabeth____, (3) Sarah____, widow of Henry Winborne and James Rascoe.

By first or another wife:

+   12   ii.   James[3] Freeman, resided in Bertie Co.

By Mary, his last wife:

+   13   iii.   Matthew[3] Freeman, d. bef. 1746, a minor, unmarried.

+   14   iv.   Hannah[3] Freeman, m. bef. 1746, John Smith, Resided Bertie Co.

---

[43]Letter Helen Leary to the author, 22 October 1984. The author contacted Helen Leary for information on North Carolina Statute or case law involving treatment of intestate estates, primogeniture and entail. Ms. Leary kindly sent photocopies of the following publications and made an excellent though unsolicited analysis of the law as it applied to the above deeds. Walter Clark, ed., *The State Records of North Carolina, Vol XXIII Laws 1715-1776* (Goldsboro, NC: Nash Brothers, 1905):67-70; Norman Adrian Wiggins, *Wills and Administration of Estates in North Carolina*, V. 1 (Norcross, GA: The Harrison Co.):323-329; and notes taken by Ms. Leary from *The Law Lectures of the Late Chief Justice, Richmond M. Pearson,*. comp by Benjamin F. Long (Raleigh: Edwards & Broughton & Co., 1879) p. 67 et seq. These notes include the Primary and Secondary Canons of Descent.

<table>
<tr><td>+</td><td>15</td><td>v.</td><td>Edie "ED"[3] Freeman, m. bef. 1746 John Davison. Resided Bertie Co.</td></tr>
<tr><td>+</td><td>16</td><td>vi.</td><td>Elizabeth[3] Freeman, m. bef. 1746 Benjamin Hollaman.</td></tr>
</table>

4. THOMAS[2] FREEMAN (John[1] Freeman) appears to have been the youngest of the known children of John and Hannah. Although his brothers moved to Chowan County, he remained in Norfolk. Despite the fact that this branch of the family remained in the same community and despite Thomas's long life, his family remains the most obscure and difficult to track. They had few land transactions and appear only occasionally in county records. No probate records of any kind have been found for him. He and his sons did not achieve the prominence in community affairs that his brothers and their families in North Carolina achieved.

Thomas was not yet living independently in 1711 when his brother, William, deeded him 50 acres of land. In 1715 He and his brother John along with William Perkins and Thomas fforgison were ordered to be taken into the Sheriff's custody until they could make security to answer the presentment of the grand Jury for "killing Hogs contrary to law."[44]

Thomas must have married about 1716. His eldest son, Thomas, Jr, first appears on tithable lists in 1733 and so was probably 16 years old by that date.[45] The first wife of Thomas, Sr., was named Sarah, her surname unknown. In 1721, Thomas Freeman and wife Sarah added to their land holdings by purchasing, for £30 current money, 100 acres from Edward Wood and Mary his wife and John Woods and Margett his wife of North Carolina of Chowan. This land was adjacent to land of Edward Wingett and Thomas Cottell.[46]

First wife, Sarah, must have died sometime before 1733. About that time Thomas married as his second wife Sarah (Low)

---

[44]Norfolk Co., VA. Bk 9(2):139.

[45]Elizabeth B Wingo and W. Bruce Wingo, *Norfolk County, Virginia Tithables, 1730-1750* (Norfolk: By the author, 1979):91.

[46]Norfolk Co., VA. DB F:8.

Wingate. She was the widow of Samuel Wingate who wrote his will 24 November 1731, proved 16 March 1732/3, naming John Bowers and Thomas ffreeman to divide his land between his two sons (unnamed).[47] Thomas soon married the widow. In 1743 Sarah Low, widow of Henry Low/Loe, died leaving a will naming numerous children and grandchildren, including a daughter, Sarah Freeman and a granddaughter Sarah Wingate.[48] It is that will which identified Sarah, second wife of Thomas, as bearing the maiden name Low and gave the evidence that she had been married to a Wingate. Thomas and Sarah (neé Low) (Wingate) Freeman had at least two sons, John and Samuel, to whom Thomas deeded the 100 acres he had purchased in 1721 from the Edward and John Woods and their wives, "after my death the plantation I now live upon to be Divided between them."[49]

Tithable lists continued to show Thomas Freeman, Sr, with sons John and Samuel through 1759.[50] In 1761 Thomas, Sr., was excused from tithe "during his indisposition."[51] Thomas, Jr. is shown on extant lists in 1750 through 1761.[52] On 29 November 1761 a Thomas Freeman, apparently Thomas, Jr., made his will giving his son Samuel "all my moveable estate and Crop that we have made together, only five shillings a piece to the rest of my Children." The will was probated in January Court 1762.[53]

Although the will names a son Samuel and mentions other unnamed children, it is clear that this is not the will of Thomas Freeman, Senior, since on 2 November 1763 Thomas Freeman made a deed to John Powell for 50 acres "it being the same parcel of Land

---

[47]Elizabeth B. Wingo, *Collection of Unrecorded Wills, Norfolk County, Virginia, 1711-1800* (n.p.: By the author, 1961):125.

[48]Norfolk Co., VA. Bk H:85.

[49]Norfolk Co., VA. DB 14:155.

[50]Elizabeth B. Wingo, *Norfolk County, Virginia Tithables, 1751-1765* (Norfolk: By the author, 1981):23, 61, 84, 133.

[51]Norfolk Co., VA. Court Orders 1759-63:92.

[52]Wingo, *Tithables, 1750-65*:23, 61, 84, 104, 134, 169.

[53]Norfolk Co., VA. WB 1:74; Order Bk 1760-63:144.

that William Freeman gave by Deed of Gift to Thomas Freeman which doth appear by Bearing Date the 2nd Day of October 1711 Likewise is part of a Patent of four hundred acres & **granted unto my Father John Freeman Deceasd....**" Thomas Freeman, son of the immigrant, was alive to acknowledge this deed on the 19th of January 1764 and thus could not have been the Thomas who died in 1762.[54]

In 1767, 1768 and 1770 a Thomas again appears on the tithable lists and in 1772 Martha Wallace was charged for Thomas Freeman and negro Milly and 100 acres of land. It is probable that this man was a grandson of Thomas Freeman, Senior. Sarah Freeman, apparently the widow of Thomas, Sr., was taxed for negro "Bow" in 1770, 1771 and in 1772 Bow was declared levy free.[55]

Thomas must have died sometime soon after his acknowledgement in 1764 of a deed to Powell, however, no will or administration has been found, possibly because he had already disposed of personal estate and his remaining land was already obligated by deed to his sons John and Samuel. Sarah's last appearance on the tax lists was in 1772. In 1768 her son John Wingate wrote his will leaving a family and leaving to his mother, Sarah Freeman, the house where she lived and 1 acre of land where the house stands during her life.[56]

A very close association existed between the Cottell/Cottle, Freeman and Wingate families from at least 1720 through 1770. Thomas Cottell and Edward Wingate were adjacent owners to the land Thomas bought from the Woods. In 1731 Thomas Cottel, Jr., was a tithable of Thomas Freeman. In 1736 Thomas Freeman, Jr., was a tithable of Thomas Cottel, Jr.[57] Thomas Cottle's last appearance on Norfolk Tithable lists was in 1754.[58]

---

[54]Norfolk Co., VA. DB 21:116.

[55]Letter Elizabeth Wingo to the author giving Freeman tithables in Norfolk County from 1766-1780; Norf. Order Bk 1770-1773:73, 22 May 1772.

[56]Pamela McVey, comp. *Norfolk County Will Book II, 1772-1788,* (pub. by author, 1986):13.

[57]Wingo, *Norfolk Tithables,* v. 1: 36, 184.

[58]Wingo, *Norfolk Tithables,* v. 2:44, 61, 84.

Thomas Cottle apparently died about then, and his widow Elizabeth died in September 1758, leaving a will which named her children Philip Cottle, Freeman Cottle, Hannah Cottle, and Catron Cottle. Elizabeth named John Wingitt as her executor. John Wainwright and Martha Freeman were witnesses.[59] On 19 October 1758, the Court ordered the Church Wardens of Elizabeth River Parish to bind Hannah Cottle to John Freeman and her sister Catherine to Samuel Freeman[60] In 1761 Philip Cottle was a tithable of Martha, widow of John Freeman.[61] Elizabeth Cottle was probably either a daughter of Thomas Freeman or a daughter of Samuel and Sarah Wingate and thus a step-daughter of Thomas. However, sufficient evidence seems lacking at this time to identify which relationship is correct.

Issue of Thomas Freeman.

By 1st wife, Sarah ___.

+   17   i.   Thomas[3] Freeman, b.c. 1717; d. testate 1762.
                       m. ___.

By 2nd wife, Sarah (Low) Wingate.

+   18   ii.   John[3] Freeman, b.c. 1734; d. 1761; m. Martha
                       (Wingate?).

+   19   iii.   Samuel[3] Freeman, b.c. 1734; d. 1784; m.
                       Judith ____.

---

[59]Norfolk Co., VA. WB I:219; Appraisements and Sales 1:27; Audits 1:32.

[60]Norfolk Co., VA. COB 1755-1768:207, 208.

[61]Wingo, *Norfolk Tithables* v. 2:170.

St. Paul's Church, Edenton, North Carolina, built
1736-1760.

GENERATION THREE

DESCENDANTS OF WILLIAM FREEMAN

5. **JOHN³ FREEMAN** (William², John¹ Freeman) has often been confused with his cousin John³ Freeman #11, and another John Freeman who died in Beaufort County in 1752.[1] Land records make it clear that our subject remained a resident of Chowan County while his cousin moved west across the Chowan River to Bertie County.

John, son of William, was born before the move to North Carolina, probably about 1710.[2] He married about 1733 to Tabitha, whose surname has been reported by some as Hoyter (Hoter, Hiter, Hayter), daughter of Thomas Hoyter.[3] The only such man in the area was a "Chiefman" of the Chowan Indians.[4] A law passed in 1741 which prohibited such marriages would have been too late to have effect.[5] At present, no evidence has been found to support that identification, but John Freeman did purchase land from the Chowan Indians and was co-grantee of

---

[1]Austin, *The Georgians:*122-124 states that John, son of William, was the one who died in Beaufort Co; Reese, "Freeman Ancestors," *Rees Genealogy, v.13* confuses the cousins, naming John of Bertie as son of William.

[2]Estimate of birth date is based on the fact that William Freeman's three oldest sons were of an age to be living independently by 1736 when William wrote his will. His service as a Vestry reader in 1733 is the first evidence that he had probably reached his majority.

[3]Neva Bolton, Cortez, CO, reported in LDS International Genealogical Index, 1989 that her surname was Hoter/Hoyter, daughter of Thomas Hoyter, gives no source. Patricia Garmon, Escondido, CA, in LDS Ancestral File lists her as Tabitha Hoter, source was research records of another, name not remembered. Phone queries to them elicited no data as to source.

[4]*Records of the Executive Council, 1664-1734* (Raleigh: Dept of Cultural Resources, Div. of Archives and History, 1984)70, 73; Haun, *Chowan Court Minutes,* v. 1:3; Saunders, *Colonial Records* v. 4:33-35. John Hayter/Hoyter/Hiter was the chief of the Chowan Indians c. 1717-30; Thomas Hoyter was one of the Great Men of the Chowan Nation; No other of the surname found.

[5]George Stevenson, "Marriage and Divorce Records," in Helen F.M. Leary and Maurice R. Stirewalt, eds, *North Carolina Research, Genealogy and Local History* (Raleigh: The North Carolina Genealogical Society, 1980): 288. "...from 1741 until the 1960's, marriages between whites and Indians and between whites and blacks were forbidden by the public laws of North Carolina."

land with them.

> [3 Aug 1733] James Bennett, **Thos Hiter,** & Jeremiah Pushing of the precinct of Chowan...One hundred & twenty pounds current money by John Freeman...200 acres part of Chowan Town y^t was formerly granted by Honb^le Gentlemen of the Province....
>
> Jam^s IB Bennet
> Thos TH Hoyter
> Jer: 3 Pushin
> Chas CB Beasley[6]

In 1737 John sold 100 acres of this land to his brother Thomas Freeman.[7] On 26 March 1733, and again on 29 March 1735, John was paid by the Vestry of St. Paul's Parish for serving as a reader, and in 1748 his neighbors successfully petitioned for his appointment to that position. In 1750 he was elected a Vestryman of the parish, serving in that capacity during much of the building of the church at Edenton.[8]

Deeds made by John to each of his brothers make it abundantly clear that John Freeman with wife Tabitha, of Chowan County, was son of William.

> 18 August 1741. **John ffreeman of the County of Chowan and Tabitha his wife to William ffreeman Brother** of same county. Out of **Natural Love** Good Will and Effection...in full **compliance of Last will and Testament of William ffreeman**...deceast...being Lawfull father...75 acres in the county Popular neck on south side of Catherine Creek Swamp adjacent to land of Thomas ffreeman Brother of John ffreeman and Wm ffreeman, adjacent to Walter Draughan and tract in occupation of Richard ffreeman and Brother to both parties...by Epaphroditus Brinkley sould to Wm: ffreeman....Wit: Thos Walton, John Walton, Richard Bond.
>
> /s/ JohnFreeman
> Tabitha (I) Freeman[9]

---

[6]Chowan Co., NC. DB W:216. Beasley signs but is not mentioned in body of deed.

[7]Chowan Co., NC. DB G:358.

[8]Fouts, *Vestry Minutes of St Paul's*:46, 52, 96, 105-108, 113.

[9]Chowan County, NC. DB A:70.

16 January 1744. **John ffreeman of County of Chowan and Tabitha his wife to William ffreeman being lacfull Brother to afsd John.** Out of Natural Love., and in full **compliance of last will of his father William ffreeman**...and also for valuable consideration of £50 current silver money paid by William ffreeman to their Brother Thomas ffreeman 75 acres Catherene Creek adjacent to land whereon sd William now lives in Popler Neck....Wit: Thomas Rountree Senr, Richard ffreeman

/s/ John ffreeman
Tabitha (T) ffreeman[10]

John Freeman served as Constable in 1748 and was directed by the Justices of the County to supervise the taking of the levy for that year.[11] In January of 1754 James Bennet and John Robins, Chowan Indians and John Freeman, Planter, for £ 20 sold to Richard Freeman 200 acres beginning at Blanchard's line, Bennets Creek, etc., hereby granted by Bennet, Robins and Freeman.[12] In July of that year Henry Hill of Chowan and James Bennet and John Robins, Chiefmen of the Chowan Indians, sold another tract to Richard Freeman.[13]

In 1762 John and Tabitha for £ 100 current money of North Carolina deeded to his son Jacob 100 acres in Chowan County at the Mouth of Juniper Branch, up said branch to a bridge called Aarons Bridge adjacent to Thomas Garrett and down Catharine Creek; and to his son John, Junior, for £ 40 Proclamation Money 300 acres in Chowan County on Juniper Swamp to Aaron's Bridge....[14]

---

[10]*Ibid*:309; Similar deeds were also made by John to his brother Richard (*Ibid*:312) and to his brother Samuel (Bertie Co., NC DB G:65). See following sections on Richard and Samuel.

[11]Chowan Co., NC. Tax lists, 1748. C.R. 024 701.2. John Freeman is shown with 3 tithables.

[12]Chowan Co., NC. DB G:137. No explanation is given for the fact that John Freeman is a co-grantor with the Chowan Chiefmen. This deeds gives the only evidence which might support the identification of Tabitha as a Chowan Indian.

[13]Chowan Co., DB G:344. Richard Freeman, grantee in these deeds is probably brother of John whose son Richard was probably still quite young.

[14]Chowan Co., NC. DB K:254 and M:221.

The formation of Hertford County placed some of the Freeman holdings in the new county. Unfortunately fire destroyed most of the records of the county which would have shed light on family relation ships. The act forming Hertford County passed in 1759 and became effective 1 May 1760. The county included the portion of Chowan County north and west of Bennett Creek, the Northern part of Bertie County, and the eastern portion of Northampton County. In 1779 Gates County was formed from Chowan, Hertford and Perquimans, taking in all that part of Hertford on the North East side of Chowan River and taking the slice of Chowan County that lay on the north side of Katherine Creek and Warwick Creek.[15] Fortunately, some of the Freeman lands which had fallen into Hertford County now were within the boundaries of Gates County whose records survive.

John Freeman, still a resident of Chowan, wrote his will on 13 April 1776. To his sons William, Jacob, and John and daughters Zilpah Outlaw, Tabitha Mansfield and Prisciller Hinton, he left only 5 shilling more than what they had already received. To his son Richard and daughter Cathrine he left each a bed and bedding and directed that on his wife Tabitha's death the remainder of his goods and lands were to be divided between Richard, Cathrine and his daughter Sara. Richard and Everard Garrett were Executors. Witnesses were Thos Garrett Senior and Junior and Joel Britt. The will was proved at the June Court in 1777.[16]

Issue of John and Tabitha ( ) Freeman in the order listed in his will:

+	20	i.	William[4] Freeman, will pr. 1802, Surry Co., NC; m. Sarah ____.[17] Resided Hertford 1760-70.[18] Bought land Surry

---

[15] David Leroy Corbitt, *The Formation of the North Carolina Counties, 1663-1943* (Raleigh: State Dept. of Archives and History, 1950);122-123.

[16] Chowan Co., NC. Original Wills. NC Archives. LDS Film 018476.

[17] Surry Co., NC. WB 3:48.

[18] Chowan Co., NC. DB K:133; O:331.

1778 from Samuel Freeman.[19] Issue: 10 children.

21   ii.   Jacob[4] Freeman, resided Hertford Co. 1771.[20] He is probably the Jacob who received a Grant in 1780 for 200 acres on Hogans Creek in Surry County and appears there on the 1790 census.

22   iii.   John[4] Freeman, resided Chowan County 1777.[21] No evidence has been found to identify him in later records.

+   23   iv.   Zilpah[4] Freeman, m. as his second wife Lewis Outlaw.[22]

+   24   v.   Tabitha[4] Freeman, m. Mr. Mansfield.[23]

+   25   vi.   Priciller[4] Freeman, m. William Hinton who d. test. Gates Co. 1 Jan 1806.[24] Issue: 4 children.

---

[19]Surry Co., NC. DB A:251. A connection of William to Chowan Co. is found in Surry Co. DB C:310-311 when John Garret, of Chowan, made a power of Attorney to his "trusty friend" William Freeman.

[20]Chowan Co., NC. DB R:69. Jacob Freeman, Hartford Co., to Robert Sumner.

[21]Chowan Co., NC. DB T:105. John Freeman to Richard Freeman.

[22]Gates Co., NC. DB 2:25. Benjamin C. Holtzclaw, "The Outlaw Family of Virginia and Other Southern States," in *Historical Southern Families*, v. 15, Mrs. John Bennett Boddie, ed. (Baltimore: Genealogical Publishing Co., 1971):54.

[23]Gates Co. records show a Thomas Mansfield who was executor of will of Garrett Davis. James Freman was witness. See Marilyn Poe Laird and Vivian Poe Jackson, *Gates County, NC, Court Minutes, 1779-1787* (Dolton, IL: Poe Publishers, n.d.):36. Chowan Co. Estate Files, NC Archives C.R. 024.508, shows a Zebulon Mansfield, died 1797, purchasers include William Freeman.

[24]Gates Co., NC. WB 1:228-230.

+	26	vii.	Richard[4] Freeman, adm. granted Feb 1787 Gates Co., NC. m.29 Sep 1778 Christian Hinton.[25]Issue: James.
	27	viii.	Cathrine[4] Freeman, no further data.
	28	ix.	Sara[4] Freeman, no further data.

6. WILLIAM[3] FREEMAN (William[2], John[1] Freeman) was born in Norfolk County, Virginia, about 1712 and died in Gates County, North Carolina, in 1781. At the time his father wrote his will, William was resident on the plantation willed him. In 1741 William received the first part of his inherited land from his brother John, and in 1744 John deeded him another 75 acres. He continued to live and do business in Chowan County, appearing on extant tithable lists from 1740-1756 and again from 1765-1778,[26] serving as grand juror, road overseer,[27] and in 1750 elected Vestryman of St. Paul's Parish.[28] In 1754 he appears on Chowan militia lists.[29]

On 3 August 1741, William purchased from John Wynne a 300 acre tract on "Quoykoson Swamp" in Bertie.[30] Just two weeks later, his brother John deeded to him 75 acres left him by

---

[25]Gates Co., NC. Estate Records. NC Archives, C.R. 041. 508.35-36; Jordan R. Dodd,ed., *N. Carolina Marriages Early to 1800* (Bountiful, UT: Precision Indexing, 1990):153.

[26]Chowan Co., NC. Tax lists, NC Archives C.R. 024.508;

[27]Weynette Parks Haun, *Chowan County North Carolina County Court Minutes (Court of Pleas & Quarter Sessions) 1730-1745* (Durham, By the author, 1983)v. 1:23,25-27, 58, 107, 129; Haun, *Chowan Minutes 1735-1738 : 1746-1748* v. 2:118.

[28]Fouts, *Vestry Minutes of St Paul's*: 105-107.

[29]Murtie June Clark, *Colonial Soldiers of the South, 1732-1774* (Baltimore: Genealogical Publishing Co., 1983):690.

[30]Bertie Co., NC. DB F:281.

his father's will. In 1744 John deeded William another 75 acres adjacent to the first parcel.[31]

While remaining a resident of Chowan County, William acquired several tracts in Bertie, apparently in order to provide plantations for his sons.[32] When Gates County was formed in 1779 it took in all of the Freeman land which had previously been in Chowan.

Starting in 1758, another William Freeman with wife Tabitha, of Norfolk Borough, bought several tracts in Bertie Co. That William finally made the move from Norfolk to Bertie County about 1775, and died there testate in 1782. Care must be taken not to confuse records of these two apparently unrelated families.[33] A discussion of that family appears in a later section on "Other Early Freeman Families."

In 1700 William Freeman bought 50 acres in newly formed Gates County from George Outlaw.[34] William wrote his will on 17 April 1781, proved in August Court of that year.[35] The will was witnessed by Lemuel (X) Taylor, Nathaniel Taylor and Christian (X) Outlaw. This latter name is interesting in that the wife of William Freeman has traditionally been identified as Christian Outlaw. However, Benjamin Holzclaw's research on the Outlaw family does not include mention of her.[36] Nonetheless, extant records indicate a very close relationship between William Freeman and the Outlaw family.

---

[31]Chowan Co., NC. DB A₁:70, 309. The will of William Freeman was "now mislaid or accidentally lost." The will must eventually have been located since the original is now on file at the North Carolina Archives.

[32]Bertie Co., NC. DB H:351; I:43; K:377.

[33]Bertie Co., NC. DB "I":114, 415; WB C:33. The widow Tabitha died in Warren Co., leaving a huge estate. Orange Co. probate records also have large files on the estate.

[34]Gates Co., NC. DB A:50.

[35]Gates Co., NC WB 1:20.

[36]Holtzclaw, "The Outlaw Family," *Historical Southern Families,* v. 15. The association between this Freeman family and the Outlaw family was very close and such a marriage would not be unlikely.

Issue of William and his wife Christian (Outlaw?) Freeman:

+ 29 i. John[4] Freeman, d. testate, Bertie Co., 1793; m.(1) bef. 1760 ____ dau. of Charles Rountree; m.(2) widow Sarah (Gordon) Norfleet who d. test. 1807 Bertie Co. Issue: 11 children.[37]

+ 30 ii. Joshua[4] Freeman, d. testate, Bertie Co., 1794; m. Mary ____. Issue: 8 children.

+ 31 iii. Moses[4] Freeman, b. by 1740; resided Bertie 1785; m. Courtna ____; Often called Moses, Sr., resided Bertie Co; older than his cousin Moses # 55.

+ 32 iv. King[4] Freeman, d. testate, Bertie Co., 1793; m. prob. bef. 1779 to Sarah (Perry) widow of William Rice. Daughter Christian m. Blake Baker.

+ 33 v. James[4] Freeman, inv. Gates Co. 1807; m(1) Selah ____; m(2) Mary Barber. Issue: By m(1) 4 children; by m(2) 2 children b. before marriage of parents.

+ 34 vi. William[4] Freeman, m. Sarah ____; Resided Gates Co.; Appears to be the William who d.test. Orange Co., NC. Issue: 8 children.[38]

+ 35 vii. Sarah[4] Freeman, m. Hardy Hayes/Haise who d. test. 1784, Bertie Co.; Issue: 7 children.

---

[37]Chowan Co., NC. Original Wills. Will of Charles Rountree names grandson Charles Freeman. This is the only Freeman with son Charles in this time period. John #29 is often called a "planter" in Bertie Co. records to distinguish him from John #11, a wheelwright or millwright,

[38]Orange Co., NC. WB D:43. William sold Gates Co. land 1792 and 1797 (5:30,34); bought in Orange Co. (DB 7:357-8) 1798. Polly (Freeman) Trotman a daughter named in will m. 27 Jan 1797 Gates Co. to Thomas Trotman. George oldest son m. in Gates 1807 Christian Hofler.

+	36	ix.	_____ m. Mr. Hinton; had son Reuben Hinton.
	37	x.	Susanna m. Mr. Spruel.[39]
+	38	xi.	[(A)mellisent?][4] Freeman, d. test. Bertie Co. 1822; m. Josiah Perry who d. test. 1820; Issue: 14 children.
	39	xii.	Mary[4] Freeman, m. Mr. Ward.[40]

7. THOMAS[3] FREEMAN (William[2], John[1] Freeman) born in Norfolk Co., Virginia, probably about 1715, since he was of age at the time of his father's death. His father left him the land "he now lives on in Indian Neck" and a negro named Emperour.

On 6 August 1737, a week before his father's will was probated, John and Tabitha Freeman sold to brother Thomas 100 acres in Catherine Creek Swamp which John had bought from the Indians in 1734.[41] In 1744 he sold 200 acres to his brother Richard which Thomas Freeman had bought of the Indians.[42]

Thomas is listed as the grantee of a 640 acre tract in Bertie which was actually purchased in 1733 by his father William. The deed, however, was not recorded in Bertie County until 13 August 1737, the same date as the probate of William's will. The tract was willed to Aaron and Samuel and seems never to have been in Thomas's possession.[43]

Thomas appears on the extant Chowan County Tithable lists from 1740 through 1754 except for the years 1748-1749 when

---

[39]Possible wife of Samuel Spruel/Sprewel or John Spruel who resided in Bertie Co.

[40]Weynette Parks Haun, *Bertie County, North Carolina, County Court Minutes (Court of Pleas & Quarter Sessions) 1788 thru 1792* (Durham: By the author, 1984):4. Mary Ward, widow of Philip Ward petitioned for dower in February 1788. A James Ward is also a very close associate of the Bertie County siblings of Mary Ward.

[41]Chowan Co., NC. DB W:358.

[42]Chowan Co., NC. DB A:308. No deed has been found from the Indians to Thomas Freeman.

[43]Bertie Co., NC. DB E:143.

he apparently moved across the Chowan River to Bertie County.[44] In 1748 Thomas Freeman, of Bertie County, carpenter, bought of his cousin John Freeman, Bertie, Wheelrwright, 150 acres on the Northern side of Barbeque Swamp. A year later he sold land on Barbeque Swamp to James Holly and another tract to John Reed.[45]

He returned to Chowan County and is listed as a private on the Muster Roll of Capt James Farlee's Company, 15 November 1754.[46] The last record found showing him a resident of Chowan is a deed dated 21 April 1757 when he sold to William Baglon 209 acres on west side of Barbecue Swamp in Bertie County.[47]

Thomas Freeman with son Thomas Freeman, Jr., appears on tax lists of Shoco District of Granville County in 1761 and 1762 near his younger brother Samuel who had moved there in 1752.[48] Thomas is listed an insolvent on the 1762 list. Granville deeds show no record of any land purchase by him, and there is no probate record there for him.

A Thomas Freeman received a patent for 400 acres in Bladen County in 1735[49]. Although no Thomas Freeman is listed in Bladen deed indexes, one Thomas appears on tax lists of 1763.[50]

The name of his wife has not been found nor has his further place of residence and death. The 1760 will of Jacob

---

[44]Chowan Co., NC. Tax Lists, NC State Archives C.R. 024.701.2

[45]Bertie Co., NC. DB G:226, 232.

[46]Clark, *Colonial Soldiers*:690.

[47]Bertie Co., NC. DB K:89.

[48]Granville Co., NC. Tax Lists, NC Archives, C.R. 044.701.19

[49]William L. Saunders, ed., *The Colonial Records of North Carolina*, v. 4 1734-1752 (Raleigh, P.M. Hale, 1886):56.

[50]Bladen Co., NC. Tax Lists, NC St. Archives.

Hinton names a daughter Mary Freeman. She may have been wife of Thomas or of one of his nephews.[51]

Issue of Thomas Freeman:

40   i.   Thomas[4] Freeman, born at least by 1745.[52]

41   ii.   Sarah[4] Freeman, born before 1756.[53]

Possible other children, names unknown.

8. RICHARD[3] FREEMAN (William[2], John[1] Freeman) may have been the first of the children born in North Carolina. He must have been born about 1718/9 since he appears on the list of Jurymen for Chowan County dated 25 February 1739/40 (old style).[54] In July 1743, John Freeman and wife Tabitha deeded to brother Richard for Love and affection in compliance with the missing will of William Freeman 150 acres on south side of Catterene Creek, "now in occupation of William Freeman." The first other business he is known to have transacted was purchase in 1744 of 100 acres on the South side of Catrine Creek from William Bly. This was land his father had purchased from Thomas Garrett and then sold to Michael Ward who sold to Bly. Shortly thereafter, Richard's brother Thomas sold him 200 acres which Thomas had bought of the Chowan Indians.[55]

---

[51]Chowan Co., NC. Original Wills, NC Archives.

[52]He must have been 16 by 1761 to have appeared on Granville Tax lists as a tithable of his father.

[53]N.C. Sec of State Original Wills, LDS film #1605224. Will of Thomas Falconar, written 31 Jan. 1756. He apparently had no children. He left, among other bequests, a Cow and Calf, two yearling "Herfirs" and three pounds two shillings to Sarah Freeman Daughter of Thomas Freeman.

[54]Saunders, *Colonial Records of North Carolina, v. 4, 1734-52*:516.

[55]Chowan Co., NC. DB A:312, 304, 308.

In 1752, Richard Freeman, like his brothers William and Thomas, purchased land on Barbeque Swamp in Bertie County.[56] In 1757 he purchased land from William Downing and in 1759 he purchased another 540 acres from Downing. He sold 50 acres in 1760 to William Steptoe and in 1761 sold a tract to David Phelps.[57]

Richard Freeman served as a private in the Chowan Militia in 1754 and sometime around 1760-61 was commissioned as Lieutenant in company of Capt. Timothy Walton.[58]

Richard married Ruth, surname unknown. Richard wrote his will 13 July 1761, proved in the July court of that year, naming his three children and granddaughter Christian Rountree and making his brother William Freeman executor.[59] Elisha Hunter, father in law of Richard's eldest son, was made guardian of the youngest son Demsey.[60] The widow Ruth married secondly to John Benbury and resided in Edenton. On 25 October 1774 she became a signer of the resolution made at the famous Edenton Tea Party, supporting the Provincial Deputies of North Carolina, not to drink any more tea, nor wear any more British cloth.[61] Ruth Benbury died testate in 1793, naming numerous grandchildren, including a granddaughter Ruth Freeman.[62]

Issue of Richard and Ruth (?) Freeman:

---

[56]Bertie Co., NC. DB G:495. John Wells to Richard Freeman of Chowan.

[57]Chowan Co., NC. DB K:238, 125, 82, 15.

[58]Clark, *Colonial Soldiers*:691, 804.

[59]Chowan Co., NC. NC Archives Chowan Original Wills.

[60]Chowan Co., NC. Guardian Bonds, 1762, NC Archives.

[61]Edenton Women's Club, *Historic Edenton*:4, 5.

[62]Chowan Co., NC. Original Wills. It is not known whether Ruth was daughter of Amos or of Demsey.

+	42	i.	Amos[4] Freeman, b. bef. 1740; m. Sarah Hunter; resided Hertford Co., probably died there.[63] Had daughter Ann Lay.[64]
+	43	iii.	Demsey[4] Freeman, b.c. 1746; m. Sarah; d. before 1786. Issue: Son Richard who moved to Orange Co.,NC, and daughter Mary.[65]
+	44	ii.	Mary[4] Freeman, m. bef 1761 to Thomas Rountree who d. test. in Gates Co., 1781. Issue: 7 children.[66]

10. SAMUEL[3] FREEMAN (William[2], John[1] Freeman) was born in Chowan County, probably about 1725.[67] In 1747 Samuel, probably just reaching his majority, was a resident of Bertie County.

12 June 1747. **John Freeman of Chowan Co to Samuel Freeman now of Bertie** in consideration of Naturall Love good will and Effection that I bear toward my beloved Brother...and more Especially out of the full Complying & fulfilling of the Last will & Testament of my **Father William Freeman, Late of Chowan County Deced.** Which sd will was proved & by the Secretary of clerk Mislaid or accidentally Lost...& is not to be found which said will did give & bequeath Six hundred & forty acres of Land to my two Brothers **Aaron & Samuel Freeman & Aaron now being deced before he was of Lawfull age & dieing intestate**

---

[63]Gates Co., NC. DB 4:112. Deed of Amos Freeman and Sarah, his wife, to Elisha Hunter, 1764.

[64]Gates Co., NC. Will of Elisha Hunter 1786. Names Granddaughter Ann Lay daughter of Amos Freeman.

[65]Chowan Co., DB Q:271, 272; R:56.

[66]Sandra L. Almasy, *Gates Co., NC Wills, Book 1, 1779-1807* (Rothschild, WI: 1984):15-16.

[67]Bertie County Court records show that another nearly contemporary Samuel Freeman was born 22 December 1730 to Ann Thomas and bound out in Bertie County at age 2 years to John Beverly and wife Margaret to learn husbandry. No further record has been found of him. Weynette Parks Haun, *Bertie County, North Carolina, County Court Minutes, 1724 thru 1739* (Durham, NC: By the author, n.d.):105.

his Inheritance Descending to me the said John Freeman beith the Eldest Brother & heir at Law...grant...640 acres in bertie Co. on Cypress Swamp adjacent to Wm Mauls, being a Patent formerly granted Henry Roads of Bertie...who conveyed to **William Freeman being the lawfull father of afsd John & Sam**[1] by deed dated 22 Sept 1733. Wit: Thos Walton, Thomas Rountree Jr., Thos Rountree Sr.   /s/ John Freeman[68]

Although Samuel remained a resident of Bertie for a short period, he traveled, apparently in company with Jethro Rountree, to Granville County and, on 2 February 1750, purchased from John Richards of Northampton Co. a 200 acre tract on the Peter Hill's Branch of Shocco Creek. The same day, Rountree purchased a nearby tract from Samuel Tarver.[69]

It must have been about this time that Samuel Freeman married, since his first child was born 11 September 1751. His wife was Elizabeth whose surname has traditionally been given as Alexander. A number of the male descendants of Samuel and Elizabeth bear the first or middle name Alexander. It has been stated that she was part of the Mecklenburg County family. No evidence has been found that Samuel was in the western part of North Carolina that early and the first Granville Grants to Alexanders in Anson Co, parent of Mecklenburg, were not surveyed until 1750. Much closer to Samuel's Bertie County residence was another large group of Alexanders who moved into Tyrrell County in the early 1750's.[70] A search of the extant Alexander wills in both counties prior to 1800 has failed to produce any connection to the Freeman family.

7 March 1752. Samuel Freeman, Bertie, carpenter, to Peter Evans, carpenter, for 25 £ current money of Virginia for 640 acres on Cypress Swamp adjacent to Coll William Maule.

---

[68]Bertie Co., NC. DB G:65.

[69]Zae Hargett Gwynn, *Abstracts of the Early Deeds of Granville County, North Carolina, 1746-1765* Rocky Mount, NC: Joseph W. Watson, 1974):27, 26.

[70]Margaret M. Hofmann, *The Granville District of North Carolina 1748-1763*, v.1 (Weldon, NC: Roanoke New Co., 1986):3; v.2 (1987):104.

Wit: Richard Brown, John Smith.[71]

Samuel must have moved soon after making this deed, since he appears on the tax list of Granville County for the year 1752 and succeeding years.[72] He appears on a muster roll as a private in the Granville County Militia in 1754.[73] In 1760 he added to his holdings by purchasing from Daniel Butts 237 acres adjacent to his previous holding.[74] His financial condition must have declined, since, in 1763, he is one of many on the list of insolvents.[75]

In 1764 Bute County was formed from the part of Granville in which Samuel lived.[76] During the next six years, Samuel engaged in the purchase and sale, with his wife Elizabeth, of over 850 additional acres. The sales of his last holdings in the county were made by Samuel Freeman, still listed as a resident "of Bute" in November and December of 1770.[77]

Also credited by some to Samuel Freeman #10 was the purchase on 15 July 1767 from William and Elizabeth Young of 52 acres on the North side of the Yadkin.[78] However, the Rowan Tax List for 1759 shows a John Freeman with a "Samuel Freeman and Jona." as a tithables, at a time when Samuel #10 was resident of Granville County. The 1778 list shows a Samuel Freeman,

---

[71] Bertie Co., NC DB H:146. Abstracted by the author. Although Samuel was married by this date, no relinquishment of Dower has been found.

[72] Granville Co., NC. Tax Lists, NC Archives 044.701.27.

[73] Clark, *Colonial Soldiers.*:725.

[74] Gwynn, *Deeds of Granville* :145.

[75] N. 71., *Supra.*

[76] Corbin, *Formation of NC Counties* :48-49. In 1779 Bute County became extinct when the area was divided into Franklin and Warren Counties.

[77] Bute Co., NC. DB A:211, DB 1:156, 236, 238, 381, 383, 448; DB 2:1; DB 3:152, 198.

[78] Rowan Co., NC. DB 6:453.

probably the same man as on the 1759 list, who may be the grantee of the deed from the Youngs.[79]

When Surry County was established from Rowan County in 1771, one of the first land transactions was a deed from Morgan Bryant to Samuel Freeman for 250 £ Virginia money for 417 acres of land at the mouth of Morgans Creek. A month later, Samuel Freeman purchased from Valentine Vanhouser 459 acres acres on the north side of the Yadkin River about two miles above the Tararat River at the mouth of Hogans Creek. Both had originally been part of Morgan Bryant's 1752 Granville grant.[80]

In 1774 Samuel Freeman was serving as Captain of Surry County Militia and became a member of the Commission of the Peace of Surry County.[81] Dissatisfaction of the colonists with the government in England grew, and in 1775 Samuel was appointed to the newly formed Committee of Safety for the County.[82] His involvement in government continued and in 1780 and 1781 he served in the North Carolina House of Commons.[83] Among his supporters were the Moravians at Bethabara who supported him, stating on 9 January 1781, "Mr. Samuel Freeman, one of the Assemblymen for our County, passed on his way thither; he was friendly, and promised to speak in our behalf there if it should be necessary."[84] That same month, following Ferguson's defeat at the Battle of King's Mountain, Freeman was appointed by the

---

[79]Mrs. Stahle Linn, Jr., C.G., *Abstracts of Wills and Estates Records of Rowan County, North Carolina, 1753-1805 and Tax lists of 1759 and 1778* (Salisbury, NC: By the Author, 1980):13, 138.

[80]Surry Co., NC. DB "A":5, 6.

[81].Clark, *Colonial Soldiers*:834; Walter Clark, ed. *State Records of NC* v. 23 (1904):994.

[82]William L. Saunders, ed. *The Colonial Records of North Carolina*, v. 10 (Raleigh: Josephus Daniels, 1890):228.

[83]Clark, *State Records* v. 19 (1901): 384, 388.

[84]Adelaide L. Fries, M.A., *Records of the Moravians in North Carolina* v. 4 (Raleigh, State Dept. of Archives and History, repr. 1968): 1529, 1666, 1716.

House of Commons as one of the Commissioners to collect, value and give receipts for arms captured in the battle.[85]

In 1778 Samuel sold 100 acres of his land to his nephew, William Freeman. He made love and affection deeds of land to his sons James and Joshua and sold land to others. At the time of his death, tax lists show him owning 367 acres and owning four blacks.[86] His will, written on 8 March 1796 and proved in May of that year, named his wife, Elizabeth, and five children. Also named is Nancy Huett, not identified as a relative, who received £15.[87] Many have believed her to be a daughter. However, a list was found in the Revolutionary Pension file of Jeremiah Early, husband of Samuel's daughter Rachel, which gives the names and birth dates of the five named by Samuel in his will as his children. That list does not include Nancy.[88] Samuel's grave is located near Siloam on a Knoll overlooking the Yadkin River Valley. A stone marker with bronze plaque erected by the Daughters of the American Revolution mark the site.

Issue of Samuel Freeman and his wife Elizabeth:

+ 45 i. Aaron[4] Freeman, b. 11 Sep 1751, Bertie Co.; resided Surry Co., m. Nancy Hawkins, "of Hillsboro". Issue: 9 children.[89]

---

[85] Clark, *State Records* v. 17 (1899): 748.

[86] Surry Co., NC. Tax Lists. NC Archives.

[87] Surry Co., NC. Original Wills. NC Archives.

[88] Rev. War Pension file of Jeremiah Early R319a p.0066. LDS Film #970,886; Brent H. Holcomb, *Surry County, North Carolina, Marriages, 1779-1868* (Baltimore: Genealogical Publishing Co., 1982):98 "Horn, Stephen & Nancy Hewett, 14 Nov. 1797; Abraham Stoe, bm [bondsman]; Jo White Linn, *Surry County, North Carolina, Will Abstracts, Vols. 1-3, 1771-1827* (Salisbury: by the author, 1974):43 "2:10a Deed of gift from Andrew Booth out of love & affection for Nancy Huitt £50 hard money after my death. 6 Dec. 1782. Wit: Samuel and Jacob Freeman, Revess. prvd by Andrew Booth. Rec. may Ct. 1783.

[89] Hester Bartlett Jackson, *The Heritage of Surry County, North Carolina, V. 1 - 1983* Winston-Salem: Surry Co. Genealogical Assn, 1983):188 (#239), 419, 639. The several articles in this volume relating to the Freeman family all continue the myth of Mayflower descent.

+ 46 ii. Joshua[4] Freeman, b. 14 April 1754, Granville Co.; d. Knox Co., TN betw. 4-22 Sept. 1832; m.(1) Lucy (traditionally King) m(2) Margaret. Issue: 5 children by m.(1), 1 child by m.(2).[90]

+ 47 iii. Rachel[4] Freeman, b. 7 Apr. 1755, Granville Co.; d. 11 Nov 1840, Surry Co.; m. 12 Nov 1791 Jeremiah Early. Issue: 5 children.[91]

+ 48 iv. James[4] Freeman, b. 10 Jan 1757, Granville Co.; d. test. Sept 1827, Blount Co., TN; m. Lucy ___ ; Issue from will: 6 children.[92]

+ 49 v. Nanny[4] Freeman, b. 13 Jan 1759, Granville Co.; d. TN; m. James Badget who d.test. Knox Co., TN.[93]

---

[90]Knox Co., TN. WB 5:162. Certified Copy of Bible Record of children of Joshua Freeman and wife Lucy in possession of author, original in 1925 in Possession of Mrs. Tennie Hardin, Colfax, Washington.

[91]Samuel Freeman left ½ his land to Rachel's children. Jeremiah Early Pension File. R.H. Early, The Family of Early (Lynchburg, VA: 1920):83.

[92]Blount Co., TN WB "1":248.

[93]Knox Co., TN. WB 5:356.

GENERATION THREE

DESCENDANTS OF JOHN² FREEMAN

11. JOHN³ FREEMAN (John², John¹ Freeman) born between 1711 and 1721,[1] was probably several years younger than his cousin, John #5, of Chowan Co., with whom he is often confused. There is no evidence that he transacted any business before 1739 when William Gray assigned to him rights to a patent of 350 acres in Bertie County[2] Shortly thereafter he sold a Chowan tract.

> 10 October 1740. **John Freeman** sold to James Sumner for £ 28 the 50 acres which...Goodwin conveyed by deed 14 July 1722 to **John Freeman and by his last will to his son Jno Freeman,** party to these presents. Wit: Jaˢ Costen, Jnº Gordon, Chaˢ Dent.
>
> /s/ John Freeman[3]

No relinquishment of dower accompanies this deed and so it is possible that John had not yet married by this date. This deed is followed by two others which make it clear that this John, a millwright, resided in Bertie and make him clearly distinguishable from his cousin John of Chowan County. These deeds are discussed in detail in the section on his father John # 3. John #3 left by his will a tract to his youngest son Matthew who died intestate. Matthew's two older brothers were half brothers but his sisters were full sisters and as such inherited Matthew's land. The sisters with their husbands sold the land in Matthew's estate to half brother John #11 who then sold to Patrick Hicks that land plus another 50 acres left undevised by his father's will to which John was entitled as heir at law of his father.[4]

John remained a prosperous, active resident of Bertie. He increased his land holdings on 7 April 1742 by purchase of 290

---

[1]See discussion of his age in section on his father John #3.

[2]Bertie Co., NC. DB F:126.

[3]Chowan Co., NC. DB C:98.

[4]Chowan Co., NC. DB E:167, 190. See also *Generation Two*, Note 30.

acres from Thomas Parker[5] and is identified in later deeds as a carpenter, millwright, wheelwright, blacksmith, and in 1767 as Captain. His cousin, John #29, also a resident of Bertie, was referred to in County records as a planter, sometimes called John, Jr., or John the younger.

Judging from the fact that John's son David first appears as a tithable on the tax lists of 1758 and is, therefore, presumably at least 16 old, John must have been married about 1740/41. His wife in 1758 was named Ann. The only evidence of her existence is the statement in the Revolutionary War widows pension application of Judith (Fleetwood) Freeman, widow of John's son Aaron who states that he was born January 30, 1758, in Bertie, son of John and Ann Freeman.[6] Judith Fleetwood was a Bertie resident whose family had a particularly close relationship with John Freeman #11 and who had every reason to know the identity of her mother-in-law. It was not until 24 Jan 1778 that John sold any land. He had apparently married a second time by this date, since the deed to James Fleetwood (probably a close relative of Judith) was joined in by wife Elizabeth.[7] On 9 February 1778, he and Elizabeth made love and affection deeds to sons Solomon, Elisha and Moses.[8] Elizabeth may have died soon after the making of these deeds since no wife is listed when he made deeds on 1 Feb 1780 to James Lain and gave a slave to his son Elisha.[9]

In 1783 John made a gift of a slave to Charlot Fleetwood, orphan of William Fleetwood, with directions that if the slave should have a child it should be given to Penelope Fleetwood, another orphan of William.[10]

---

[5]Bertie Co., NC. DB F:353.

[6]National Archives. Rev. War Pension file W.8833 service of Aaron Freeman.

[7]Bertie Co., NC. DB M:370. Elizabeth may have been the widow of William Fleetwood whose daughter m. 1777 to Aaron Freeman. This would account for the several deeds from John Freeman to Fleetwood children.

[8]Ibid: 371, 372.

[9]Ibid.: 480.

[10]Ibid:596.

John Freeman made his will on 7 Dec 1782 naming what must have been his third wife, Sarah, his daughter Elizabeth Baker and sons Solomon, Elisha, John, Moses and Aaron. The will was proved on 9 May 1785.[11] Sarah had been previously married twice, first to Henry Winborne and second to James? Rascoe. John's heirs believed that by a premarital agreement she had agreed to forego her dower right in exchange for the will giving to her all the property she owned by her previous marriages. Sarah, however, sued for her dower right and in August 1785, Aaron Freeman answered her petition laying out the reasons he felt she should not be allowed dower.[12] However, the court in the May term 1786:

> pr. Cur. Sci.fa to issue to Jas Wilson & Solomon Freeman Exors of John Freeman to shew Cause why a former Judgt. of the Court in favour of Sarah Freeman should not be complied with in order that the Sheriff may summon a Jury on the premisses to lay off the Dower of the said Sarah.[13]

Issue of John Freeman, probably all by m(1) to Ann _____ :

	50	i.	David[4] Freeman, b.c. 1742, d.c. 1765, Bertie Co. Tithable of father on tax lists of 1758, 1759, 1761 and on same list as father in 1764.[14] No known issue.
	51	ii.	Elizabeth[4] Freeman, m. James Baker.
+	52	iii.	Solomon[4] Freeman, b.c. 1743; d. test Bertie Co., 1788. m.(1) ____ Speight, m(2)

---

[11] Bertie Co., NC. Original Wills. NC State Archives.

[12] Bertie Co., NC. Estate Records NC State Archives, 010.504.1 box 29. Bertie Co. Estate files are undated and badly mixed. The file for John Freeman contains several estates including those of John #11 and John #29. but includes the answer of Aaron Freeman to petition of the widow Sarah. Another Freeman file has mixed papers most from 1816 but includes a petition from Sarah 1785 for Dower in estate of John on 360 acres.

[13] Haun, *Bertie Orders, 1781-1787* Bk 5:102.

[14] Died before his father. Last on tax lists 1764; Probably the one who witnessed deed 1760 from Paul Bunch to John Freeman (Bertie DB K:10); David should not be confused with his cousin, David #57, son of James who survived and d. testate in Mecklenburg Co. 1806.

Martha (neé Cherry) her 2nd; she d. test 1815 Bertie Co. 5 chn by m(1)[15]; 3 chn by m(2)[16]

+ 53 iv. Elisha[4] Freeman, b.c. 1749; d. test, Onslow Co., NC. proved 1793; m. Elizabeth ____. Issue 8 children.

 54 v. John[4] Freeman, b.c. 1751; d. post 1783. No further information.[17]

+ 55 vi. Moses[4] Freeman, b.c. 1754; d. post 1800. appears to have left Bertie Co.; m. Mary ____. Issue at least 2 children.[18]

+ 56 vii. Aaron[4] Freeman, b. 30 Jan 1758, Bertie Co; d. 26 Nov. 1821, Livingston Co., KY. m. 9 Sep. 1777, Judith Fleetwood. Issue: 13 children.[19]

12. **JAMES[3] FREEMAN,** (John[2], John[1] Freeman), still a minor in 1729 when his father wrote his will, was probably very close in age to his older brother John. It is not possible to say whether they were full brothers, but neither was a full brother to Matthew or their sisters. As a second son, James did not inherit land from

---

[15]Gates Co., NC. Guardian Bonds, 5 oldest children under guardianship of Joseph Speight. See his will Gates Co., 1792.

[16]Bertie Co., NC. Estate File of Solomon Freeman shows two youngest children and posthumous child under guardianship of Solomon Cherry.

[17]Bertie Co. records contain numerous records to John Freeman, it is not possible to distinguish between references to John #53, John #29, John s/o #29, John s/o Solomon and possible unknown issue of Thomas #8, John #22,

[18]Called Moses Freeman, Junior, in county records. Estate records: Moses Freeman files suit brought by Carney Freeman, Indorsee of Moses Freeman, against Moses Freeman, Junr. Moses Freeman, Junior, not to be found. 31 Nov. 1806. Haun, *Bertie Court Minutes*, v. 6:9 shows Moses Freeman making deeds for slaves to son Josiah and daughter Betsey on oath of Aaron Freeman.

[19]Rev. War Pension File W8833, Nat. Archives. Some claim Aaron who moved to Rowan Co and m. 1769 to Mary Bently was this man, but the pension record clearly identifies Aaron b. in Bertie as the man who m. Judith Fleetwood and died in Kentucky and Bertie Co. records show him as resident in Bertie until at least 1790.

his father but was willed a bed and "the furniture belonging to it," twelve pounds good pay of this government, a long gun, six pewter plates marked MT and three iron wedges.[20]

On 7 April 1742, James and his brother John each purchased a tract in Bertie County in St. John's Neck from Thomas Parker, "Turner." James paid Parker 33 £ for 166 acres "near the mouth of Tumbling at Gumbling Branch."[21] This apparently was his only land holding.

James was much less active in the affairs of the county than most of the other Freemans, never once appearing as a juror. He appears consistently on extant tax lists from 1755 through 1768. In 1758 his son David, apparently just reaching 16 yrs, first appears as his tithable. His son Michael appears as his tithable in 1764.[22] In 1772, a third son "William Freeman the orphin [sic] of James Freeman be aged about fourteen," was apprenticed to his cousin Solomon Freeman to learn the trade of a Carpenter.[23]

In October 1762, James, along with William Hardy, Adam Harrell and Jacob Lassitor was appointed to divide the Estate of his brother-in-law, John Davison, and in February of 1763 the above group exhibited the division in Court.[24]

In 1767 James deeded the 166 acre land tract "where James Freeman now dwells" to his brother John for 50 £. He appears on a tax list the following year but disappears after that, probably dying about this time, certainly dead when his son William was apprenticed in 1772. No will, probate or estate file has been found for him.

No evidence survives to identify his wife who had probably died before 1767 when he sold his land without a release of dower.

Known issue of James Freeman:

---

[20]Chowan Co., NC. NC Archives, Sec. State Wills. Will of John Freeman probated 1732.

[21]Bertie Co., NC. DB F:353.

[22]Bertie Co., NC. Tax Lists. NC Archives C.R.010.702.1.

[23]Haun, *Bertie Court Minutes,* v. 4:1.

[24]Haun, *Bertie Court Minutes,* v. 2:100; v. 3:3.

+	57	i.	David[4] Freeman, b.c. 1742; d. test. 1806 Mecklenburg Co., NC; m (1) Mary ___, m(2) Jean (Hayes?). Issue: 6 children.[25]
	58	ii.	Michael[4] Freeman, b.c. 1748; prob. disappears from Bertie tax lists after 1768. No other information.
+	59	iii.	William[4] Freeman, b. 26 Oct. 1759, Bertie Co.; d. 27 or 28 Jan 1838, Greene Co., MO; Rev. War. pension W-10042; m. Mary Bryan, 1786, Martin Co., NC. Issue: 9 children reached adulthood.

14. HANNAH[3] FREEMAN, (John[2], John[1] Freeman) was probably the oldest of the daughters of John Freeman. Named after her paternal grandmother, she is first of the daughters named in his will. She was a child of the last marriage, probably born about 1720 or later. Evidence of her marriage to John Smith is found in the 1747 deed which she and her sisters made to her half brother John of land inherited by them from their deceased full brother Mathew.[26]

No other mention is found of Hannah. The couple lived on the South side of Chinkapin Swamp near the mouth of Miery Branch on land they purchased in 1749 of brother-in-law John Davison (husband of Edith Freeman) and John Evans. John Freeman and brother-in-law Benjamin Hollyman also lived in the area. John Smith was named executor of the will of his brother-in-law John Davison written on 10 October 1768, proved March 1772 by John Smith and the widow Edey Davison.[27]

There are numerous John Smiths in Bertie County tax lists.[28] Wills and probate records were searched without success

[25] His original signature appears as witness on 1768 will of his uncle John Davison in Bertie Co and matches the signature on his original will. His oldest son, Michael, received a Rev. War Pension S-30426.

[26] Chowan Co., NC. DB E:167. See discussion in section on John #3.

[27] Bertie Co., NC. Original Will of John Davison. NC Archives C.R. 010.801.4; Haun, *Bertie Court Minutes* v. 4:1.

[28] Bertie Co., NC. Tax Lists. NC Archives. As many as five men of the name appear in some years.

in hopes of finding Hannah listed as a wife or widow. She may have predeceased her husband. John Smith died after the 1772 proving of Davison's will.

Will of one John Smith, written 10 March and proved May court 1783, was found which names a wife "Anna" and children Josiah, John, Sarah West, Henry, Mallacai, and Mary. Sons Josiah and John Smith were named executors. Ages of the older sons named in this will were estimated by their first appearance on tax lists as tithables of their father.[29] These sons appear to be of an appropriate age to be the children of Hannah (Freeman) Smith. However, witnesses to that will, Andrew Oliver, Thomas Rhoades and George Clements, were not resident of the area around Chinkapin where the subject John Smith and the rest of the family lived but were all resident of the area around Roquist, where another one of the John Smiths lived.

It appears that insufficient evidence exists to identify which John Smith was husband of Hannah or to identify any of their issue.

15. **EDIE[3] FREEMAN**, (John[2], John[1] Freeman)named in her father's will as "ED" has been omitted by most researchers as a daughter of John, probably either because reader's believed the letters to be a false start for the name Elizabeth which follows or because the initials were not recognized as an abbreviated spelling of Edie or Edith. She married sometime before September 1746 to John Davison of Bertie County with whom she was co-grantor with her sisters and their husbands to John Freeman of the land inherited by them from their brother Matthew.[30]

John Davison bought 600 acres from John Wynns on Chinkapin Swamp and was joint owner with Wynns of other land nearby.[31] In 1749 Wynns and John Davison sold 100 acres on

[29]Bertie Co., NC. Tax Lists.

[30]Chowan Co., NC. DB E:167.

[31]Mary Best Bell, *Colonial Bertie County, North Carolina, Deed Books A-II, 1720-1757*, (Easley, SC: Southern Historical Press, 2nd ed. 1977):179.

south side of Chinkapin Swamp at Myery Branch to his brother-in-law, John Smith.[32]

'This John Davison made his will 10 October 1768 naming his wife "Edey" and children William, John, Amos and Elizabeth. "My loving friend" John Smith was named coexector with the widow.[33] The will was witnessed by Humphrey Hardy and David Freeman (# 57) and proved 24 March 1772. Edey Davison and John Smith presented the will in court.[34] The will reserved the plantation "whereon 1 now live," negroes, stock and household furniture to the Edey during her widowhood and after that the land was to be equally divided between the three sons, Amos to receive the mansion house. On 3 May 1796 survey was made to divide the land, 496 acres going to John who had purchased William's share and 248 acres to Amos. This division was probably triggered by the death of their mother.

Issue of John and Edie (Freeman) Davison:

60	i.	William[4] Davison, b.c. 1747, Bertie Co.[35] No further information.
61	ii.	John[4] Davison, b.c. 1748, Bertie Co; Died after 3 May 1796. No further information.[36]
62	iii.	Amos[4] Davison, b.c. 1756, Bertie Co; Died after 3 May 1796. No further information.[37]

---

[32]*Ibid:203.*

[33]Bertie Co., NC. Original Wills. NC Archives 10.801.4

[34]Haun, *Bertie Court Minutes,* v. 4:1.

[35]Bertie Co., NC. Tax List. NC Archives. First appearance of William as tithable of father John Davison was 1763.

[36]*Ibid.* First appearance as tithable with father 1764.

[37]*Ibid.* Amos appears as a tithable of his mother in 1772 following his father's death. In 1775 he appears in his own right.

63   iv.   Elizabeth[4] Davison. No further
information.[38]

16. ELIZABETH[3] FREEMAN, (John[2], John[1] Freeman) was the last of the daughters named in her father's will. She married before 1746 to Benjamin Hollaman and with him was one of the cograntors with her sisters and their husbands of the estate of her full brother Matthew to her half brother John.[39]

Hollaman had land on Loosing (Luesin) Swamp and on Chinkapin Creek adjacent to John Smith.[40] He died before 10 February 1752 when an inventory of his estate was filed by the widow Elizabeth. On 3 August 1753, a division of the estate was made to "John Hollaman son of Binj[n] Holliman"; to William Hollaman son of Binj[n] Hollaman; to Marey Hollaman daughter to Binj[n] Hollaman by James Droughan, John Sovell, and John Smith. Edward Outlaw was named guardian to the three orphans with John Freeman and Ralph Outlaw his securities.[41] Nothing more is known of the widow.

Issue of Benjamin and Elizabeth (Freeman) Hollamon:

64   i.   John[4] Hollaman, no further data.

65   ii.   William[4] Hollaman, no further data.

66   iii.   Mary[4] Hollaman, no further data.

---

[38] One Elizabeth Davison m. 16 Sept 1779 to Absolom Knott. Since there are other Davison families in the area, further research would be required to determine if the Elizabeth, daughter of John and Edey was the one who m. Knott.

[39] Chowan Co., NC. DB E:167.

[40] Bell, *Bertie Co. Deeds*:200 (DB F:563), 216 (G:193).

[41] Bertie Co., NC. Estate Records. NC Archives C.R. 10.504.1.44; The Inventory bears the original mark of John Smith.

Will of Thomas Freeman, Jr., #17, Norfolk Co., Virginia WB 1:74.

GENERATION THREE

DESCENDANTS OF THOMAS[2] FREEMAN

17. THOMAS[4] FREEMAN (Thomas[2], John[1] Freeman) first appeared as a tithable of his father in 1733 and so was probably born circa 1717, a son of the first marriage. In 1736 he was a tithable of Thomas Cottel, Jr. The first extant list on which he was listed in his own right was 1750 and he continues to be listed until 1761. He shows no other male tithables on any extant list.[1]

He seems not to have owned property in his own right.[2] His father, Thomas #4, probably intended that Thomas, as heir at law, would inherit the 50 acres which William #2 deeded to Thomas #4 in 1711. When Thomas #17 wrote his will, proved at January Court 1762, he mentions no wife and was probably a widower.

> In the Name of God, Amen. I Tho[s] Freeman of Norfolk being in my senses and Memory and gives God thanks for it, do make this my last Will and testament in manner and form following. I give unto my Son Samuel Freeman all my moveable Estate and crop that we have made together, only five shillings apiece to the rest of my Children and I leave my Son Sam[l] Freeman my whole Executor by my last Will and Testament sd Witness my hand and Seal the 29th day of November 1761.

James Jolleff	his
Jno (X) Wesson	Thos Freeman and seal
Wm (X) Hobgood	mark[3]

Two records in Norfolk refer to a Thomas Freeman with wife Sarah. In November 1756, one Thomas Freeman and Sarah his wife were adjudged guilty in a suit for slander brought by Benjamin Johnson and Mary his wife. A month after the proving of Thomas's will, a petition (of unspecified subject matter) filed

---

[1]Wingo, *Norfolk Co., Tithables, 1730-1750*:91, 140, 184. Lists for 1737-1749 are missing.

[2]Norfolk Co., VA. Deed Index shows no deeds to or from him and his will mentions no devise of land.

[3]Norfolk Co., VA. WB 1:74.

by a Sarah Freeman was rejected by the county court.[4] These references could be to Thomas, Sr, and his second wife, but the possibility exists that both Thomas, Jr., may also have had a wife named Sarah.

Thomas Freeman's brother John had died intestate in 1761. In 1765 his widow, Martha, was taxed for a Thomas Freeman. It is unlikely that this Thomas was her son, since John appears to have been only about 17 at the time of this Thomas's birth. It seems more probable that this Thomas was one of the younger children mentioned but unnamed in the will of Thomas # 17.

Issue of Thomas Freeman:

67	i.	Samuel[4] Freeman, No further mention of him found in the records.[5]
68	ii.	Probably Thomas[4] Freeman, tithable in 1765 of Martha Freeman. Taxed in 1767, 1768, 1770. Witnessed will of John Ellis 1774.[6]

Others. Referred to but unnamed in will of father.[7]

18. JOHN³ FREEMAN (Thomas², John¹ Freeman) must have been a child of Thomas's second marriage. He first appears as a tithable of his father on the tithable lists in 1750, indicating a birth date about 1734. In 1749 Thomas Freeman made a deed to John and his brother Samuel of the 100 acres of land which Thomas and his first wife, Sarah, had purchased of Edward Wood and Mary his wife and John Wood and Margett his wife, the deed was to be effective on the death of their father Thomas. In May of 1756 the

---

[4]Norfolk Co., VA. COB 1755-59:97; COB 1759-63:150 18 Feb 1762.

[5]One Samuel died in Norfolk in 1784. That was probably Samuel #19 who became possessor of land once in possession of Thomas Freeman, Sr. This Samuel probably either died soon after his father, or left the county.

[6]Wingo, *Tithables, 1751-1765*. Norfolk Co., VA. WB ll:fol 44.

[7]Later tithable lists show none who might be his sons.

Churchwardens bound Rachael Johnson to John Freeman and in 1758 Hanah Cottle was also bound to him.[8]

John Freeman married sometime before 1758 to Martha.[9] She may have been a Wingate step sister, daughter of Samuel and Sarah. On 17 September 1761, administration of John Freeman's estate was granted to Martha Freeman and recorded in the Norfolk Order Book.[10] Robert Bower, James Jollif, John Winget and John Jollif were ordered to appraise the estate. Martha (Patsey) was taxed for Philip Cottle in 1764 and for a Thomas Freeman and 150 acres of land in 1765. If he was a son of John and Martha, he must have been born c. 1749/50 to be 16 years old and a tithable, but John Freeman would appear to have been too only about 17 years old by that date, not impossibly young to father a child, but more likely this Thomas was a younger child of Thomas # 17, placed with an aunt as farm help. Possibly Martha had the care of the orphans of Thomas # 17. Martha continued to appear on Norfolk tax lists with 50 acres of land through 1771. Lists are missing for 1772 through 1780. A "Patsy" Freeman appeared with 50 acres on Land tax lists in 1787 through 1790.[11]

Issue of John and Martha (Wingate?) Freeman:

69   i.   William[4] Freeman, prob. b.c. 1759; d. before 18 Oct. 1784.[12]

70   ii.   Elizabeth[4] Freeman, b.c. 1761; m. bef. 1784 to James Taylor.

---

[8]*Ibid* :53, 207.

[9]She signed as Martha Freeman when witnessing the will of Elizabeth Cottle.

[10]Norfolk Co., VA. COB 1759-1763:120. This administration is not listed in Torrence's, *Virginia wills and Administrations, 1632-1800*.

[11]Wingo, Letter to author giving data in Norfolk Tithables v. 3. Norfolk land and personal property tax lists at VA State Archives.

[12]Norfolk Co., VA. DB 28:162. On that date, Martha Freeman, James Taylor and Elizabeth his wife sold 4 acres to Willis Winget which descended to the said Elizabeth Taylor by the death of her brother William Freeman as being his heir at law.

19. SAMUEL³ FREEMAN, (Thomas², John¹ Freeman) must have been the youngest of the three sons, but must have been quite close in age to his brother John, since he appears with his brother John as a tithable of their father in 1750.[13] In 1758 Catherine Cottle, orphan of Thomas and Elizabeth Cottle was bound to him by the Churchwardens of Elizabeth River Parish.[14] Samuel first appears on his own in the tithable lists in 1759.[15]

In 1763, Samuel was listed with 50 acres of land.[16] Deed indexes do not show him purchasing any land, nor had he inherited it from his father who was still living. In 1767 he had 100 acres which may indicate that he had received his inheritance but subsequent years listed him with 50.[17] Abstracts of Norfolk wills do not show him as devisee in any estate.[18] Perhaps he had received this tract through marriage. His father Thomas had deeded him and his brother John 100 acres to divide on Thomas's death.[19] John died before their father and it is probable that John's share eventually went to his widow Martha and the children who were taxed for 50 acres, leaving 50 acres for Samuel.[20]

Norfolk Burrough was a thriving port city until its destruction in January 1776 by Lord Dunmore. While the family did not live in the town itself, the destruction and the skirmishes in the county must have had a frightening and destructive effect on life in the area. No account survives of the activities of the family during these years.

---

[13]Wingo, *Norfolk Tithables, 1730-50*:206.

[14]Norfolk Co., VA. COB 1755-59:208.

[15]Wingo, *Norfolk Tithables, 1751-65*:189, 214.

[16]*Ibid*:189.

[17]N. 10, *supra*.

[18]Elizabeth B. Wingo, *Norfolk County, Virginia, Will Book 1, 1755-1772*; Pamela McVey, *Norfolk County Will Book II, 1772-1788 (1986)*.

[19]Norfolk Co., VA. DB 14:155.

[20]Wingo, *Norfolk Tithables* v. 2:

Samuel apparently married about 1762 since his oldest son George must have been 21 when taxed in his own right in 1784.[21] He died intestate before 31 May 1783. Willis Winget was Administrator of his estate.[22] A Judith or Juda with 50 acres, presumably Samuel's widow, shows on tax lists through at least 1809.[23] In 1783, her son George appears as her tithable and in 1785 Samuel, presumably her son, appears with her.[24]

Issue of Samuel and Judith ( ) Freeman:

71	i.	George[4] Freeman, b.c. 1763; m. 2 Jan. 1790, Mary Pullen.[25]
72	ii.	Samuel[4] Freeman, b.c. 1768; No more data.
73	iii.	Patience[4] Freeman, b.c. 1771; m. bond 12 Mar 1792, Hilary Ethridge.[26]

[21]N. 10, *supra*.

[22]Norfolk Co., VA. Appraisals and Sales, Bk 2:14, 31 May 1783; Audits BK 1:186, Dec. 1784.

[23]VA State Archives, Land Tax Lists.

[24]*Ibid*.

[25]Elizabeth B. Wingo, *Marriages of Norfolk County, Virginia, 1706-1792*, v. 1 (Norfolk: by the author, 1761):25.

[26]Wingo, *Norfolk Marriages*:22 " Bond March 12, 1792 Patience Freeman, orphan of Samuel Freeman"; Dr. Benjamin C. Holtzclaw, "Ethridge Genealogy" in Boddie, *Historical Southern Families* v. 16:82.

In the name of god amen I John Freeman Sen[r] being
sick and weak and the memb[er] that it is appointed for
all persons once to die do take this Opportunity to dispose
of such worldly good as I am possessed with in Manner and form
following but first I Recommend my Soul to God that gave
it when he shall call for it and my Body to be decently Buryed
after the discretion of my Executors not doubting a joyfull Resur-
rection

After all Just debts being paid I give to my Son william Freeman five shilling More then he hath allready Rec[d] I give to my
Son Jacob freeman five shilling proc with what he hath allredy Rec[d]
I give to my Son John freeman five shilling proc and also the dett
owed of he[r] I give to my daughter Zilpah outlaw five shilling
proc with what she hath Rec[d] allredy I Give to my daughter Tabitha
outlaw five shilling proc with what she hath Rec[d] I Give to my
daughter prisciller hinston five shillings proc with what she
hath already I give to my Son Rich[a]rd freeman one bed bolster
and pair of Sheets to him and his heirs forever I Give to my daughter Pa Berice freeman one bed and bolster and pair sheets to
Sarah hinson forever I Give and bequeath to my Loving wife tobitha
all the Remainder of my goods Chattles Lands or tenements
to be freely and undisturbedly possessed by her During her Natural
Life and after her death my will is that what shall Remain
after her death should be Equally be devided between my
Son Richard my daughter Cathirine and my daughter
Sarah and Lastly I do ordain and appoint my Son Rich
ard freeman and Richard Garrett Executors to this my Last
will and testament Confirming this to be my Last will
will as witness my hand and Seal this thirtienth day of
April 1776 and do pronounce and declare this to be my
Last will and testament   John Freeman [seal]

In presence of
Tho[s] Garret Sen[r]

Jno Garrett Jun[r]

Joel Boyett
mark

GENERATION FOUR

DESCENDANTS OF JOHN FREEMAN # 5.

20. WILLIAM[4] FREEMAN (John[3], William[2], John[1] Freeman) was probably born circa 1738 in Chowan County.[1] He is probably the William Freeman, Jr, who appears on the Chowan Militia Roll of 1754.[2]

In 1760 William Freeman, "of Hertford County" bought 50 acres of land in Chowan County from Hardy Griffin. Witnesses were Everet Garret, John Freeman (either William's father or brother) and William's brother Jacob.[3] In 1770 William sold his Chowan County land, now totaling 150 acres to his brother John Freeman, Junior, of Chowan. His father, John, Sr., was one of the witnesses to the deed.[4]

In 1777 his father, John, died in Chowan County, leaving William only 5 shillings more than he had already received.[5] William soon moved to Surry County where in 1778 he purchased 100 acres from his uncle, Samuel Freeman.[6] In 1782 he received a North Carolina Patent for 167 acres on the Yadkin River, below

---

[1]Some have believed that William Freeman, son of John # 5, was the man who resided in Norfolk and died in Bertie in 1781 who m. Tabitha Wilson. For data on that William see section, "Other Freemans of North Carolina." William # 20 was resident in Chowan and Hertford in the 1760's while the other was in Norfolk.

[2]Murtie June Clark, *Colonial Soldiers of the South, 1732-1774* (Baltimore: Genealogical Publishing Co., 1983:692.

[3]Chowan Co., NC. DB K:133.

[4]Chowan Co., NC. DB O:331. Hertford records are destroyed for this period.

[5]Chowan Co., NC. Original Wills.

[6]Surry Co., NC. DB A:251. Surry Co. tradition erroneously identifies William as brother of Samuel. Deeds of Chowan Co. clearly show that William, brother of Samuel, retained his property in Chowan (the portion which later became Gates Co.) and died in Gates Co. in 1781. See Generation Three, #6 William Freeman.

the mouth of the Tarrarat River.[7] Ties to Chowan County must have remained strong, as the following year John Garret of Chowan County made a Power of Attorney to his "Trusty Friend" William Freeman to collect moneys due Garret.[8]

A William Freeman, probably this man, received a Revolutionary War voucher #3959 for a public claim for £5.0.0, signed by the Auditors of Salisbury District 26, August 1783.[9]

Filed among the Bastardy Bonds of Surry County is the following:

> Know all men by these Presents that we Wm Freeman & Joseph Williams of the County of Surry are held and firmly bound unto Wm Meredith Sheriff of said County in the Just and full sum of fifty pounds [illeg.] Currancy of Said State for payment of which we bind outselves Our Heirs Assignes &c firmly by these Presents Sealed with Our Seale & datd this 10th day of Oct[r] 1782.
>
> ___The Condition of the Above Obligation is such that if the above bound Wm Freeman do make his personal Appearance at the next Court held for this County on the Second Munday in Nov[r] Next than & there to answer the Grand Jury to abide the Judgm[t] of said Court that then the above Obligation to be Void Else to Remain in force & virtue --
> Test - Sign[d] & Acknowledg[d] by us - Wm Freeman Seal
> [blank] Seal[10]

No further information has been found to indicate the resolution of this case, but it appears clear that William may have fathered an illegitimate child.

William wrote his will 25 March 1802, probated in May Session of the Surry Court.[11]

---

[7]Surry Co., NC DB B:51.

[8]Surry Co., NC. DB C:310.

[9]NC State Archives, *Revolutionary War Pay Vouchers and Certificates.*

[10]Surry Co., NC. Bastardy Bonds & Records, 1782-1829. NC State Archives C.R. 092.101.1. This document is obviously a copy. Text and signature is in the same hand.

[11]Surry Co., NC WB 3:48.

He left his wife Sarah the use of two negros for her lifetime, household furniture and use of his plantation. To each of his sons Josiah and William and his daughters Kiddy Mitchel and Penelope Hains he left a negro. His son Tyre was to inherit the negros and all his lands and plantation where "I now live", also a still and all necessary utensils. The remaining part of his estate he left to be equally divided between Noah, John, Richard and David &c. No relationship is mentioned to these last four, but they were probably also his children.

This family seems to have left fewer descendants in Surry County than that of his uncle, Samuel Freeman. Census records show only sons Tyre and David as residents and no mention of the family has been found in *The Heritage of Surry County, North Carolina*.[12]

Josiah, the first named son, was probably the eldest. In 1783 he bought 320 acres on the N. side of the Yadkin adjacent to Samuel Freeman & Mears from Frederick Greene who had given a power of attorney to Samuel Freeman to sell the land.[13]

The identity of William's wife Sarah is not known, nor is it known whether this was his only marriage.

The children of William Freeman:

74	i.	Josiah[5] Freeman, b.c. 1762 probably in Hertford Co., NC. Bought 320 acres in Surry Co. He does not appear on the 1790 or 1800 Surry Co. census.[14] Received Revolutionary War Voucher #2296.
75	ii.	Kiddy[5] (Christian?) Freeman, m. ____ Mitchell. No more data.
76	iii.	William[5] Freeman, no more information.

[12] Surry County Genealogical Society, *The Heritage of Surry County, North Carolina, North Carolina* v.1 (Winston-Salem: Hunter Publishing Co., 1983).

[13] Surry Co., NC DB C:46, 47.

[14] *Ibid.*

77	iv.	Polly[5] Freeman, no more data.
78	v.	Penelope[5] Freeman, m. ____ Haines.
79	vi.	Manoah (Noah)[5] Freeman, m. 1 Jan 1790, Surry Co., Nancy Brown.
80	vii.	John[5] Freeman, may be the John who m. 9 Aug 1796, Surry Co., Elizabeth Isbell.[15]
+ 81	viii	Richard[5] Freeman, b.c. 1770/74; may be one who d.t. 18 January 1841, Franklin Co., GA; m.1797 Oglethorpe Co., GA, Elizabeth Haggard.
82	ix.	David[5] Freeman, b.c. 1781; Probably the David on the 1820 - 1850 Surry Co., census. Age 69 in 1850.[16]
83	x.	Tyre[5] Freeman, b.c. 1790-1800, probably the youngest since he inherited the home plantation; m. 8 Mar 1808, Surry Co., to Elizabeth Stoe. In 1830 Surry Co. census.[17]

23. ZILPAH[4] FREEMAN (John[3], William[2], John[1] Freeman) became the second wife of Lewis Outlaw. They resided in Gates County. in 1788 Lewis deeded to his son James all of his land and slaves, to be his after the death of his parents.[18] Lewis had a daughter Ann by his first marriage to a daughter of John Rice of Chowan County. Lewis was much older than Zilpah, probably having been born c. 1729.[19]

---

[15]Brent H. Holcomb, *Marriages of Surry County, North Carolina, 1779-1868* (Baltimore: Genealogical Publishing Co., 1982):70.

[16]1850 Census, Surry Co., NC, p.345.

[17]1830 Census. Surry Co., NC, p.123.

[18]Gates Co., DB 2:25.

[19]Benjamin C. Holtzclaw, "The Outlaw Family of Virginia and Other Southern States," in *Historical Southern Families*, v. 16, Mrs. John Bennett Boddie, ed. (Baltimore: Genealogical Publishing Co., 1971):54.

| 84 | i. | James[5] OUTLAW. |

24. TABITHA[4] FREEMAN (John[3], William[2], John[1] Freeman) married a Mr. Mansfield. He was probably the Zebulon Mansfield who died intestate in Chowan Co in 1797. Estate papers show no widow.[20] Ophans were:

85	i.	Kader[5] MANSFIELD.
86	ii.	Ruth Celia[5] MANSFIELD.
87	iii.	Docter[5] MANSFIELD.
88	iv.	John[5] MANSFIELD.
89	v.	Mary[5] MANSFIELD.
90	vi.	Miles[5] MANSFIELD.
91	vii	Barnabas[5] MANSFIELD.

25. PRECILLER[4] FREEMAN (John[3], William[2], John[1] Freeman) was the wife of William Hinton of Gates County. He left a will, probated in 1806, in Gates County. In it he named his wife, Presciller, and four children.[21]

92	i.	Elizabeth[5] HINTON, m. ___ Forster
93	ii.	Sally[5] HINTON
94	iii.	William[5] HINTON
95	IV.	John[5] HINTON

---

[20]Chowan Co., NC. Estate Records. NC State Archives C.R. 0024.508.

[21]Gates Co., NC WB 1:228-30.

69

26. RICHARD⁴ FREEMAN (John³, William², John¹ Freeman) was apparently the youngest of the sons of John Freeman, probably born about 1750-55. He married on 9 April 1778 in Chowan County to Christian Hinton.[22] Apparently his land fell within the boundaries of Gates County, formed in 1779. He appears on tax lists of Gates, through 1786, with 100 acres of land, one white and one black poll, through 1786.

One Richard Freeman appears in the Halifax District military records. He died by 1784 while this Richard appears to have survived until about 1787.

Administration was granted on Richard's estate in February 1787. Kedar Hinton was appointed guardian for Richard's orphan, James Freeman. Another James Freeman, probably #33, was security for Hinton. Later a William Berryman was guardian for James, the orphan.[23] An audit of the account of the Estate of James Freeman decd, a minor orphan of Richard Freeman was made by an order of the court in February 1801.

Christian (Hinton) Freeman, the widow, may be the one who married on 28 November 1787 to Robert Taylor who signed the bond with a mark.[24] Jonas Hinton was bondsman. Taylor did not live long, He made a will 26 October 1790 which he signed with a mark. He names his wife Christian and several children, some adults, including a daughter Sarah Freeman. Executors were two sons-in-law and James Freeman. It was probated in May Court of 1792.[25]

Issue of Richard and Christian (Hinton) Freeman:

> 96   i.   James⁵ Freeman, b. bef. 1787; d. before 1801, a minor.

---

[22]Liahnona Research, Inc., comp., Jordan R. Dodd, ed., *N. Carolina Marriages* (Bountiful, UT: Precision Indexing Publishers, 1990):154.

[23]Gates Co. Estate Records, NC State Archives C.R. 041.508.35. File of Richard Freeman, 1788.

[24]Genealogical Society of Utah, *Gates County, North Carolina, Marriage Bonds* (Salt Lake City: n.p., 1943):179.

[25]Almasy, *Gates Co., Will Book 1*: 88-89.

GENERATION FOUR

DESCENDANTS OF WILLIAM FREEMAN #6.

29. JOHN[4] FREEMAN (William[3], William[2], John[1] Freeman) must have been born in Chowan County circa 1735. He married, first, sometime before 1760 to a daughter of Charles Rountree, who died in 1760, naming in his will a grandson, Charles Freeman.[1] John married a second time to Sarah (Gordon) widow of Abraham Norfleet.[2]

John, a planter, lived in Bertie County. He first appears on the 1757 tax list taken by Ralph Outlaw.[3] John is sometimes designated in records as John Freeman, Jr, to avoid confusion with his uncle, Capt. John Freeman # 11, a millwright, or wheelright. In August 1763 his father, William Freeman, yeoman of Chowan Co. deeded to John Freeman planter of Bertie a tract joining Swamp Branch adjoining John Wynns. The deed was witnessed by Moses and Aaron Freeman.[4] In November of the same year John Freeman, Junior, purchased for £20 a tract of 100 acres on Loosing Swamp from Benjamin Warrin, with Joshua Freeman, William Outlaw and Thomas Ward as witnesses.[5] In 1767 "Young John Freeman the son of William" purchased from John Campbell for £64 a tract of 640 acres between "Barbique and Quoicison Swamps."[6] In August of 1764 Joshua Freeman, Mathew Hubbard, John Freeman, John Rainer, Edward Outlaw, and John Outlaw

---

[1] Chowan Co., NC Original Wills. Will of Charles Rountree. This is the only Freeman in this time period with a son Charles.

[2] Bertie Co., NC. WB F:55; Bertie Co., NC. Original Will of Sarah Freeman, NC State Archives 010.801. Will of Sarah Freeman (probated Nov. 1807) names her children Benjamin and Isaac Norfleet and Mary, John and Elizabeth Freeman. The daughter, Mary, was by Sarah's marriage to Mr. Norfleet. Mary Norfleet married her step brother, Jeremiah Freeman on 2 Oct 1792. See also N. 20, *Infra*. gives data on Norfleet family gives Sarah's maiden name.

[3] Bertie Co., NC. Tax Lists. NC State Archives C.R. 010.702.1

[4] Bertie Co., NC. DB K:377. Aaron cannot be #45 nor #56 who were both too young to witness. Perhaps John #5 or William #6 had a son Aaron who predeceased his father.

[5] Bertie Co., NC. DB K:358.

[6] Bertie Co., NC. DB L2:159.

John Freeman, John Rainer, Edward Outlaw, and John Outlaw were assigned to work on "Quioccoson Road" in the District of Thomas Outlaw.[7] Finally in 1784 he purchased from Josiah Outlaw 120 acres on West side of of "Quyokoson swamp".[8]

During the Revolutionary War, John Freeman "Quiocheson" submitted a claim for to the government for £291. The claim was allowed but, unfortunately, no evidence remains to help determine the nature of the claim.

N° 196. . . £291
State of North Carolina
Edenton District Board of Auditors March 24th 1781
There may certify that John Freeman (Quiocheson) claims being exhibited were allowed _[hole]_ hundred and Ninety _[hole]_unds Currency.
Test   Will[m] Righton
Ja[s] Webb Jun[r] Secty   Edw[d] Everigin[9]

John's will was proved in the November Term 1793.[10] He left a tract of land to each of his sons by his first marriage: Charles, Hardy, Jeremiah, Josiah. To his daughters by his first marriage: Rachel Outlaw, Leach Lurry (Leah Leary), Melicant Perry, Christian Norfleet, Deliah Ward, he left to each a negro and what they had already received. To his son John and daughter Elizabeth he left four negros, 2/3 of his stock and household furniture and personal estate after death or widowhood of his wife, Sarah, to be equally divided between them. His children Charles, Rachel Outlaw, Leach Lurry, Melicant Perry and Christian Norfleet and Deliah Ward to equally divide the residue of his negros that he had not mentioned. Executors were his brother Joshua Freeman, son Charles, son Hardy and Friend Timothy Walton.

---

[7]Haun, *Bertie Minutes, 1763-1771*, v. 3:677.

[8]Bertie Co., NC. DB M:648.

[9]NC State Archives, *Revolutionary War Pay Vouchers and Certificates.* Certificates were cancelled by punching several holes in them. Often the holes obscure data on the certificate.

[10]Bertie Co., NC. WB D:228.

Issue of John Freeman by his wife _____ Rountree.[11]

97	i.	Charles[5] Freeman, born before 7 Oct 1760.[12] First appears as a tithable of John Freeman, Esq. in 1775.[13] In May 1784, he was appointed a patroller in Capt. Watford's District.[14] He appears in the Bertie 1790 Census with 2 white males under 16 and 5 females. No will or estate papers found.
98	ii.	Hardy[5] Freeman, b. 1755-1774.[15] Married 4 Apr 1796 to Senith Hunter.[16] Had a Revolutionary War Claim.[17]
+ 99	iii.	Jeremiah[5] Freeman, b. 1755-1774.[18] Married 2 Oct 1792 to Mary Norfleet,[19] daughter of his step mother, Sarah (Gordon) and her first husband, Abraham Norfleet.[20] Will probated Bertie Co. in 1810.[21] Names wife Mary and children:

---

[11]That Charles was by the first wife, _____ Rountree, is certain. It is probable, but not certain, that all but the two youngest children were also by that marriage.

[12]N. 1, _supra._

[13]Bertie Co., Tax List, 1775. NC State Archives 010.702.1.

[14]Haun, _Bertie Minutes, 1781-1787_ v. 5:57.

[15]1800 Census, Bertie Co., NC:44.

[16]Liahona Research, Inc. _NC Marriages_:153.

[17]NC State Archives. Treasurer and Comptroller Records- Military Papers, Vols. 40-66, Index to Revolutionary Army Accounts, Vol I-XII [vol. 55-66]. Vol. VI:31 folio 3. Revolutionary Pay Vouchers and Certificate # 162, 4 Nov. 1782 for £10.14.

[18]1800 Census, Bertie Co., NC.

[19]Liahona Research, _NC Marriages_:153.

[20]Marilu Burch Smallwood, comp. _Some Colonial and Revolutionary Families of North Carolina_, Vol. II (Published by the Author, 1969):343-344.

[21]Bertie Co., NC. Original Wills. NC Archives. Recorded Bk F:136.

		Saley Spivey, Jacob Freeman and Christian Freeman.
100	iv.	Josiah[5] Freeman, m. 23 Dec 1796 to Sarah Moore.[22] An undated estate record, inventory dated 1800, Moses Freeman admr. Mixes several accounts but may belong to this man.[23]
+ 101	v.	Rachel[5] Freeman, m. James Outlaw.[24]
102	vi.	Leah/Leach[5] Freeman, m. Chowan Co. 24 Mar 1778 to William Lurry or Leary.[25]
103	vii.	Mellicent[5] Freeman, m. Mr. Perry.[26]
104	viii.	Christian[5] Freeman, m. Mr. Norfleet.
105	ix.	Deliah[5] Freeman, m. Mr. Ward.

Issue of John Freeman by m(2) widow Sarah (Gordon) Norfleet.[27]

106	x.	John[5] Freeman, a minor in 1793.
107	xi.	Elizabeth[5] Freeman, a minor in 1793.

30. JOSHUA[4] FREEMAN (William[3], William[2], John[1] Freeman) was a resident of Bertie County, as was his brother, John. He

---

[22]Liahona Research, *NC Marriages*:153.

[23]Bertie Co., NC Estate Records. NC State Archives 010.504.1 Box 2.

[24]Benjamin C. Holtzeclaw, "The Outlaw Family," in *Historical Southern Families* v. 15 (Baltimore: Genealogical Publishing Co., 1971):30-32, Mrs. John Bennett Boddie, ed.

[25]Liahona Research, *NC Marriages*:153; Miss Hazel Ahrens, Oskaloosa, KS requested data on descendants in 1955 in *The North Carolinian*.

[26]Melicent (Amelicent) #38, aunt of this Mellicent, married Josiah Perry. Josiah is named as son-in-law in will of William Freeman # 6. Identity of Mr. Perry, husband of this Mellicent is unknown at present.

[27]N. 20, *supra*. States that Sarah Gordon was daughter of John Gordon (whose will was probated Feb. Term 1793 in Gates Co.) and his wife Mary.

bought 210 acres on "Quoyockason Swamp" in 1760 from William Wood.[28] His wife was named Mary, but her surname has not been found. Joshua's will was proved in Bertie County in 1794.[29] There is an estate file containing an inventory and sale dated 30 September 1796, for the estate of "Mary Freeman." Buyers at the sale are the children of Joshua and indicate that this is the estate of his widow, but the Division of Joshua's estate in September 1797 shows a distribution to Mary Freeman and also one to Mary Copeland, indicating that Mary Freeman, the widow was still alive.

This is probably the Joshua who appears in the Index to Revolutionary Army Accounts in the Edenton District and for whom two Pay Vouchers survive.[30] The other Joshua Freeman in NC who was of age during the Revolutionary War was Joshua # 46 son of Samuel and a resident of Surry County in Salisbury District.

Issue of Joshua and Mary ( ) Freeman.

+   108   i.   Christian[5] Freeman, m(1) James Wood, m(2)_____ Moring. James Wood's will was probated in Northampton Co., NC, in March 1797.

       109   ii.   Mary "Polly"[5] Freeman, d. post July 1824; m(1) Samuel Harrell, m(2) William Copeland.[31]

       110   iii.   William[5] Freeman, d. testate in Bertie Co., 1824; m. Celia ___. He became the guardian for his brother James Freeman and by 1816 for the orphans of his brother

---

[28]Bertie Co., NC. DB K:16.

[29]Bertie Co., NC. Original Wills. NC State Archives 010.801.

[30]See Appendix.

[31]Bertie Co., NC. Will of William Freeman written 9 Jul 1824. Original Will. NC State Archives 010.801. The will of Joshua Freeman # 30 identified the husband of Mary as Samuel Harrell. At the time of an 1805 petition to ratify title of a negro deeded by James Freeman to William Freeman, she was the wife of William Copeland (Estate file of James Freeman # 115.)

Jacob Freeman.[32] No Issue. Named his sisters, neices and nephews.

+ 111 iv. Joshua[5] Freeman, d. post Nov. 1805, ante 1816; Joshua "of Bertie" m. 11 Feb. 1793 in Gates Co., to Mary Pipkin.

+ 112 v. Jacob[5] Freeman, d. post Nov. 1805, ante 1816; Jacob "of Hertford" m. 30 June 1798 Gates Co., to Sarah Pipkin.

113 vi. Sally[5] Freeman, d. ante 1824; m(1?) 12 Aug 1791 in Bertie Co., to Cullen Wood who died in Northampton Co. May 1792; m(2) Thomas Sutton.

114 vii. Celia[5] Freeman, d. ante 1824; m. 23 Mar 1793 in Bertie Co., to John Campbell; m.(2) Mr. ___ Daughtee[33]

115 viii. James[5] Freeman, a minor at his father's death; d. circa 1800. No issue.[34]

31. MOSES[4] FREEMAN (William[3], William[2], John[1] Freeman) first appears as a tithable in his own right in Bertie County in 1762 and so must have been born about 1741 or before. Sometimes referred to as Moses, Sr., he was older than his cousin Moses #55. Several Revolutionary War records mention a Moses Freeman, but do not specify to which Moses they refer. The only reference to his wife is found in a deed of 2 October 1778 by which Moses and Courtney his wife sold to John Askew a tract of 230 acres adjacent

---

[32]Bertie Co., NC. Original Will. NC State Archives C.R.010.801.1. Will of William Freeman written 9 July 1824, probated Nov. 1830, contested by John Freeman, jury says is writing of William Freeman and ordered recorded.

[33]Bertie Co., NC. Original Wills, NC State Archives C.R.010.801. Will of brother, William Freeman, written 9 Jul. 1824, named heirs of John Campbell he had by sister Celia and Heirs of Celia Daughtee that she now have of hereafter may have.

[34]Bertie Co., NC. Estate File of James Freeman. NC State Archives C.R.010.504.1. His estate generated an assignment of title to his brother William in 1805 and a petition for division of land of James which provide much of the data on his siblings and their issue.

to John Stallings.[35] The 1800 Federal Census lists one Moses over age 45 and one 26 to 45 as resident in Bertie County. A third Moses appears in Iredell County. By the 1810 census the only Moses in North Carolina is in Buncombe County, and appears to be the man previously in Iredell.[36] An 1806 Estate file for Moses Freeman contains a document from a suit brought by "Carney Freeman Indorsee of Moses Freeman against Moses Freeman Jun[r.] of a plea that he render unto him the sum of fifty pounds which he owes & unjustly detains to his Damage £20. [The Sheriff] returned the writ that the Body of the said Moses Freeman Junior was not to be found." An attachment was issued.[37]

32. KING[4] FREEMAN (William[3], William[2], John[1] Freeman)
resided in Bertie County. He married before 1779. to Sarah apparently surnamed (Perry) Rice, daughter of John and Sarah Perry, and the widow of William Rice. On the 1779 tax list King is shown as the guardian of William and James Rice, indicating that he had probably married their mother by that date.[38]

King Freeman served in the militia during the Revolutionary War. Pay voucher #3413 for him survives.[39] No detail remains to indicate the term or type of service he rendered.

---

[35] Bertie Co., NC. DB M:401.

[36] Elizabeth Petty Bentley, Comp., *Index to the 1800 Census of North Carolina* (Baltimore: Genealogical Publishing Co., repr.1982):83; *Index to the 1810 Census of North Carolina* (Baltimore: Genealogical Publishing Co., repr. 1990):87.

[37] Bertie Co., NC. Estate File of Moses Freeman. NC Archives C.R. 10.504.1.29. Bertie Estate files have no dates. An administator was appointed in 1829.

[38] Bertie Co., NC. Tax Lists. NC State Archives. C.R.010.702.1.; Bertie Co., NC. Estate Record of Sarah Perry, October 1761. NC State Archives. She appears to be widow of John Perry who died 1758. Distribution gives child's share to Will[m] Rice who appears to have married one of her daughters; Will of William Rice, 29 Mar 1762, Bertie Co., NC. Names wife Sarah and children: William, James, Mary and Sarah.

[39] NC State Archives, Revolutionary Pay Vouchers and Certificates; Treasurer's and Comtroller's Records, Book B. See Appendix.

King wrote his will on 2 February 1793. It was proved at the May Court of that year. He left his estate to his daughter, Christian, wife of Blake Baker, and to her children and left bequests to his stepson William Rice and to John Rice the son of his stepson James Rice. Executors were his wife Sarah and her son James Rice.[40]

Issue of King and Sarah ( ) (Rice) Freeman.

+   116   i.   Christian[5] Freeman, m. Blake Baker. Removed to Caldwell County, KY.[41]

33. JAMES[4] FREEMAN (William[3], William[2], John[1] Freeman) lived in Gates County, North Carolina. His first wife was Selah, surname unknown. By her he had, at least, four children. Selah died after 1801.

He is appears to be the only candidate to be the James Freeman who received Pay Voucher # 2801 for sundries as allowed by the auditors of Edenton District.[42]

James and Selah deeded lands to each of his sons in turn. The first deed, to Timothy, for 320 acres was made in November 1796.[43] The next to receive lands were Thomas and William who each paid £25 for tracts of 125 acres.[44] William had married in 1793 to the widow of John Rountree, and been taxed for 151½ acres beginning in 1794.[45] In 1798 William and his father, James, deeded the 125 acre tract to Reddick Trotman for 50 Spanish

---

[40]Bertie Co., NC. WB D:217.

[41]Caldwell Co., KY. WB A:39-41. An account of the estate of Sarah Freeman and King Freeman decd, by Blake Baker guardian of his children.

[42]See Appendix.

[43]Gates Co., NC. DB 4:110. Timothy appears on the Gates Co. Tax Lists starting in 1794 with this tract, however the deed was not made until 1796. This deed was not for a consideration of £150 not "love and affection."

[44]Gates Co., NC. DB 4:169,170.

[45]Gates Co., NC. Tax Lists. NC State Archives C.R. 041.701.1.

Dollars "being the same that James Freeman gave his son William Freeman."[46] In 1799 James and Selah made another deed to Thomas for a tract of 150 acres at the mouth of Juniper Branch, Aron Blanshard's Bridge, the line of Thomas Garrett, Cathren's Creek.[47] In 1801 Thomas Freeman deeded to Josiah the 125 acre tract that James and Selah had first deeded to Thomas.[48] Finally, on the 22 of August 1801 Josiah Freeman made an agreement with his parents, James and Selah, to lease His property to his parents for the full term of their Natural Lives.[49]

James Freeman had two illegitimate daughters by Mary Barber, Milly born about 1789 and Betsy born about 1792. He also had an illegitimate daughter, name unknown, born about 1796 to Elizabeth Eure.[50] Because Milly and Betsy were born before the marriage of their parents, they could not be considered legitimate without a specific petition to the court by their father. No such action was taken and so the girls could not inherit from their father. Mary, the widow, filed a petition in Nov. 1810 stating that James had died in August of that year without a will. Elisha Bond was administrator of his estate. She asked for dower from her husband's land holding of 125 acres, a years maintenance, and mentioned her daughters, Milly and Betsy, born out of wedlock.[51] She was awarded a years maintenance.

James Freeman's son William died shortly after 1800. William's son James Trotman Freeman had inherited property from his half brother, John Rountree. James T. Freeman's guardian for this monetary estate was his father, William and then

---

[46]Gates Co., NC. DB 4:182.

[47]Gates Co., NC DB 5:173.

[48]Gates Co. NC. DB 5:203.

[49]Gates Co., NC. DB 5:421.

[50]Gates Co., NC Bastardy Bonds. NC State Archives. C.R. 041.102.1.

[51]Gates Co., NC. Estate File of James Freeman. NC State Archives. C.R. 041.508.35.

after William's death, his grandfather became guardian of the orphan and of the inherited estate.[52]

Selah must have died sometime after 1801, since, on 22 September 1803, James Freeman married Mary Barber, the mother of his two daughters, born 1789 and 1792.

Issue of James and Selah ( ) Freeman.

+	117	i.	William[5] Freeman, m. 19 Oct. 1793 in Gates Co., to Mary (Trotman ?) Rountree, widow of John Rountree; d.c. 1804.[53]
	118	ii.	Timothy[5] Freeman, b.c. 1771, d. 12 Sep 1825; m(1) 14 Oct 1790 in Gates Co., to Perthena Bond, m(2) 27 Feb 1799 in Gates to Celah Valentine.[54]
	119	iii.	Josiah[5] Freeman, b.c. 1780
+	120	iv.	Thomas[5] Freeman, b. May 1773, d. 9 Nov 1859, Monroe Co., GA; m(1) 4 Jul 1806, Gates Co., to Rachel Hurdle; m(2) Chowan Co., Hannah Hurdle.[55]

Issue of James and Mary (Barber) Freeman, born before marriage of parents.

| | 121 | v. | Milly Barber, b.c. 1789. |
| | 122 | vi. | Betsy Barber, b.c. 1792. |

---

[52]Gates Co., NC. Estate File of John Rountree, 1800. NC State Archives. C.R. 041.508.104. Estate file of William Freeman 1802, C.R. 041.508.1, contains guardianship petition 17 May 1808 of James Freeman for James Trotman Freeman orphan of William Freeman. Estate papers of James Freeman, in file misdated 1801. C.R. 041.508.35 distributes to Thomas Freeman by virtue of his guardianship of Jas T. Freeman. and an amount paid to the widow "in virtue of her legal right." Signature on the Guardianship papers of James for James T. match the signatures on the Bastardy Bonds.

[53]Liahona Research, *NC Marriages*:153; Gates Co., NC. Estate Record. NC State Archives, C.R. 041.508.35.

[54]*Ibid.*

[55]Letter, 21 January 1985, from descendant, Helen Freeman Taylor, Box 8025, Dallas, TX 75205, to the author.

Issue of James and Elizabeth Eure.

Child, name and sex unknown, b.c. 1796.

34. **WILLIAM⁴ FREEMAN** (William³, William², John¹ Freeman) was one of several of the name who lived in Gates County toward the end of the 18th century. William # 34 and his father, William # 6, both had land which fell into Gates at the time of its formation in 1779. William the father, died in 1781. William # 34 inherited the home plantation by the will of his father.[56] He appears on the Gates County tax lists in most years through 1798. Starting in 1794, this William is known as William, Senior, and a William, Junior, also appears on the tax lists. William Freeman, Junior, appears to son of #34 James Freeman.[57]

William Freeman, with his wife Sarah, sold a Gates County tract in 1792 to Daniel Reddick of "Nansimond" Co., Virginia. In 1797 William and Sarah sold to Richard Rawls 150 acres on Cathrin Creek Swamp at a "Pint called Freemans Pint."[58] Witnesses were James Freeman and William Freeman, Junior. William, Sarah and their family left the land on which William's grandfather had settled and moved west to Orange County.

William purchased land in 1798 and 1799 in Orange County.[59] He appears to have followed the lead of Richard Freeman, son of Demsey, who left Gates for Orange County about 1798. William did not live long after the move. He made his will on 4 December 1800. It was proved in the May Court of 1801.[60] William left land to his son George and to his sons, John and William, after his wife's decease or marriage, all the reminder of his land. His daughter Polley Trotman was to receive 20 shillings. His wife was to have all his land which he had not given away, and

---

[56]Gates Co., NC. WB 1:20; Inventory, NC State Archives, C.R. 041.508.36.

[57]Gates Co., NC. Tax Lists. NC State Archives C.R. 041.701.1.

[58]Gates Co., NC DB 5:30; 5:34.

[59]Orange Co., NC. DB 7:357,358; 9:214.

[60]Orange Co., NC. DB D:43.

his stock for the maintenance of his children, and after her death or marriage to be divided between his children Christian, Freeman, Nancy Freeman, John Freeman, Betsy Freeman, Salley Freeman and William Freeman. Executors were his widow, Sarah and his son George.

Issue of William and Sarah ( ) Freeman:

123   i.   George[5] Freeman, returned to Gates Co.; prob. the man who d. 1843, Chowan Co.[61]; prob. the man who had a marriage bond Gates Co.,12 Mar 1805 to Mary Walton, possibly also the one who had a bond, Gates Co., 24 Nov 1807 to Christian Hofler.[62]

124   ii.   Mary[5] "Polley" Freeman, m. bond Gates Co., 21 January 1797 to Thomas Trotman.

125   iii.   Christian[5] Freeman.

126   iv.   Nancy[5] Freeman, m. 20 Mar 1809, Orange Co., William Anderson.

127   v.   John[5] Freeman.

128   vi.   Betsy[5] Freeman.

129   vii.   Salley[5] Freeman.

130   viii.   William[5] Freeman, m. 14 May 1811, Orange Co., Mary Edwards.

35. SARAH[4] FREEMAN (William[3], William[2], John[1] Freeman) was named as Sarah Haise in her father's will. She is probably the Sarah, named as wife of Hardy Hayes, in his will written 7 March 1784 and proved in Bertie County.[63]

---

[61]Chowan Co., NC. Estate Records. NC State Archives C.R. 024.508

[62]NC Archives, Marriage Bonds.

[63]Bertie Co., NC. Original Wills. NC State Archives C.R. 010.801.

Issue of Hardy and Sarah (Freeman) Hayes.

131	i.	Joshua[5] Hayes, m. 9 May 1792, Bertie Co., Ann Hayes.[64]
132	ii.	Penelope[5] Hayes, m. 23 May 1786, Bertie Co., John Franton.[65]
133	iii.	Elizabeth[5] Hayes, m. 13 Nov 1797 Bertie, James Norfleet.[66]
134	iv.	Sally[5] Hayes.
135	v.	Tempy[5] Hayes.
136	vi.	Judah[5] Hayes, m. 25 July 1800, Bertie, Reuben Higgs.[67]
137	vii.	Susannah[5] Hayes.

35. DAUGHTER (William[3], William[2], John[1] Freeman) married Mr. Hinton. Her father, William Freeman named a grandson, Reuben Hinton, in his will. Reuben was to be the residual legatee to the plantation on which Sarah Haise was living and also a negro in her posession. It is possible that Sarah married first to a Hinton and had a son, then married Hardy Hayes/Haise.[68]

138	i.	Reuben[5] Hinton.

38. [(A)MELICENT?][4] FREEMAN (William[3], William[2], John[1] Freeman). This daughter was probably born circa 1750 since

---

[64]International Genealogical Index, Latter Day Saints, 1992, ed.

[65]*Ibid.*

[66]*Ibid.*

[67]*Ibid.*

[68]Gates Co., NC. Original Will of William Freeman. NC State Archives C.R. 041.801

appearance on tax lists show that her eldest brother was born by 1735 and brother Joshua about 1740, Moses by 1741/42 and King by 1742 and she is the fourth daughter named in the will of her father. She married Josiah Perry who was named as a son-in-law in the will of William Freeman. William did not state the name of his daughter who was wife of Josiah Perry, but left a negro named Jacob to his grandson, William Perry, and a bed and furnishings and two cows and calves to "Sun in law" Josiah Perry. The fact that Freeman does not name this daughter raises the possibility that the girl was dead by this date. Other married daughters are mentioned by name.

To further confuse the issue, # 29 John Freeman (above), had a daughter Mellicent who married a Mr. Perry. Some researchers have concluded that Josiah Perry married first to a daughter of William Freeman and secondly to a neice, a daughter of John Freeman. Josiah Perry's youngest child, Amellisant, is said to have been born in 1794.

Census records of 1800, 1810, 1820 all show the oldest female in Josiah's household, presumably his wife, as over 45, thus born before 1755. If John Freeman #29 was born circa 1735 it seems highly unlikely that he had a daughter born before 1755. Furthermore, John Freeman's (#29) will names four sons and then five daughters by his first marriage and then a son and daughter by his second marriage. Mellicent is named as the third of the daughters and that was probably her birth order of the female children.

Thus it is certain that a daughter of # 6 William Freeman, name uncertain, married Josiah Perry and possible though unlikely that he married secondly to Amellicent daughter of John Freeman.

Josiah Perry wrote his will in Bertie County, 25 Apr. 1820 and a codicil in June that year, naming his wife "Amelicent," and numerous children and grandchildren. Melicent also died testate. Her will is dated 18 October 1822, in Bertie. Both wills name a number of grandchildren and should be consulted for further descendants.[69]

Issue of Josiah and Melicent (Freeman) Perry:

---

[69] Bertie Co., NC. Original Wills. NC State Archives C.R. 010.801

139	vi.	William[5] Perry.
140	vii.	Salley[5] Perry, m. Mr. Stephens
141	viii.	Christian[5] Perry, m. Mr. Walton.
142	ix.	John[5] Perry.
143	x.	Josiah[5] Perry.
144	xi.	Bersheba[5] Perry, m. Mr. Garrett.
145	xii.	Mary[5] Perry, m. 15 Dec 1788 Bertie Co., to Samuel Jenkins.[70]
146	xiii.	Nancy[5] Perry, m. Mr. Belflour.
147	xiv.	Celia[5] Perry, m. Miles Rayner.
148	iii.	Freeman[5] Perry.
149	iv.	Frusanna[5] "Furzy" Perry, m. Mr. Mercer.
150	v.	James[5] Perry m. 7 Jun 1809, Bertie Co., to Sarah Parker.[71]
+ 151	i.	Penelope[5] Perry, m. 12 Aug 1806, Bertie Co., to Nathan Sessoms.[72] Children named in will of Amillicent Perry.
+ 152	ii.	Amillicent[5] Perry m. John Simons. Children named in will of Amillicent Perry.

---

[70]International Genealogical Index, Church of Jesus Christ of Latter-day Saints, 1993 ed; A query in 1957 in *The North Carolinian* from Miss Cora D. Jenkins, 3200 16th N.W., Apt 510, Washington D.C. states that she m.(2) Dempsey Jenkins and m.(3) husband's name unknown.

[71]*Ibid.*

[72]*Ibid.*

GENERATION FOUR

DESCENDANTS OF RICHARD FREEMAN #8.

40. AMOS[4] FREEMAN (Richard[3], William[2], John[1] Freeman) was the oldest of the three children of Richard Freeman and was named a co-executor of his father's will with William Freeman, brother of Richard, and Timothy Walton. He inherited from his father the "ferry Plantation and all the Land and appurtenances thereunto Belonging and the Land and Plantation whereon William Beaglen now Lives." He also was willed a third of the marsh and property in the "wild Percosen" lying in Hertford County.[1]

Amos first resided in Chowan County and was involved in a number of land transactions in Chowan and in Bertie Counties.[2] Between February and June of 1765 he moved his residence to Hertford County.[3] The loss of Hertford records makes description of this part of his life impossible. He is listed on the tax list of Surry County in 1782 with 100 acres 2 horses and four cows[4] and in 1783 was security with Chris Lay for Edward Smith's application for a tavern licence.[5] No further record is found of him in Surry County. Since there is no probate record for Amos in Surry County, it is probable that he moved from there prior to his death, possibly returning to Hertford County.

No Revolutionary War record has been found for Amos Freeman. Several documents make reference to "A. Freeman" but those records may refer to Allen, Aaron, or Archibald Freeman for whom there are numerous other military records.

---

[1] Chowan Co., NC. Original will of Richard Freeman. NC State Archives.

[2] Chowan Co., NC. DB K:127; M:216; N:239; Bertie Co., NC. DB K:233; L-2:68, 192.

[3] Chowan Co., DB M:216; N:239.

[4] Surry County Tax List 1782. NC State Archives, L.P. 46.1 (GA) Tax List. Capt Dyer's Dist.

[5] Mrs. W.O. Absher, *Surry Co., North Carolina, Court Minutes, 1768-1785,* Vol. 1:52. Perhaps Chris Lay was the husband or a relative of the husband of Amos's daughter Ann who married prior to 1786 to a Mr. Lay.

Amos married Sarah Hunter, daughter of Elisha Hunter, who was named guardian of Amos' younger brother, Demsey. Elisha Hunter named in his will a granddaughter, Ann Lay, daughter of Amos Freeman, to whom he had already given her full part of his estate.[6] The marriage of Amos and Sarah must have taken place before 15 November 1764 when Amos and his wife Sarah of Chowan County deeded to Elisha Hunter 130 acres in Hertford County received from the will of Richard.[7]

Known Issue of Amos and Sarah (Hunter) Freeman.

153   i.   Ann[5] Freeman, m. (Chris?) Lay before 1786.

43. DEMSEY[4] FREEMAN (Richard[3], William[2], John[1] Freeman) was younger than his brother, Amos. On 27 July 1762, Elisha Hunter was appointed his guardian.[8] Demsey reached his majority by 21 January 1767 when he released and forever quit claimed Elisha Hunter from any claim for any act done by him "as my guardian."[9]

Demsey continued to live on the home plantation in Chowan County willed him by his father, Richard. His land fell into Gates County when that county was formed in 1779. In 1771, Elisha Hunter, having already bought Amos's part, bought Demsey's portion of the "marsh and Pecosan" land purchased by his father Richard from William Downing on the North East side of Chowan River.[10]

Demsey married to Sarah whose surname has not been found but who signed a deed to George Outlaw with a "W".[11]

---

[6]Almasy, *Gates Co, Wills- Book 1:57*.

[7]Gates Co., NC. DB 4:112. Although made in 1764, this deed was recorded with deed dated c. 1796.

[8]Chowan Co., NC. Guardian Bond. NC State Archives, C.R. 024.508.39.

[9]*Ibid*.

[10]Chowan Co., NC. DB P:22

[11]Chowan Co., NC. DB Q:239.

Demsey made deeds of gift for love and affection to his son Richard a negro girl named Lucy and her increase and to his daughter Mary a Negro Girl named Hannah and her increase.[12] In July 1777 Demsey Freman deeded to his son Richard for love and affection "the plantation whereon I dwell on Catherine Creek joining the land of William Freman and George Outlaw after my decease and his mother's" clear from all other former gifts.[13]

Demsey served in the Militia during the Revolution. He received voucher # 2504 for £2.0.0 specie for a gun.[14] Note the holes punched in the voucher as a means of cancellation.

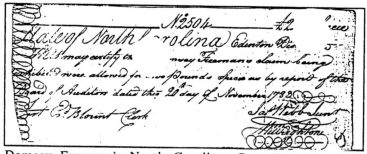

Demsey Freeman's North Carolina, *Revolutionary Pay Voucher*.

Demsey died before October 1786 when the State of North Carolina granted land to William Freeman on Catherine Creek, joining William Freeman and Demsey Freeman, deceased.[15] George Outlaw was guardian for Richard Freeman and exhibited an account 16 Febraury 1789 and annually thereafter.[16] In 1795, Richard of Gates Co. sold to Charles Powell the tract on

---

[12]Chowan Co., NC. DB Q: 271, 272.

[13]Chowan Co., NC. DB R:56.

[14]NC State Archives. *Treasurer and Comptrollers Records, Revolutionary Army Accounts Book C (Vol. 42) p. 27*

[15]Gates Co., NC. DB 2:4.

[16]Marilyn Poe Laird & Vivian Poe Jackson, *Gates Co., NC, Court Minutes, 1788-1803.* (Dolton, IL: Poe Publishers, n.d.):16, 31, 49, 71, 87.

Catherine Creek "whereon my Father Demsey Freeman formerly lived, containing by estimation 100 acres."[17]

Richard moved to Orange County before January 1798 and as Richard Freeman "of Orange County" sold his negro slave "Lewcy" to John B. Walton. The same day he purchased of Walton another negro woman, Peny and her child Agatha.[18]

Issue of Demsey and Sarah ( ) Freeman.

154	i.	Richard[5] Freeman,b.c. 1774, moved to Orange Co., NC.
155	ii.	Mary[5] Freeman.

44. MARY[4] FREEMAN (Richard[3], William[2], John[1] Freeman) married Thomas Rountree. The marriage must have taken place before 1760, since Richard Freeman named his daughter Mary Rountree in his will.[19] The couple lived in Chowan and later Gates County. Thomas Rountree wrote his will in Gates County, on 18 April 1781. The will was proved in May Court of that year.[20] The children named in this will match the children named as grandchildren in the will of Ruth ( )(Freeman) Benbury. Another Thomas Rountree died in Chowan in 1773, leaving an orphan Christian but not the other grandchildren listed in their grandmother's will.

Issue of Mary Freeman and her husband Thomas ROUNTREE.

156	i.	Seth[5] ROUNTREE, m. Gates Co., 8 March 1787, to Selah Outlaw.[21]

---

[17]Gates Co.,NC. DB 4:40.

[18]Gates Co., NC. DB 4:278, 283.

[19]N. 1. *Supra*.

[20]Almasy, *Gates Co., Wills- Book 1*:15-16.

[21]Liahona Research, *NC Marriages*: 387.

157	ii.	Christian[5] ROUNTREE, m. Gates Co., 31 August 1785, James Knight.[22]
158	iii.	Leah[5] "Leach" ROUNTREE, m. Mr. Felton.[23]
159	iv.	Levina[5] ROUNTREE, m. Simeon Brinkley.[24]
160	v.	Rachel[5] ROUNTREE, m. Gates Co., 19 May 1795, Mills Hurdle.[25]
161	vi.	Precilla[5] ROUNTREE, m. Chowan Co., 29 Mar 1793, Kader Felton.[26]
162	vii.	Peniah[5] ROUNTREE, m. Gates Co., 19 Feb 1800, Noah Trotman.[27]

---

[22] *Ibid*:386.

[23] Chowan Co., NC Original Will of Ruth Benbury. NC State Archives.

[24] *Ibid*.

[25] Liahona Research, *NC Marriages*:386.

[26] *Ibid*.

[27] *Ibid*.

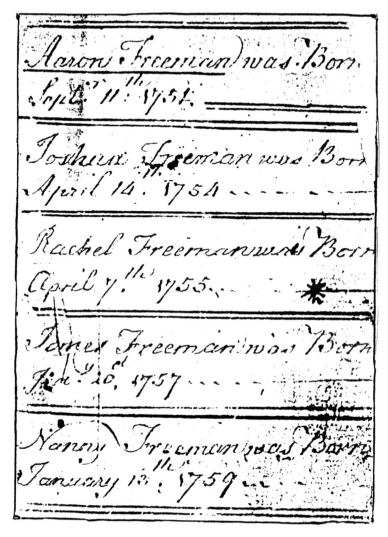

Birth record of Samuel Freeman's children found in Revolutionary War Pension file of Jeremiah Early R3191.

GENERATION FOUR

DESCENDANTS OF SAMUEL FREEMAN #10

45. AARON[4] FREEMAN (Samuel[3], William[2], John[1] Freeman) is the ancestor of most of the present day Freeman families of Surry County. He was the only one of the sons of Samuel Freeman who remained in North Carolina. He was born 11 September 1751 probably in Bertie County, and moved with his family the next year to Shocco Creek in Granville County.[1]

Records of Aaron's life are sparse. Aaron of Salisbury District received £90 for a publick claim Cert #610; and £6.10.6 specie for a public claim, Cert. #2297; and £3.16.0 for public claim, cert # 5201.[2]

In October 1783, he witnessed a power of attorney from John Garret of Chowan County to William Freeman.[3] This is the only reference found to him in Surry deed books of 1770-1797. He was taxed in 1782 with 200 acres, one slave named Tobe, 2 horses and 7 cows.[4]

Aaron does not appear in Surry county in the 1790 census but is on the tax list for that year on the list of Capt. Edward with 300 acres and 2 poles. He is listed on the 1800 census with males: 2 und/10, 2 10/16, 1 16/26, 1 over/45; females: 1 und./10, 1 10/16, 1 26/45. He married, probably about 1776, to Nancy. Her surname is traditionally given as Hawkins. Tradition of the Surry County descendants of this couple give the place of marriage as

---

[1]Birthdates of Samuel Freeman's five children are found in the Revolutionary War Pension file of Jeremiah Early R3191 p.0068; Granville Co. tax lists show Samuel Freeman as a resident in 1752.

[2]NC State Archives. *Revolutionary War Pay Vouchers and Certificates.*

[3]Mrs. W. O. Absher, *Surry County, North Carolina, Abstracts, Deed Books A, B, and C (1779-1788)* (Easley Co., SC: Southern Historical Press, 1981):91.

[4]Surry Co., NC. Tax Lists, NC State Archives, C.R. 092.____

Hillsborough.[5] On 16 April 1809, Aaron made an agreement with his son-in-law William Cunningham to maintain Aaron and his wife Nancy in a comfortable decent manner of living for their natural life. In consideration Aaron Freeman gave unto William Cunningham a negro man called Tobias & one negro woman called Patty, 2 mairs, cattle, hogs, and furniture. Cunningham was to deliver 2 good cowes, to Aaron or to whomever he shall name. Freeman is to give to Cunningham a title in fee simple to 100 acres of land out of a tract whereon he now lives off the lower end of the said tract.[6] Aaron left no will.

Issue of Aaron and Nancy (Hawkins - trad.) Freeman.[7]

163	i.	John[5] Freeman. Went to Tennessee.[8]
164	ii.	Abner[5] Freeman, b.c. 1783; d. test. 1854 in Lincoln Co., TN. Said to have m(1) ___Cunningham; m(2) ___Underwood; m(3) Drucilla Moore.[9] 33 children.
165	iii.	Richard[5] Freeman, said to have moved to St. Louis, MO. However, Missouri Census Indexes for 1830-1850 fail to show him.[10]

---

[5]Letter, 22 February 1922 Robert Alexander Hawkins to Anna Kirk Faulkner, original in possession of author.

[6]Surry Co., NC. DB M:185.

[7]No estate record has been found naming the children. The following list is a compilation taken from the letters written by Robert A. Freeman, of Dobson, Surry Co., great grandson of Aaron and Nancy to Mrs Anna Kirk Faulkner, originals in possession of author; and data which appears in the *Heritage of Surry County.*

[8]Letter 16 Nov. 1926 Mrs. B.F. Palmer, 300 N. Randolph St., Rockingham, NC to Mrs. W. S. Faulkner. She descended from Rachel #168. She stated that John # 163 "went to Tennessee."

[9]R.A. Freeman states Abner married 3 times and had 33 children. Mrs. Palmer gives surnames of wives. 1850 census of Lincoln Co., TN gives name of wife as Drucilla; Lincoln Co., TN. WB 2:85, names wife and mentions 6 youngest children (minors). No other children mentioned.

[10]R.A. Freeman and Mrs. Palmer agree he went to St. Louis.

166	iv.	James[5] Freeman, b.c. 1780. In household of Alexander H. Freeman in 1850.[11]
167	v.	Elizabeth[5] Freeman m. John Ryser.[12]
168	vi.	Rachel[5] Freeman m. John Ryan. to Adair Co., KY.[13]
169	vii.	Polly[5] Freeman m. William Cunningham. Resided Surry Co.[14]
170	viii.	Nicholas[5] Freeman, b.c. 1799. Resided Surry in 1850, a Schoolteacher, in household of brother Alexander H.
+ 171	ix.	Alexander Hawkins[5] Freeman, b.c. 1794 d.c. 1858, Surry Co., m.c. 1818 to Sally Mosely.[15]

46. JOSHUA[4] FREEMAN (Samuel[3], William[2], John[1] Freeman) was born 14 April 1754 in Granville County, North Carolina[16]. His first wife was Lucy. Her surname has been given as King but no evidence has been found to support this tradition. Joshua must have married quite young since his first child was born 28 April 1774 when he was just twenty.[17]

---

[11]Not on Mrs. Palmer's list of Aaron's children.

[12]R.A. Freeman and Mrs. Palmer agree on husband's name.

[13]Data from R.A. Freeman. *The Heritage of Surry County:*Section # 239. Gives her husband as Jacob Beamer. Palmer lists her but names no spouse.

[14]Mrs. B.F. Palmer submitted papers to D.A.R. on service of Samuel Freeman through this line.

[15]Many descendants of this family stayed in Surry County. Data on descendants in *Heritage of Surry County.*

[16]N. 1. *Supra.*

[17]Notorized copy of bible records "certified to be a true Copy" sent in 1926 by Mae Smith McGuire to Mrs. W.S. Faulkner, in possession of author. Robert W. Hardin left the bible in care of his niece, Mrs. Sarah Jane Gallaher of Concord, Knox Co., TN, when he moved to Washington in 1889. He died Nov. 12

In May 1783 Samuel Freeman deeded to Joshua Freeman, "his son, for love" at the mouth of Hogans Creek to the old Geared Mill, adjacent to Moses Wright, Arrarat, Yadkin River; part of Granville grant to Morgan Bryan, Senr. 1752.[18] On 20 April 1789 Joshua deeded back to Samuel 267 acres which appears to be the aforementioned land.[19] In May 1789 Joshua received a grant for 200 acres on the South fork of Codys Creek adjoining Bray.[20] In 1800-1801 he received three grants. The first, on the south side of Fishers River at Rainwater's corner was issued under a duplicate warrant, the original entered 13 August 1778, as by plat annexed. The other two for 400 and 500 acres respectively.[21]

To date no evidence has been of found of Revolutionary War service. However, Joshua Freeman of Surry Co., made an affidavit in 1801, that James Yarbrough, decd, was a soldier, and that William Yarbrough was his only son and heir.[22]

In 1796 Joshua Freeman was one of the Commissioners of the Town of Rockford.[23] He appears to have been in business with Reuben Grant who was his son-in-law. In 1809 Grant died suddenly and unexpectedly at his father-in-law's house. An inquest was held which determined the death to have been by Act of God.[24] Joshua, his family and his daughter, Temperance Grant, and her young children moved to Knoxville, Tennessee by

---

1898. The bible records were sent to Mrs. Tennie Hardin 25 Nov. 1925 by Miss Callie Gallaher daughter of Mrs. Sarah Jane Gallaher, Concord, Knox Co., TN. Gives names and birthdates of children of Joshua and Lucy Freeman.

[18]Mrs. W.O Absher, C.R.S., *Surry County, North Carolina Abstracts, Deed Books A,B, and C (1770-1788)* (Easley, SC: Southern Historical Press, repr. 1981):64.

[19]Surry Co., NC. DB F:186.

[20]Absher, *Surry Deeds D,E,F*:52.

[21]Surry Co., NC. DB I:237, 471.

[22]NC State Archives. *Index to Secretary of State Revolutionary Military Papers.*

[23]Absher, *Surry Co., Deeds, D,E, and F*:127.

[24]Surry Co., NC. Minutes, 8 September 1809, Coroner's Inquest held over the body of Reuben Grant, Esq.

10 August 1810 when Joshua made a bill of sale to Reuben Tiption for a slave named Winey and her child, Jane for $350. Freeman promised to defend the title to the slaves from any claim.[25] In October of 1810 Joshua purchased from Abraham and Reuben Tipton a tract of 261¼ acres on Stock Creek.[26] Joshua, his brother James and brother-in-law James Badgett owned land on Stock Creek from:The Maryville-Knoxville pike bridge crossing on both sides of the track and adjoining Little River."[27]

On 20 February 1813 Joshua Freeman, Sr., deeded 78 acres to his grandson, James F. Grant " for the natural love and affection and for the better maintenance and preferrment of the said James F. Grant."[28] Joshua married second to Margaret ___ . Joshua Freeman, Sr., wrote his will 4 September 1832. He died shortly thereafter, as his death notice appeared in the *National Banner & Nashville Advertiser* issue of Saturday, September, 22, 1832.[29]

Issue of Joshua and Lucy (traditionally King) Freeman.

	172	i.	Elizabeth[5] Freeman, b. 28 October 1774, m. Joseph Kirby.
+	173	ii.	Temperance[5] Freeman, b. 2 Sept 1776, m(1) Reuben Grant, m(2) bond 24 Apr 1813, Knox Co., TN, Richard Kearby.

---

[25]Surry Co., NC. DB M 304. Joshua Freeman "of Knox County, Tennessee;" Knox Co., TN. DB O_1:173. It was a good thing that Tipton received an assurance of the validity of the deed, since it was not until 1813 that Jeremiah Early, the previous owner of the slaves, made clear title to Freeman. See section of Rachel (Freeman) Early, below.

[26]Knox Co., TN. DB O_1:178.

[27]Letter, W.E. Parham to Mrs. I. J. Berry, 707, 15th St., Knoxville, TN. 28 May 1925. Copy sent by Mr. Parham to Mrs. W.S. Faulkner, in possession of author.

[28]Knox Co., TN. DB O:356.

[29]Knox Co., TN. WB 5:162; The Rev. Silas Emmett Lucas, JR., *Obituaries from Early Tennessee Newspapers, 1794-1851* (Easley, SC: Southern Historical Press, 1978) 136.

174	iii.	Moses[5] Freeman, b. 5 Apr. 1780. No more data.
175	iv.	Nancy[5] Freeman b. 20 Aug. 1782, d. 4 Nov. 1862, Pikes Co., GA; m. 17 Aug. 1809, Surry Co., NC to 1st cousin Foster Freeman. Resided Griffin, Pike (Spalding) Co., GA. See #188 Foster Freeman.
+ 176	v.	Mary "Polly"[5] Freeman, b. 10 Nov. 1785, d. 12 Jan 1858; m. 16 Nov 1804, Surry Co., Rev. Jeremiah King.
177	vi.	Joshua[5] Freeman, b. 10 May 1791, d. post Sept 1832.

47. RACHEL[4] FREEMAN (Samuel[3], William[2], John[1] Freeman) was born 7 April 1755, probably in Granville County. She married Jeremiah Early but the date of the marriage is uncertian. A genealogy of the Early family gives the year as 1772 which would appear logical given her birthdate. However, the rejected pension application for her husband contains the marriage bond issued 12 November 1791.[30] This date would have made her over 36 at the date of her marriage. It would also indicate that she had 4 children before March 1796 when her father, Samuel Freeman wrote his will leaving half of his lands to the four children of his daughter Rachel Early, namely, Asa, Sion, Sarah and Elizabeth. Census records confirm that births of the children were after 1790. Her age would indicate that she may have had an earlier marriage.

Rachel and Jeremiah continued to live in Surry County, apparently suffering some financial reverses, but were aided by family members, for in 1813 the following bill of sale and agreement was executed:

> Jeremiah Early of Surry Co to Asa Early and other. Know all men by these presents that I Jeremiah Early of the County of Surry and State of North Carolina for the following consideration will and truly to be performed and executed

---

[30]National Archives. Pension File R.3191.

and complied with on the part of Asa Early, Sion Early, Sally Early, Elizabeth Early and Nancy Early of the County and state aforesaid, viz First that they the sd Earleys pay and discharge the several debts due to the persons herein after mentioned, James Badgett, Sen., the sum of $16. Christian Lamb $17, John Bryan $15, and interest currency of the United States as will appear by the notes, bonds and judgments of sd persons against the sd Jeremiah Early and the sd Jeremiah's debts due to Matthew Hughs, Esq. Secondly the sd Earlys execute to Joshua Freeman his heirs, executors or assigns a good & sufficient title to a negro woman named Winney and her 2 children Jenny and Jack heretofore in sd Freeman's possession of the value of $1000 like money as above sd to the same. 3rdly - The Earlys to give a right & title in fee simple of the mill seat & 20 acres of land to Nicholas Horn, his heirs, assigns forever. 4th Asa, Sion, Eliz[b] and Nancy (Sally not included) shall find and support J. E. and Rachel his wife with a comfortable house, food, raiment, washing and lodging suitable to their station. 5thly Whereof Asa & Sion Early have paid $100 currency to Jeremiah Early receipt acknowledged he delivers into possession of the above named 5 Earlys to share and share alike all rights, title and claim to the plantation where he now resides as a tenant under & in part gift or at will of Eliza[b] Freeman with crops, farming utensils... signed by Jeremiah Early on 2 Oct 1813 before Jas. Howard.[31]

Jeremiah Early died 31 January 1823. Rachel applied for a pension on service of Jeremiah, but her claim was "never allowed for the reason that she failed to furnish proof of the alleged services of her husband." Rachel died 11 November 1840.[32]

Issue of Jeremiah and Rachel (Freeman) Early.

178	i.	Asa[5] EARLY, b. 1790-1800, d.c. 1833, Stokes Co.; m. 22 Apr. 1821, Polly Kirby. 2 children: Samuel, b.c. 1822 and Mary, b.c. 1827.[33]

---

[31]Surry Co., DB N:60

[32]National Archives. Pension File R.3191. Microfilm frame 68-69.

[33]Stokes Co., NC. WB 3:249. NC State Arch; 1850 Census, Stokes Co., NC p.115.

179	ii.	Sion[5] EARLY, b. 1794-1796, d. 1851, Wythe Co., VA; m. 28 Feb. 1816 Sally Haines, she d. 1871.[34]
180	iii.	Sarah[5] EARLY, b. 3 Nov. 1792. Alive 1851. Mentally disabled.[35]
181	iv.	Elizabeth[5] EARLY, b. 22 May 1794, d. post 1851. m. 2 Feb 1817, Micajah Reeves. Resided Surry Co.
182	v.	Nancy[5] EARLY, b. 1 Apr 1796, alive 1851; m. 15 Jul 1818 to Joseph Howard. Said to have gone to Missouri.

48. JAMES[4] FREEMAN (Samuel[3], William[2], John[1] Freeman) b. 10 January 1757, probably in Granville County. On 7 May 1784, Samuel Freeman deeded to James, his son, for love and affection a tract above the plantation whereon Samuel Freeman now lives.[36] James married Lucy Foster, daughter of John Foster of Franklin County.[37]

James Freeman served as a Lieutenant of Light Horse in the Cross Creek Campaign in the Company of Capt. Jabez Jarves under Col. Joseph Williams of Surry County Militia.[38] This action was probably the expedition led by Rutherford against the

---

[34]R.H. Early, *The family of Early: Which settled upon the Eastern Shore of Virginia, and its Connection with other Families* Lynchburg, VA: n.p. 1920):83.

[35]Surry Co., NC, 1850 Census, Household/Family 1168/1168. Sally appears in household of sister Elizabeth Reaves., aged 57, "idiotic."

[36]Absher, *Surry Co., Deeds, A,B, and C*:62.

[37]Stephen E. Bradley, Jr., *Will Book B, Franklin Counry, North Carolina, 1794-1804,* (South Boston, VA: By the author, n.d.):37. Will of John Foster.

[38]Weynette Parks Haun, *North Carolina Revolutionary Army Accounts Secretary of State Treasurer's & Comptroler's Papers, Journal "A", (Public Accounty) 1775-1776* (Durham: By the author, 1989): 26,27,164,166.

Cherokees in September 1776, since Col. Williams itemized an expense for an Express with Colo. Rutherford's instructions.[39]

James does not appear on the 1790 or 1800 census of Surry County. He went to Oglethorpe County, Georgia, where he purchased land from Thomas Hill in 1798, described as the tract on which Freeman lived.[40] The Inferior Court of Oglethorpe had put down the name James Freeman on the list of person entitled to draws in the 1805 lottery without making a distinction between James Freeman, Sr., and James Freeman, Jr. On 2 December 1805 James Freeman, Sr., allowed James Freeman, Jr., to claim Lot 30-3 in Baldwin County which had been won in the lottery.[41] In 1811 James Freeman purchased a tract from Thomas Hill which included "a plantation whereon the said Freeman now lives. Foster Freeman, son of James Freeman, Sr., was witness to the deed.[42]

James, Senior, moved to Blount Co., Tennessee, where, on 14 May 1811, he purchased 538 acres on Little River.[43] On 27 April 1815, James Freeman of Blount Co., State of Tennessee, made a deed to Nancy Early of his 1/6 part of 260 acres willed to him by the will of Samuel Freeman deceased, where Freeman died on the Yadkin River, a little above the mouth of Hogan's Creek.[44] He lived in Blount County until his death in 1827. He wrote his will 21 August 1827, naming his wife, Lucy; sons John, Druid J., Robert, Foster, and James; and a daughter Eliza

---

[39]Helen F.M. Leary and Maurice R. Stirewalt, *North Carolina Research, Genealogy and Local History* (Raleigh: The North carolina Genealogical Society, 1980):389-390.

[40]Hollingsworth Collection, GA Dept. of Archives and History, Drawer 216, box 64.

[41]Robert S. Davis, Jr., and Rev. Silas Emmett Lucas, Jr., *The Georgia land Lottery Papers, 1805-1914* (Easley, SC: Historical Southern Press, 1979):228.

[42]Hollingsworth Collection.

[43]Blount Co., TN DB 1:___

[44]Surry Co., NC. DB N:456. Witnessed by James Howard and James Freeman.

"Davis."[45]   *The National Banner and Nashville Whig*
reported his death in the issue of Saturday, September 15, 1827.[46]

Issue of James and Lucy (Foster) Freeman:

183	i.	John[5] Freeman. May be the one who bought land in Knox Co., TN in 1795 and 1797.
184	ii.	Drued I (J?)[5] Freeman, m.bond 2 May 1820, Blount Co., TN to Betsy Thompson. He lived near Rockford. Sold several tracts in Blount and Knox Co. the last in 1837. To Georgia. Probably the D.J. Freeman in 1840 census Harris Co., GA.
185	iii.	Eliza[5] Freeman, m. 1822, Blount Co., Rev. J. Dover or Doser.[47]
186	iv.	Robert[5] Freeman.
187	v.	James[5] Freeman, b. 20 August 1782, d. 4 Nov. 1862. Griffin, Spalding Co., GA. m. Sarah Bailey.[48]
+ 188	vi.	Foster[5] Freeman, b. 5 March 1787, d. 28 June 1846, bur. near Griffin, Pike Co., GA; m. 17 Aug 1809, Surry Co., NC, 1st cousin Nancy Freeman # 174.

49. NANNY[4] FREEMAN (Samuel[3], William[2], John[1] Freeman)
was born 13 January 1759 in Granville Co., North Carolina. She
married, probably about 1775 to James Badget. The Badgett
family, like that of her brothers Joshua and James moved to
Tennessee, settling in Knox County. Nanny died and James

---

[45]Blount Co., TN. WB:1:248.

[46]Lucas, *Obits from Tennessee*:136

[47]Notes on Blount Co. marriages sent to Mrs. W.S. Faulkner by Will Parham.

[48]Letter Parham to Berry, 1925. Parham recapitulated Mrs. Berry's data.

Badgett m(2) 5 October 1822, Knox Co. to Fanny Williams.[49] James Badgett, Sr., wrote his will 15 March 1833.[50] In it he names his children and sons-in-law, stating that he had given them each their portion and leaving his estate, both real and personal to his wife, Fanny. She married again in Knox County on 2 May 1835 to J. W. Singleton.[51] As Executors of James Badgett's estate, John W. and Fanny Singleton made an account of expenses, stating that they had incurred expenses in recovering a Judgment against James Badgett, Jr. in the Circuit Court and Supreme Court at Knoxville.[52]

Issue of James and Nanny (Freeman) Badgett:

189   i.   Abraham[5] BADGETT, b.c. 1772, d.c. 1862; m(1) 13 Dec 1810, Surry Co., to Mickey Holser[53]; m(2?) 8 June 1830 Sophira Hunter.[54]

190   ii.   Samuel[5] BADGETT, d.t. will written 15 Jul 1830, Blount Co. Leaves to Brothers[55], sisters, nephew Hannibal Don Carlos.[56] The will does not make it clear whether Don Carlos is a surname or a middle name, (surname Badgett).

---

[49]LDS, IGI, 1992 ed.

[50]Knox Co., TN. WB 5:356.

[51]LDS, IGI, 1992, ed.

[52]Knox Co., TN. WB 6:304.

[53]Holcomb, *Surry Co., Marriages*:8. Abraham's brother Ransom was bondsman.

[54]Letter Parham to Faulkner, 1926.

[55]Letter Parham to Faulkner, 1926, in possession of author.

[56]Blount Co., TN. WB 1:8. Will of Sam Badget.

191	iii.	James[5] BADGETT, Jr. m. 23 Nov. 1820, Knox Co., Susana Harris. had Child Eliza B.[57]
192	iv.	Burrell Freeman[5] BADGETT, m. 19 Jan 1814, Surry Co., to Lucy Forkner.[58] Named in will of brother Samuel #190.
193	v.	Lucy[5] BADGETT, m. 29 Dec. 1794, Surry Co., NC to Edward Lovill.[59]
194	vi.	Elizabeth[5] BADGETT. m(1) 12 March 1801, Surry Co., Robert Cole Carlos/DonCarlos[60], resided Blount Co, TN; m(2) William Pryor. Possible child: Hannibal Don Carlos.
195	vii.	Ransom[5] BADGETT, m. 15 Jan 1803, Caswell Co., Nancy Carloss (Don Carlos?).[61] Named in will of his brother, Samuel Badgett, and of father, James. Possibly father of Robert Don Badgett (d. 1834 Knox Co., TN.[62]) and of Hannibal Don Carlos (Badgett?) named in will of Ransom's brother Samuel.
196	viii.	Rebecca[5] BADGETT. m. Nathaniel Horne who d. testate in Knox Co. c. 1835.[63] Only child, Nancy Gormon.

---

[57] *Ibid.*

[58] Holcomb, *Surry Co., Marriages*:8. Ransom Badgett, bondsman.

[59] *Ibid.*:127.

[60] Holcomb, *Surry Marriages*:32,39. Gives groom as Robert Cole or Don Carter but says filed under DonCarlos; Katherine Kerr Kendall, *Caswell County, North Carolina, Will Books, 1777-1814* (n.p., By the Author, 1979):63. Abstract of will of Archelaus Carlos written 10 Jul 1798. Chn include: Nancy (who m. Ransom Badgett) and Robert Cole Carlos.

[61] Katherin Kerr Kendall, *Caswell County, North Carolina, Marriage Bonds, 1778-1868* (n.p.: By the author, 1981):4.

[62] Knox Co., TN. WB 5:318.

[63] Knox Co., WB 5:368.

104

GENERATION FOUR

DESCENDANTS OF JOHN FREEMAN #11

52. SOLOMON[4] FREEMAN (John[3], John[2], John[1] Freeman) was born about 1743, probably in Bertie County. He first appeared on the Bertie Tax lists as a tithable of his father, John, in 1759, a year after the first appearance of his brother David.[1] In 1764 he was appointed an overseer of roads in the place of Hardy Hunter.[2] In March 1772, his cousin, William Freeman, age 14, orphan of James Freeman, was bound as an apprentice to Solomon to learn carpentry.[3]

By 1774 Solomon had sufficient standing in the community to be named a constable.[4] His brother Elisha replaced him in 1774. He was called for jury duty 1777 and excused in 1778 but served as a petit juror in 1780.[5]

During the Revolution, Solomon served in the militia. Several vouchers and receipts survive, including the one shown here for 18 shillings for "cloathing."[6]

In 1785 Solomon was executor of his father's will; and, the same month, was named executor of the will of Richard Rayner.[7] His will was written in April and proved in May of 1788. He named his wife Martha and children: Joseph, Francis, Ann, John, David, Sarah and James, who was to have the land that "my father, John Freeman, deced, gave me." He states that his three youngest

---

[1]Bertie Co., NC. Tax Lists. NC State Archives, C.R. 010.702.

[2]Haun, *Bertie Co., NC, Minutes* v. 3:25.

[3]*Ibid.* v. 4:1.

[4]*Ibid.* v. 4:38.

[5]*Ibid.* v. 4:81, 86, 113, 117, 118, 119.

[6]NC State Archives. Revolutionary War Pay Vouchers # 3363 and 3868 and Account Book C pp. 40, 52 for sundries furnished and cash paid the militia. See Appendix.

[7]*Ibid.* v. 5:76, 82.

children were Sarah, James and the unborn child. His friend James Cherry and James Wilson were executors.[8]

Solomon apparently married twice, first to a daughter of Joseph Speight; and, secondly, to Martha, who was probably surnamed Cherry.[9]

Solomon Cherry of Bertie County was named guardian to James, orphan of Solomon Freeman, and was also guardian of Martha (the posthumous child) and Sarah.[10] Joseph and Francis chose their grandfather Joseph Speight of Gates County as their guardian. He was appointed guardian of Anne, John and David.[11] Joseph Speight wrote his will, which was probated in Gates County in 1792. He mentioned his grandchildren: Joseph, John, and Anne Freeman.[12]

Issue of Solomon and ____ (Speight) Freeman.

197	i.	Joseph[5] Freeman, d.t. Gates Co., 1842.[13]
198	ii.	Francis[5] Freeman.
199	iii.	Ann(a)[5] Freeman, m. Gates Co., 2 Apr 1798 Henry Lee. Resided Bertie Co.[14]
200	iv.	John[5] Freeman, d. before division of estate of David Freeman.

---

[8]Bertie Co., NC. WB D:90.

[9]Guardian records in Solomon Freeman Estate Records, Bertie Co., and Gates Co.

[10]Bertie Co., NC. Solomon Freeman Estate File. NC State Archives.

[11]Gates Co., NC. Estate Records: File Solomon Freeman, 1791. NC State Archives C.R.

[12]Almasy, *Gates Co., Wills Bk 1*:105-107.

[13]Gates Co., NC. WB 3:36.

[14]Genealogical Soc. Utah, *Gates Co. Marriage Bonds*:116; Gates Co., Estate File, David Freeman 1837. NC State Archives, C.R. 041.508.35. "John F. Lee, Agent for Ann Lee" appeared at court asking an order to divide estate of David Freeman.

201   v.   David[5] Freeman, declared a lunatic, 1805, Joseph Guardian.[15] Died in Gates Co., 1837, testate but will challenged.[16]

Issue of Solomon and Martha (Cherry?) Freeman.

202   vi   Sarah[5] Freeman, m. Mr. Williford, d. after November 1839; resided Bertie Co.[17]

203   vii.   James[5] Freeman, d. after November 1839; resided Tennessee.[18]

204   viii.   Martha[5] Freeman, m. Mr. More/Moore, d. after November 1839; resided Tennessee.[19]

53. ELISHA[4] FREEMAN (John[3], John[2], John[1] Freeman) was born in Bertie County, probably about 1747, since he first appears as a tithable in his father's household in 1763.[20] He was appointed a pettit juror in September 1770.[21]

---

[15]Gates Co., NC. Estate Record, David Freeman, 1805. NC State Archives. C.R. 041.508.35.

[16]*Ibid.* File David Freeman, 1837. David died leaving a will which was presented for probate in Nov. 1837. Joseph Freeman was named Executor. In February Court of 1838 a suit by Martha Moore, et als. challenging the valitity of the will, was heard. The Court upheld the will but Martha stated her intent to appeal to the next Superior Court. In November, 1839 Joseph Freeman, now called Administrator of David's estate, together with John F. Lee, Agent for Ann Lee, James Freeman, Martha More and Sarah Williford, prayed an order to distribute the estate. The fact that Joseph was administrator rather than executor indicates that the will was not allowed.

[17]*Ibid.*

[18]*Ibid.*

[19]*Ibid.*

[20]Jeannette Holland Austin, *The Georgians, Genealogies of Pioneer Settlers* (Baltimore: Genealogical Publishing Co., 1984):122-124. Ms. Austin purports to give a genealogy of this family but presents badly muddled, undocumented data. She mixes John Freemans from several different unconnected families, misidentifying Elisha's grandfather John and his son John and naming only 5 of Elisha's children.

[21]Haun, *Bertie Co., NC, Minutes,*v.3:102.

He continued to do business in Bertie County, serving as Constable in 1774 through 1778.[22] In February 1778, Elisha's father John and his second wife, Elizabeth, deeded to Elisha 640 acres in Cypress at the mouth of Reedy branch, which John had bought of Paul Bunch. In the same month, John also gave a negro woman and 2 negro boys to Elisha.[23]

Elisha Freeman moved to Onslow County sometime before December 1786, when, as a resident of Onslow, he deeded part of his land to his brother Solomon, and part to Jacob Outlaw.[24] He married, probably in Bertie County, to Elizabeth (Betsy) whose surname has not been found. He does not appear on the 1790 census. Elisha made his will in Onslow County on 11 Nov 1789. It was not probated until 1793. The original of the will is in the Archives but no recorded copy survives. He speaks of money owed him in Bertie County and names his children.[25] He named his widow, Elizabeth, and His "Friend" Reuben Grant, executors.

His widow, Elizabeth, appears on the 1800 census with 2 males 16/26 and females 1 10/16, 16/26 and one over 45. In 1810 her household had 1 male 16/26, 1 26/45 and females 2 under 10, 1 10/16, 1 16/26 and one over 45. It appears that Elizabeth had a married son, daughter-in-law and grandchildren living with her in 1810.[26]

Issue of Elisha and Betty ( ) Freeman:

       205   i.   Isaac[5] Freeman.

---

[22]*Ibid.* v. 4:38, 78, 85.

[23]Bertie Co., NC. DB M:372, 480.

[24]Bertie Co., NC. DB O: 145, 151.

[25]Onslow Co., NC. Original Wills, LDS Film # 019437. The Reuben Grant of Onslow who is co-executor of Elisha's will was not the same person as Reuben Grant of Caswell and Surry Counties who married Temperence Freeman, #173.

[26]1800 census, Onslow Co., NC p.137; 1810 census, Onslow Co., p. 772.

206	ii.	Hannah[5] Freeman, m.bond 24 Jan 1802, Onslow Co., William Henderson.[27]
207	iii.	Nancy[5] Freeman, m.bond 24 Jan 1797, Onslow Co., Matthew Wise.
208	iv.	Ferribar[5] Freeman.
209	v.	James[5] Freeman.
210	vi.	Mark[5] Freeman.
+ 211	vii.	John[5] Freeman, m, Susannah ___ ; will probated Onslow, 1857
212	viii.	Betty[5] Freeman.

55. MOSES[4] FREEMAN (John[3], John[2], John[1] Freeman) was born in Bertie County, probably about 1756. He first appears as a taxable in his father's house in 1770. It is difficult to distinguish records pertaining to this Moses from those of his older cousin, Moses # 31. Bertie records sometimes designate this man as Moses Freeman, Jr., of Moses, son of John. The first record which can be identified as pertaining to him is the designation of Moses Freeman, Jr., as a member of the petit juror in 1778.[28]

In 1778 his father, John, deeded him 403 acres, for love and affection, which John had gotten by deed from James Freeman, who had purchased it from Jacob Parker.[29] His wife was named Mary, surname unknown. With her, he deeded to Luke White 100 acres.[30] In 1788, Moses made deeds, for love and affection, to his son Josiah and to his daughter Betsy, to each a slave. Witnesses to these last deeds were Moses' brothers

---

[27]Marriage Bonds of Onslow Co.,

[28]Haun, *Bertie Co., NC, Minutes* v. 4:89.

[29]Bertie Co., NC. DB M:372.

[30]Bertie Co., NC. DB O:66.

Solomon and Aaron, which would seem to identify this Moses as father of these children.[31]

An undated estate file labeled Moses Freeman contains papers from a law suit by Carney Freman, "indorsee" of Moses Freeman against Moses Freeman, Junior. Marked, "Moses Freeman not to be found." Property attached, administrator appointed.[32]

Issue of Moses and Mary ( ) Freeman:

213	i.	Betsy[5] Freeman.
214	ii.	Josiah[5] Freeman.

56. AARON[4] FREEMAN (John[3], John[2], John[1] Freeman) was the youngest of the sons of John Freeman. It is his Revolutionary Pension file which identifies his parents as John and Ann Freeman, giving the information of a previously unknown marriage of his father. It also gives his birthdate and birthplace as 30 January 1758, in Bertie County.[33] The pension file also states that Aaron married Judith Fleetwood on 9 September 1777 in Bertie County.

As the Revolutionary War drew to a close, troops were still needed. Aaron entered the service in Dobbs Co., North Carolina and was discharged at Ashley Hill, South Carolina, on the completion of his one year term of service. He was sick at the time of discharge and remained awhile at Camden, South Carolina, in hospital. Served as sergeant in guard at Camden.

No reason for Aaron's presence in Dobbs County at the time of his enlistment has been found.

John Freeman, Sr., left his son, Aaron, his manner plantation, whereon he lived, and his lands southerly thereof, and his saw mill. Apparently in an effort to protect his inheritance,

---

[31] Bertie Co., NC. DB O:230.

[32] Bertie Co., NC. Estate Records. NC State Archives, C.R. 010.508.

[33] National Archives, Pension File of Aaron Freeman, W 8833.

Aaron filed a petition in August 1785, seeking to enforce a prenuptial agreement, which his father had made with his third wife, Sarah, that she would accepted a settlement in lieu of dower rights.[34]

On 15 July 1786, Aaron gave an acre to the Baptist Society for the building of a house of public worship. He added to his holdings in 1788 by purchasing 370 acres from Capt. David Meredith and Sarah, his wife; and the same day, with his wife Judith, Aaron sold Meredith 788 acres, whereon he and Judith lived, and 290 acres in St. John's Neck at Cypress Swamp, near the mouth of Tumbling or Gumbling Branch.[35] He was still in Bertie County at the time of the 1790 Census and the 1800 Census.

Aaron, his wife Judith and his growing family moved to Caldwell County, Kentucky, where his cousin, Michael Freeman, son of James # 12, also settled. Christian (Freeman) Baker, daughter of Aaron's cousin King Freeman, and her husband, Blake, also moved to Caldwell County.

According to the pension application filed by Judith, Aaron died 26 November 1821 in Livingston Co., Kentucky.

Issue of Aaron and Judith (Fleetwood) Freeman:

215	i.	Alexander[5] Freeman, b. 23 Apr 1778, Bertie Co.; d. 28 May 1829,Caldwell Co., KY; unmarried. Will written 1829, names brothers: Hardy, Henry and John P.; and "the girls."[36]
216	ii.	Elizabeth[5] Freeman, b. 15 Sep 1779, Bertie Co., NC; d. 14 Nov 1805.[37]

---

[34]Bertie Co., NC. Estate Records, file of John Freeman. NC State Archives, C.R. 010.504.29

[35]Bertie Co., NC. DB N:268; O:292, 278.

[36]Pension File, Aaron Freeman, W 8833; Caldwell Co., KY, WB A:426.

[37]Pension File, W 8833.

217	iii.	John Parker[5] Freeman, b. 21 Jun 1781, Bertie Co., NC; d. 18 Apr 1786, Bertie Co., NC.[38]
218	iv.	Edmund[5] Freeman, b. 12 Feb 1785, Bertie Co., NC; d. 16 Mar 1790, Bertie Co., NC.[39]
219	v.	Ann[5] Freeman, b. 22 Oct 1787, Bertie Co., NC; m. 17 May 1810, Daniel Wormarlsdorff. 6 children.[40]
220	vi.	Christian[5] Freeman, b. 22 Mar 1790. Bertie Co., NC; m. 27 Mar 1810, William Evans.[41]
221	vii.	John Parker[5] Freeman, b. 25 Feb 1792, Bertie Co., NC; m. 9 Mar 1817, Christian Co., KY, Betsy Wolff.[42]
222	viii.	Polley[5] Freeman, 2 Dec 1794, Bertie Co., NC; m.13 Aug 1822, Caldwell Co., KY, Perryman Cannon.[43]
223	ix.	Delilah[5] Freeman, b. 3 Nov 1796, Bertie Co., NC; m. 18 Jan 1818, Caldwell Co., KY, Mathew Stephenson.[44]
224	x.	Jarsey[5] Freeman, b. 16 Oct 1798, Bertie Co., NC; m. 4 Apr 1822 Pulaski Co., KY, Nutter Scott.[45]

---

[38]*Ibid.*

[39]*Ibid.*

[40]*Ibid.*

[41]*Ibid.*.

[42]*Ibid.*; LDS, International Genealogical Index, 1992, ed.

[43]*Ibid.*

[44]*Ibid.*

[45]*Ibid.*

225   xi.   Patsey[5] Freeman, b. 4 Sep 1800; d. 29 Nov 1805.[46]

226   xii.   Henry[5] Freeman, b. 7 Jun 1802 m. 7 Sep 1824, Caldwell Co., KY, Nancy W. Thompson.[47]

227   xiii.   Hardy[5] Freeman, b. 29 Sep 1804; m. 22 Oct 1832, Caldwell Co., KY, Ruth A. Son.[48]

---

[46]*Ibid.*

[47]*Ibid.*

[48]*Ibid.*

Account of Taxables Listed with James Campbell

Name	White	Negro Men	Negro Women	Total		Name
William Harle	1			1		Brought forward & Contin
James Aaron	1			1		Isfhew Sparkman &
Thomas Aaron	1			1		Negroes Phill & Judith
John Liverman	1			1		Jeremiah Holland
Rebecca Joyner for Lewis Baulch	1			1		Aaron Askew
William Pierce	1			1		John Askew
David Freeman	1			1		John Berry & Son Neic
William Robeson	1			1		Stephen White
Adam Harleford & Son Isaac	2			2		James Burrass Senr
Joshua Evans	1			1		Negroes Pompey & Ben
James Wilson & John Wilson Robert Hendry	3			3		John Hail & Son Dem
John Meizelle & Son Henry	2			2		Edmund Glaughn
John Simmons	1			1		Luke White Senr & Son Media
Peter Parker	1		—	1		Luke Rainer
John Davison for Yolow William and John						Ross Bennett Baker
	2	1	2	6		Isaiah

Name	White	Negro Men	Negro Women	Total		Name
Sam Moll Nan						Cuff Sam 2 Males Taff
John Mades & Son James	2			2		Hagar Sall 2 females
Godfrey Askew	1			1		Capt John Freeman & Sons Henba & John
Edward Sparkman & Negroes Sarah	1		1	2		Boatswain
Benjamin Slone & Sons John and Benjamin	3			3		Cris Pompey — 4 Males Adam
James Freeman & Son Michael	2			2		Dinah
Daniel Ventress	1			1		Sadah Ann 4 females Elizabeth
John Burrass Senr and Sons Joshua and Absalom	3	1		4		
Negroes Man Lazarus						Mr James Howell & John Glaughan
Richard Rainer & Sa. Hall	2		—	2		Dick
Benjamin Hooker	1			1		Harper 3 Males Taff
Richard Sowell	1		—	1		Patt
Solomon Baker	1			1		Patt Nann 2 females
Samuel Harle	1		—	1		
Capt. William Spark man & Negroes Jo. Silas } Men Hannah, Dick } Women Silla & Jinny	1	2	4	7		
Carried forward	41	4	7	52		

Tax list, 1767, Bertie County, NC. C.R.010.702.1.2

114

GENERATION FOUR

DESCENDANTS OF JAMES FREEMAN #12

57. DAVID[4] FREEMAN (James[3], John[2], John[1] Freeman) appears, from tax records, to have been the oldest son of James Freeman. David, was almost a contemporary of his cousin, David #50, son of John #11. Both appeared on tax list with their fathers through 1761. In 1764 each appeared as a taxable in his own right, but on the same list with his father.[1] In 1765 one David only appears on the lists. John, named no son David in his 1785 will.[2] But, a David whose signature matches that made by a David of Bertie County, died in 1806 in Mecklenburg County. Although James left no will and no probate record exists naming his issue, it seems certain that the David who survived until 1806 was son of James.

Signature of David Freeman in 1768 witness to John Davison will, Bertie Co; Signature on his will 1805, Mecklenburg Co.

David bought of Susanna Howell a tract of 150 acres in Chincopen Swamp. Witnesses included James Freeman, probably David's father.[3] David married to Mary, whose surname has not

---

[1]Bertie Co., NC. Tax Lists. NC State Archives, C.R. 010.702.

[2]Bertie Co., NC. Original Will of John Freeman, 1785. NC State Archives, C.R. 010.801.

[3]Bertie Co., NC. DB K:389.

been found.[4] In 1768 David witnessed the will of his uncle John Davison. The original will bears his signature.[5]

On 7 November 1770 David and his wife Mary sold their land in Bertie to James Howell of Hertford County.[6] He disappeared from the Bertie County tax lists in that year.

On 17 October 1779 Joseph Taggart of Mecklenburg County sold to David Freeman a tract of 200 acres on Shugar Creek in Mecklenburg County.[7] He appears to have lived in Mecklenburg County until the end of his life. He seems to have married a second time since his will names a wife Jean and a stepdaughter Elizabeth Hayes.[8]

Issue of David and Ann ( ) Freeman.

+	228	i.	Michael[5] Freeman, b. 1 Mar 1764, Bertie Co., NC; d. 9 Feb 1842, Caldwell Co., KY; Rev. War, Pensioner.[9]
	229	ii.	Reuben[5] Freeman.
	230	iii.	James[5] Freeman.
	231	iv.	Sarah[5] Freeman, m. Mr. Bigham.
	232	v.	Ann[5] Freeman, m. Mr. Berryhill.
	233	vi.	Jemimah[5] Freeman, m. Mr. Stephenson.

---

[4]Bertie Co., NC. DB L:275.

[5]Bertie Co., NC. Original Will of John Davison. NC State Archives, C.R. 010.801.4.

[6]Bertie Co., NC. DB L:275.

[7]Brent H. Holcomb, C.A.L.S. and Elmer O. Parker, *Mecklenburg County, North Carolina Deed Abstracts, 1763-1779* (Easley, SC: Southern Historical Press, 1979):200

[8]Mecklenburg Co., NC. Original Will of David Freeman. NC State Archives, C.R. 065.801.17.

[9]National Archives, Rev. War Pension file of Michael Freeman, S-30426.

59. WILLIAM⁴ FREEMAN (James³, John², John¹ Freeman) was born on 26 October 1759 in Bertie County. He was much younger than his brothers who were born in the 1740's and is possibly the child of a second marriage. William was orphaned before the age of fourteen and at that age was indentured to his cousin, Solomon Freeman, to learn the trade of carpentry.¹⁰

He enlisted in Bertie or Martin County as a private with the North Carolina troops in 1776, for a three months period in Capt. Andrew Oliver's company, Col Hogan's Regiment; from 20 July 1778 he served nine months in captain Child's Company in Col Hart's regiment; in 1781 he served three months in Captain Taylor's company in Col. Eaton's regiment and was in the battles of Guilford and Camden.¹¹

He was a resident in Martin County in 1786 when he married Mary Bryan, daughter of Robert Bryan.¹² He is probably the William Freman, who owned land in Martin County, selling to Mason Lee, Chistopher Hines and Thomas Watson.¹³ He was living in Burke Co., North Carolina, in 1832, when he applied for and received a pension.¹⁴

He moved to Greene County, Missouri about 1835 and died there 27 or 28 July 1838. Mary, his widow, died 5 November 1845.¹⁵

Issue of William and Mary (Bryan) Freeman:¹⁶

---

¹⁰Haun, *Bertie Minutes* v. 4:1.

¹¹National Archives, Pension File of William Freeman, W 10042.

¹²*Ibid.*

¹³Martin Co., NC. DB B:181; C:311, 178.

¹⁴Pension File. W10042.

¹⁵*Ibid.*

¹⁶List of Children, their ages and residences and marriages taken from pension file W. 10042, except as otherwise noted.

234	i.	Reddick[5] Freeman. b. 8 Apr. 1783,[17] d. 17 August 1783, bur. Saraduc Cem. Caldwell Co.;[18] m. 2 Feb 1815, Burke Co., Rebecca Ellis.[19] Resided Caldwell Co., NC, 1850.[20]
235	ii.	John[5] Freeman, aged 54 in 1850; may be the one who m. Lavicy Williams on 16 Nov. 1815 in Burke Co. Resided Greene Co., MO in 1850.[21]
236	iii.	Larry[5] Freeman, aged about 52 in 1850, resided Owen Co., IN; m. 12 Aug 1822, Burke Co., Nancy Colyer.
237	iv.	Lemuel H.[5] Freeman, aged 49 in 1850, resided in Greene Co., MO.[22]
238	v.	Elizabeth[5] Freeman, twin of James age about 47 in 1850 wife of Isaac Smith , resided Caldwell Co., NC.
239	vi.	James[5] Freeman, twin of Elizabeth, age about 47, resided Owen Co., IN in 1850.
240	vii.	Nancy[5] Freeman, about 45 years in 1850 wife of Green Austin. Resided Greene Co., MO.[23]

---

[17]Note birthdate in 1783 and marriage date of parents is reported as 1786.

[18]NC Cemetery Index. LDS film #822,951. Rebecca, b. 8 June 1783, d. 21 Oct 1861, bur. Saraduc Cem. Caldwell Co.

[19]NC Archives. Marriage Bonds Index.

[20]"Rederick" Freeman died testate in Caldwell Co., 1873. WB I:103. Original in Archives.

[21]LDS, IGI, 1992, ed; 1850 Census Greene Co., MO. p. 257. Household 194/Family 194. 8 children in household.

[22]1850 Census Greene Co., MO p.254, Campbell Twp. Household 153/Family 153. 7Children in household.

[23]1850 census, Greene Co., MO p. 265. Household 302/ Family 302. Nancy listed as age 43. 5 Children in household.

241 viii. Frances[5] Freeman. about 41 years wife of Jacob Painter in 1850. Resided Greene Co., MO.[24]

242 ix. Rachel[5] Freeman, d. by 1849; m. John Austin. had daughter Asenath.[25]

Others who died without issue.

---

[24] 1850 Census, Greene Co., MO, p. 268. Household 347/ Family 347. Frances age 38 in Census. 5 Children listed.

[25] 1850 Census, Greene Co., MO, p. 175. Household 454/ Family 454. Rachel not listed in family, probably dead by this date. 3 children listed.

241   viii.   Frances[5] Freeman. about 41 years wife of Jacob Painter in 1850. Resided Greene Co., MO.[24]

242   ix.   Rachel[5] Freeman, d. by 1849; m. John Austin. had daughter Asenath.[25]

Others who died without issue.

---

[24]1850 Census, Greene Co., MO, p. 268. Household 347/ Family 347. Frances age 38 in Census. 5 Children listed.

[25]1850 Census, Greene Co., MO, p. 175. Household 454/ Family 454. Rachel not listed in family, probably dead by this date. 3 children listed.

GENERATIONS FIVE & SIX

82. RICHARD⁵ FREEMAN (William,⁴ John,³ William,² John¹ Freeman) is probably the one of the name who was married in Oglethorpe County, Georgia, on 3 May 1797 to Elizabeth Haygood (Haggard) daughter of Samuel Haggard and Nancy Hix of Surry County, North Carolina. Richard Freeman died in Franklin Co., Georgia in 1841. He is presumed to be the son of William Freeman of Surry. Several of his siblings also apparently moved to Georgia.[1]

Issue of Richard and Elizabeth Haggard.

243	i.	Sydney⁶ Freeman
244	ii.	Richard⁶ Freeman
245	iii.	Elizabeth⁶ Freeman
246	iv.	Frances "Franky"⁶ Freeamn
247	v.	James⁶ Freeman
248	vi.	John⁶ Freeman
249	vii.	Sarah⁶ Freeman
250	viii.	Nathaniel H.⁶ Freeman
251	ix.	William S.⁶ Freeman

99. JEREMIAH⁵ FREEMAN (John⁴, William³, William², John¹ Freeman) lived in Bertie County. He married 2 Oct 1792 to Mary Norfleet, daughter of his step-mother, Sarah ( ) (Norfleet)

---

[1]Data on this family has been received from Victor Lewis Rainey, Rt 1 Bx 1887, Lovonia, GA 30553.

Freeman.[2] Jeremiah's father died in 1793 and willed Jeremiah the home plantation, and a Brandy still after Sarah's death or widowhood. He also gave Jermiah a tract bought of Michel Briton, a negro man and girl, a feather bed, livestock and blacksmiths tools.[3] Sarah, his step-mother, made her will in 1807.[4] It was only three years later, on 4 January 1810 that Jeremiah wrote his own will, which was probated the next month. He named Hardy Freeman and Aron Askew executors.[5]

Issue of Jeremiah and Mary (Norfleet) Freeman:[6]

252	i.	Saley or Sary[6] Freeman, m. Mr. Spivey.
253	ii.	Jacob[6] Freeman.
254	iii.	Christian[6] Freeman.

101. RACHEL[5] FREEMAN (John[4], William[3], William[2], John[1] Freeman) married James Outlaw. He died in 1783, in Hertford County.[7]

Issue of James and Rachel (Freeman) Outlaw:[8]

255	i.	James[6] OUTLAW.

---

[2]NC State Archives, Marriage Bonds, Grooms list.

[3]Bertie Co., NC. Original Will of John Freeman. NC State Archives, C.R. 010.801.

[4]Bertie Co., NC. Original Will of Sarah Freeman. NC State Archives, C.R. 010.801.

[5]Bertie Co., NC. WB F:136.

[6]All data on heirs from will of Jeremiah.

[7]Holtzeclaw, "The Outlaw Family" in *Historical Southern Families* v. 15:30-32.

[8]All data on Descendants from Holtzeclaw.

256   ii.   Lewis[6] OUTLAW.

257   iii.   William[6] OUTLAW.

108. CHRISTIAN[5] FREEMAN, (Joshua[4], William[3], William[2], John[1] Freeman) married first to James Wood. He wrote his will in Northhampton Co., on 3 April 1795. It was proved in March 1797. She married second to Mr. __ Moring. Her will was written on 28 May 1814 and states that she was a resident of Northampton County. It was probated in Bertie County in 1816.[9]

Issue of James and Christian (Freeman) Wood:[10]

258   i.   Mary[6] WOOD.

259   ii.   Elizabeth[6] WOOD.

260   iii.   Freeman[6] WOOD.

261   iv.   John Edwards[6] WOOD.

262   v.   Sarah[6] WOOD.

263   vi.   Celia[6] WOOD.

264   vii.   John[6] WOOD.

Issue of __ and Christian (Freeman) (Wood) Moring.

265   viii.   William[6] MORING.

111. JOSHUA[5] FREEMAN (Joshua[4], William[3], William[2], John[1] Freeman), a resident of Bertie County, married 11 February 1793

---

[9]Bertie Co., NC. Original Will of Christian Moring. NC State Archives, C.R. 010.801.

[10]Margaret M. Hofmann, *Northampton County, North Carolina, 1759-1808: Genealogical Abstracts of Wills* (Weldon, NC: The Roanoke New Company, 1975):100.

in Gates County to Mary Pipkin.[11] He died between November 1805[12] and 1816.[13]

Issue of Joshua and Mary (Pipkin) Freeman:[14]

266	i.	Nancy[6] Freeman, m. Malachi Weston.
267	ii.	Richard[6] Freeman.
268	iii.	Isaac[6] Freeman.

112. JACOB[5] FREEMAN (Joshua[4], William[3], William[2], John[1] Freeman), a resident of Hertford County, married 30 June 1798, Gates County to Sarah Pipkin.[15] He died between the dates of the 1805 agreement and the 1816 petition.[16]

Issue of Jacob and Sarah (Pipkin) Freeman:

269	i.	Isaac Pipkin[6] Freeman.
270	ii.	John[6] Freeman.
271	iii.	Celia[6] Freeman.

116. CHRISTIAN[5] FREEMAN (King[4], William[3], William[2], John[1] Freeman) married Blake Baker who was named as her husband in King Freeman's will. Blake and Christian Baker moved to

---

[11]NC State Archives, Marriage Bonds.

[12]Bertie Co., NC Estate File of James Freeman. NC State Archives, C.R.010.504.29. Signator of an agreement to confirm title to a negro girl of James Freeman to his brother William.

[13]*Ibid*. Petition for division of a tract belonging to James Freeman.

[14]*Ibid*. All data on children from Petition.

[15]NC State Archives, Marriage Bonds.

[16]N. 10 *Supra*.

Caldwell County, Kentucky. In April 1813 an account was recorded for 1811-1813 for the estate of Sarah Freeman decd and King Freeman, decd was recorded in Caldwell County.[17] Blake Baker was guardian for his children for the property left them.

Issue of Blake and Christian (Freeman) Baker:[18]

272	i.	Betsey[6] BAKER, m. ___Sprague.
273	ii.	Sally[6] BAKER, m. ____Holly.
274	iii.	John F.[6] BAKER.
275	iv.	Celia[6] BAKER.
276	v.	Polly[6] BAKER.
277	vi.	Thomas L.[6] BAKER.
278	vii.	Blake[6] BAKER, b. 26 Jun 1804, d. 29 Aug 1852, Trigg Co., KY; m. Edna J. Gresham.[19]
279	viii.	Christian[6] BAKER.
280	ix.	Tinsey[6] BAKER

117. WILLIAM[5] FREEMAN (James[4], William[3], William[2], John[1] Freeman) married 19 October 1793 in Gates County to Mary (Trotman) Rountree, widow of John Rountree.[20] On 25 June 1801, William deeded for love and affection to his son, James T.

---

[17]Caldwell Co., KY. WB A:39-41.

[18]*Ibid.* Children listed as named in account.

[19]Birth, death and marriage dates from the record of Patricia Garmon of Escondido, CA.

[20]Gates Co., NC. Estate File of John Rountree, 1793. NC State Archives, C.R. 041.508.104. "In Obedience To and Order of Court hereto annext withe Subscribers have Audited & setled the Accounts of Miles Rountree Administrator & **William Freeman who intermarried mary rountree Administratrix to the Estate of John Rountree.** Dated February 13th 1796."

Freeman a tract formerly given by Thomas Trotman to his daughter Mary Rountree.[21] William died circa 1804 and his father, James Freeman became guardian of William's son.[22]

Issue of William and Mary (Trotman) (Rountree) Freeman:

> 281   i.   James Trotman[6] Freeman, 16 October 1819 Gates Co., to Mary Hinton; d. testate Gates Co., 1842.[23]

120. THOMAS[5] FREEMAN (James[4], William[3], William[2], John[1] Freeman) was born in May of 1773.[24] He became guardian to his nephew, James T. Freeman, in 1810, after the death of James's grandfather.[25]

Thomas married first in Gates County, 14 July 1806 to Rachel Hurdle who must have died very shortly after the wedding, before the birth of any children.[26] She must have had an estate in her own name, since Thomas Freeman made bond for $2000 as her administrator.[27] On 24 January 1807, just six months after his marriage to Rachel, Thomas married in Chowan County to Hannah Hurdle.[28]

---

[21]Gates Co., NC. DB 5:411.

[22]Gates Co., NC. Estate File of William Freeman. NC State Archives, C.R. 041.508.

[23]Gates Co., NC. WB 2:47.

[24]Information from descendant in 1985, Helen Freeman Taylor, Box 8025, Dallas, TX 75205. Age on tombstone, Cabiness- Burner Cem., Monroe Co., GA. Died November 9, 1859, 86 yrs 6 mo.

[25]Gates Co., NC. Estate File of William Freeman, 1808. NC State Archives, C.R.041.508.35.

[26]NC State Archives, Marriage Bonds.

[27]Gates Co., NC. Estate File of Rachel Freeman. NC State Arhives, C.R.041.508.35

[28]NC State Archives, Marriage Bonds.

Thomas and his family were living in Freeman's District in Wilkes Co., Georgia at the time of the 1821 Land Lottery. He moved to Monroe Co., Georgia on 5 December 1822, starting from Jones County. Thomas died 9 November 1859 and is buried in Cabiness-Burner Cemetery in Monroe Co., Georgia.[29]

Issue of Thomas and Hannah (Hurdle) Freeman:[30]

282	i.	Alexander[6] Freeman, b. 1809, NC, m. 5 Aug 1849, Elizabeth D. Miller.
283	ii.	Josiah Beauregard.[6] Freeman, b. 25 Nov. 1811, NC, d. 5 Aug 1882, Indian Springs, Butts Co., GA; m. 16 Aug 1849, Sarah White Hearne.
284	iii.	Eliza[6] Freeman, b. 1813, NC; d. 25 Feb 1856, Monroe Co., GA; m. 10 Dec 1828, Albert Harvey.
285	iv.	Thomas Paul[6] Freeman, b. 16 Jan 1815, NC; d. 24 Dec 1887, Monroe Co., GA; m. 24 Apr 1851, Mary Elizabeth Walker.
286	v.	Rachel[6] Freeman, b. 1820; m. 2 Jun 1842, Michael G. Brady.
287	vi.	Elizabeth A.[6] Freeman, b. 1823, GA; m. 11 Jan 1844, Marion M. Dicken(s).
288	vii.	William H.[6] Freeman, b. 1823, GA; m. 25 Apr 1854, Susan G. Garr.

151. PENELOPE[5] PERRY (Melicent[4], William[3], William[2], John[1] Freeman) married 12 Aug. 1806 in Bertie to Nathan Sessoms. Named in their grandmother's will were six children and provision for future children born to Penelope.

---

[29]Letter 21 January 1985, Helen Freeman Taylor to the author.

[30]All data on descendants from Helen Freeman Taylor.

Issue of Mr. Nathan and Penelope (Perry) Sessoms:

289	i.	Emily[6] SESSOMS.
290	ii.	Elanson[6] SESSOMS.
291	iii.	Peneniah[6] SESSOMS.
292	iv.	Harrell[6] SESSOMS.
293	v.	Selah[6] SESSOMS.
294	vi.	Laviny[6] SESSOMS.

152. (A)MILLISANT[5] PERRY (Melicent[4], William[3], William[2], John[1] Freeman) married John Simons. Three children were named in their grandmother's will with provision for future born issue.

Issue of John and Millisant (Perry) Simons:

295	i.	Laviny Catherine[6] SIMONS.
296	ii.	Elizabeth Millisant[6] SIMONS.
297	iii.	Mary Louise[6] SIMONS.

171. ALEXANDER HAWKINS[5] FREEMAN (Aaron[4], Samuel[3], William[2], John[1] Freeman) was born about 1796[31] in Surry County and died there in 1858.[32] He married Sally Mosely and they are the ancestors of most of the present day descendants of Aaron Freeman who still reside in Surry County. County records and histories are have much data on descendants of this couple.

---

[31]1850 Census, Surry County, p.313. Household #654, family #654.

[32]Hester Bartlett Jackson, ed., *The Heritage of Surry County, North Carolina, Vol. 1 --1983* (Winston-Salem: Surry Co., Genealogical Assn., 1983):Section 517.

Issue of Alexander Hawkins and Sally (Mosely) Freeman:

298   i.   West(ly) M.[6] Freeman, b.c. 1825; d. 1857; m. Virginia Franklin.[33]

299   ii.   Hawkins[6] Freeman, b.c. 1822;d. bef. Nov. 1857; m. 27 Dec 1851, Mary Cave.[34]

300   iii.   Henry[6] Freeman, b.c. 1826. To Missouri.[35]

301   iv.   Rebecca[6] Freeman, b.c. 1827.[36]

302   v.   Mary[6] Freeman, b.c. 1829; m. 26 Feb 1855, Dalton Forkner.[37]

303   vi.   Nancy[6] Freeman, b.c. 1834.[38]

304   vii.   Alexander Hamilton[6] Freeman, b.c. 1836; d. 1915; m. Elizabeth (Martin) Waugh, widow of Dr. James Waugh. Twin of Nicholas.[39]

305   viii.   Nicholas[6] Freeman, b.c. 1836. Twin of Alexander.[40]

---

[33] Jackson, *Heritage of Surry. Sect. #517.*; Surry County, NC. Estate File of West. M. Freeman, NC State Archives, C.R. 092.508.

[34] 1850 Census, p. 313; Surry Co., NC. Marriage Bonds; Surry Co., NC. Estate file of Hawkins Freeman. NC State Archives C.R. 092.508. Petition of widow Mary for years support.

[35] 1850 Census, Surry Co., p.313; Letter 22 Feb 1922 Robert A. Freeman, son of Alexander Hamilton Freeman, to Mrs. W.S. Faulkner. Original in possession of author.

[36] 1850 Census, Surry Co., p.313.

[37] 1850 Census, Surry Co., p.313; Surry County Marriage Bonds. *Heritage of Surry,* Sect. #517.

[38] 1850 Census, Surry Co., 1850, p.313.

[39] Letter, R.A. Freeman to Faulkner; *Heritage of Surry,* Sect.#517.

[40] 1850 Census, Surry Co., p.313.

306	ix.	Samuel Aaron[6] Freeman, b.c. 1842, d. 1876; m. 26 Jan 1864 Susane Waugh.[41]
307	x.	Abner[6] Freeman?[42]
308	xi.	Edward[6] Freeman?[43]
309	xii.	Sally[6] Freeman?[44]

173. TEMPERANCE[5] FREEMAN (Joshua[4], Samuel[3], William[2], John[1] Freeman) was born to Joshua Freeman and his wife, Lucy, on 2 September 1776. Her first husband was Reuben Grant, son of James and Ann (Diskin) Grant of Caswell County, North Carolina. He was a young businessman who moved to Surry County about 1793, and married soon after to Temperance. Reuben bought lots in the newly formed town of Rockford and built and became the proprietor of a large hotel there. He was also engaged in the buying and selling of Iron with his father-in-law, Joshua Freeman.

Reuben Grant served as witness in a case between Joshua Freeman vs. Jesse Lester on 8 March 1808; and Reuben and Temperance Grant were witnesses for the State in the case of The State vs. Benjamin Lee for Pettit Larceny on 9 March 1809.[45]

Reuben Grant died unexpectedly on 27 March 1809 at the home of his father-in-law, Joshua Freeman. An inquest was held which decreed that the death was by Act of God.[46] Joshua Freeman moved to Tennessee about 1810 or 1811, taking with him his daughter Temperance Grant, and her young family.

---

[41]1850 Census, Surry Co., p.313; *Heritage of Surry*, Sect. #517.

[42]Letter R.A.Freeman to Mrs. W.S. Faulkner. Not in census, or will of Aaron Freeman.

[43]*Ibid.*

[44]*Ibid.*

[45]"Surry County, North Carolina, Superior Court Minutes," in *Journal of Surry County Genealogical Association*, Vol 10, #3:4; Vol. 11, #2:8; #3:6

[46]Surry Co., NC. Crt Minutes, 8 Sept. 1809.

On 24 April 1813 in Knox County, Tennessee, Temperance Grant married Richard Kearby.[47] Tradition is that the couple moved to Kentucky where Kearby, a drunk, quickly spent the money left by Reuben Grant.[48] All efforts to trace Temperance and Richard Kearby have failed. Several of her children did live for a time in Shelby County, Kentucky, but tax lists and deeds show no Kearby/Kirby family there.

Issue of Reuben and Temperance (Freeman) Grant:

310	i.	Joshua D.[6] GRANT, m. 3 Dec 1822, Shelby Co., KY to Nancy A. Foree.[49]
311	ii.	"Polly"[6] GRANT, m. M. H.[Michael?] Hinch.[50] Resided Randolph Co., GA 1830 Census; Hinch was Sheriff of Randolph and later Stewart Co., 1830; Chambers Co., AL 1840-1850 Census. She apparently d. bef. 1850 census.
312	iii.	Lucinda Ann[6] GRANT, b. 15 Aug 1799, d. 15 Apr 1833, Rockville, Monroe Co., TN; m. 2 Apr 1820, Blount Co., TN, John McCrosky.[51]
313	iv.	Elizabeth Caroline[6] GRANT, b. 19 Mar 1804, d. 23 Aug 1824, Monroe Co., TN; m. 4 Jul 1822, Samuel McCrosky (his second wife).[52]

---

[47]Knox Co., TN, Marriage Bond.

[48]A.K. Faulkner, Notes.

[49]Shelby Co., KY. Marriage Records.

[50]Letter, James Freeman Grant, Columbus Georgia, Mar 17 1832, to his sister Lucinda Ann McCrosky. Copy in possession of author. Letter speaks of "Sister Polly" and Mr. Hinch.

[51]Genealogical Notes of Anna Kirk Faulkner (Mrs. Wm Scott Faulkner), grandmother of the author. and letters, Sally Lynn, Tacoma, Washington, to the author.

[52]A.K. Faulkner Notes.

314	v.	Jacob[6] GRANT, b.c. 1805. Resided Shelby Co., KY.[53]
315	vi.	Matilda Dandridge[6] GRANT, b. 2 Feb 1807, Rockford, Surry Co., NC; d. 6 Jan 1864, Near Reads AL; m. Thomas R. Mangham.[54] Resided Randolph Co., GA 1830; 1840 Russell Co., AL; Benton Co, AL 1850.
316	vii.	James Freeman[6] GRANT, b. 29 Dec 1808, Rockford, Surry Co., NC; d. 10 Oct 1878, Jacksonville, Calhoun Co., AL; m. 15 May 1834, Monroe Co., TN, Elizabeth Lefevre Riley. He was owner and editor of the *Jacksonville Republican* and served as Treasurer of the State of Alabama.[55]

176. MARY "POLLY"[5] FREEMAN (Joshua[4], Samuel[3], William[2], John[1] Freeman) was born 10 November 1785. She married the Reverend Jeremiah King on 16 November 1804 in Surry County. The Reverend King was a minister of the Methodist Episcopal Church. He joined the ministry on probation in 1799 and was in Virginia District. He was sent to Goshen and Newbern in North Carolina; in 1800 to Salisbury; in 1801 to Camden, 1802 to Williamsburg. At the 1804 Conference held at Salem, VA, on April 10, he was ordained and appointed to Yadkin, NC.[56]

The family moved from Surry county to Knox Co., TN about 5 miles from Knoxville. Polly King, died 12 January 1858.

Issue of Jeremiah and Polly (Freeman) King:

---

[53]A.K.Faulkner Notes; Shelby County Ky Deeds and Tax lists.

[54]A.K. Faulkner Notes; Letters to her from descendants.

[55]Thomas McAdory Owen, LL.D., *History of Alabama and Dictionary of Alabama Biography*, v. 3, (Chicago: The S.J. Clarke Publishing Co., 1921):692. James Freeman Grant is great great grandfather of the author.

[56]Data sent by Wm J. Campbell, Pastor of M.E. Church, Rochester, Michigan, to Judge Maloney, circa 1891-92. Sent by Mrs. Alexander Harris, Knoxville, TN from Judge Maloney's letters, to Mrs. W.S. Faulkner.

317	I.	Joshua Horton[6] KING, b. 1 Feb 1810, d. 12 Feb 1864; m. c. 1838 Lousa Jane McCray.
318	ii.	Robert[6] KING.
319	iii.	Lucinda[6] KING, m. George Gallaher.
320	iv.	Mary "Polly"[6] KING, m. William Gallaher.
321	v,	Amanda E.[6] KING, m. 25 Jan 1844, Robert W. Harden.
322	vi.	Minerva E.[6] KING, m(1) Josiah Leith George, m(2) ___ Howell, m(3) James Maloney.
323	vii.	Nancy F.S.[6] KING, b.c. 1808, d. 24 Sep 1831, Hawkins Co., TN; m. Henry Burim.[57]

188. FOSTER[5] FREEMAN (James[4], Samuel[3], William[2], John[1] Freeman) was born 5 March 1787. He moved with his father to Oglethorpe County, Georgia and lived there a number of years. He returned to Surry County where he married on 17 August 1809 to his cousin, Nancy Freeman #174, daughter of Joshua and Lucy Freeman.

The couple moved to Knox County Tennessee and then to Griffin, in the portion of Pike County which became Spalding County, Georgia. Foster Freeman died 28 June 1846 and his wife Nancy died 4 November 1862.

Issue of Foster and Nancy (Freeman) Freeman:

324	i.	Francis Asbury[6] Freeman. died 1898, Griffin, Spalding Co., GA.
325	ii.	Dr. Robert King[6] Freeman, buried Holly Springs Cemetery, 2 miles from

---

[57]Knoxville Register 12 Oct 1831.

Harrisburg, Arkansas; m. Mary Elizabeth Sessions.

326   iii.   James⁶ Freeman.

211. JOHN⁵ FREEMAN (Elisha⁴, John³, John², John¹ Freeman) died testate in Onslow County, North Carolina. His will is undated but was filed for probate in 1857. He names a wife Susannah.

Issue of John and Susannah (?) Freeman:[58]

327   i.   John S.⁶ Freeman.

328   ii.   Elisha W.⁶ Freeman, m(1) 12 Oct 1847, Elisabeth Canady; (2) 30 Aug 1866, Mary J. Marshall.[59]

329   iii.   Edward B.⁶ Freeman, b.c. 1833; m. 8 Dec 1853, Onslow Co., Martha J. Coston.[60]

330   iv.   Isaac J.⁶ Freeman.

331   v.   Susan J.⁶ Freeman, m. Mr. Morton.

332   vi.   Betsy Ann⁶ Freeman, m. 30 Nov. 1842, Onslow Co., Isaac Taylor.[61]

333   vii.   Mary M.⁶ Freeman.

334   viii.   Nancy E.⁶ Freeman, m. 7 Feb. 1861, Onslow Co., John Jarman.[62]

335   ix.   Clarissa C.⁶ Freeman, m. Mr. Jones.

---

[58]Names and order of children from Will of John Freeman.

[59]LDS, IGI, 1992 ed.

[60]*Ibid.*

[61]*ibid.*

[62]*Ibid.*

228. MICHAEL⁵ FREEMAN (David⁴, James³, John², John¹ Freeman) was born 1 March 1764 in Bertie County. He moved with his father, David, to Mecklenburg County where, on 1 March 1780, he enlisted for 6 months in Capt. Polk's Company, Col. Davis, Regt. Enlisted 20 August 1780, served 8 months in Capt. J. Tagert's Co., Col. Irwin's Regt. In battles of Friday's Fort, Orangeburgh Courthouse, and Shubric's Plantation. Discharged last of March 1782.

He left North Carolina for Caldwell County Kentucky in 1806, just after the death of his father. and was pensioned in 1832. He died 9 February 1842. No evidence of the name of his wife has yet been found.

Issue of Michael Freeman:

336	i.	Polly⁶ Freeman, d. bef. 3 Dec. 1840; m. Mr. Fite.
337	ii.	Jannett B.⁶ Freeman, m. Mr. Wood.
338	iii.	Penniah⁶ Freeman, m. 23 Jan 1812, Caldwell Co., KY, Andrew Dunn.[63]
339	iv.	Matilda (Malilon)⁶ Freeman, m. 5 Dec 1815 Caldwell Co., KY, John Mercer.[64]
340	v.	Eliza B.⁶ Freeman, m. 9 Sep 1816, Caldwell Co., Johnah Bigham. [65]
341	vi	Michael Washington⁶ Freeman.

---

[63] *Ibid.*

[64] *Ibid.*

[65] *Ibid.*

OTHER

EARLY FREEMAN FAMILIES

OF

NORTH CAROLINA

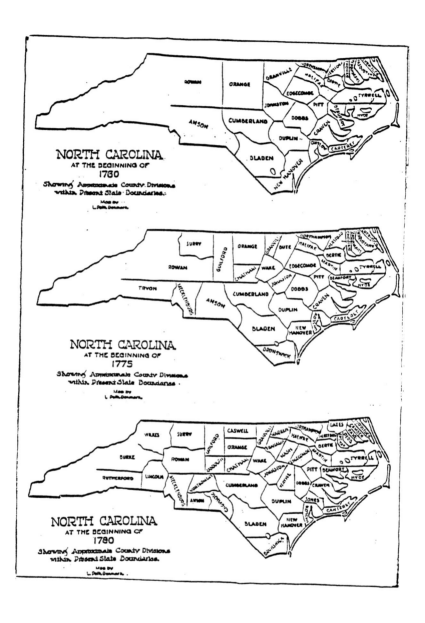

NORTH CAROLINA
AT THE BEGINNING OF
1730
Showing Approximate County Divisions
within Present State Boundaries.
Map by
L. Polk Denmark.

NORTH CAROLINA
AT THE BEGINNING OF
1775
Showing Approximate County Divisions
within Present State Boundaries.
Map by
L. Polk Denmark.

NORTH CAROLINA
AT THE BEGINNING OF
1780
Showing Approximate County Divisions
within Present State Boundaries.
Map by
L. Polk Denmark.

138

OTHER EARLY FREEMAN FAMILIES
of
North Carolina

The purpose of this section is to provide a documented basis for researchers seeking connection to eighteenth century Freeman families of North Carolina. No effort has been made to carry research into the nineteenth century.

There were 78 heads of household surnamed Freeman in the 1790 census and 99 Freeman families in the 1800 census of the state.[1] The census was used to identify counties where Freeman families were resident. A survey was made of deed indexes and will indexes of those counties in which several families resided.

Descendants of John Freeman of Norfolk County constituted the largest group of Freemans in early North Carolina. Twenty-three of the seventy-eight Freemans on the 1790 census and twenty-six of the ninety-nine on the 1800 census can be identified as part of that family and were discussed in the previous section. There were, however, many others of the surname resident in the state. The Freeman families covered in this section fall into two groups.

The first group is composed of those who may be, as yet, unidentified descendants of John Freeman of Norfolk who had migrated to other parts of North Carolina. Little is known of descendants of Thomas Freeman #7, and nothing is known of the families of Jacob #21, John #22, Moses #31, or of John #54. Surely, some of the other Freemans of North Carolina must be descendants of these men. However, the author has not been able to locate records which would positively identify any of the families covered in this section as descendants of that family.

The second group of North Carolina Freeman families discussed in the following pages have no connection to the family covered in section one and unless otherwise noted, they have no apparent connection to each other.

---

[1]United States Bureau of the Census. *Heads of Families at the First Census of the United States Taken in the Year 1790* (Repr. 1978.); Elizabeth Petty Bentley, *Index to the 1800 Census of North Carolina* (Baltimore: Genealogical Publishing Co., 1982). A listing, not found in the above, was found in the 1800 census of Onslow County for a Lizebeth Freeman.

The sketches in this section vary in length and detail. In many cases insufficient evidence exists to make a sketch of the makeup of a family possible. In some cases a large number of records exist to give data relevant to the activities of a family, in others the records are sparse, allowing only the briefest of summary.

It is hoped that the information in these sketches, when combined with the material in the main part of this book will make it possible for future researchers to connect to the correct families.

ALLEN FREEMAN OF MECKLENBURG COUNTY

Allen Freeman, a man of considerable means, appears to have been a relatively late arrival on the North Carolina scene. On 10 January 1780 he purchased from John Polk for £800 North Carolina money, four tracts of land on the mouth of Clear Creek and Rocky River in the east part of Mecklenburg County. The first tract was of 77 acres at the mouth and on both sides of Clear Creek and Rocky River, the second for 85 acres joining the first, the third for 121 acres on Rocky River and the fourth for 270 acres on both sides of Clear Creek adjacent to Charles Polk and the River.[2]

In 1787 Rees Shelby sold Allen 40 additional acres on Clear Creek adjacent to Freeman's other lands. Gideon Freeman and Thomas Polk were witnesses to the transaction. Shelby and his wife Mary also sold Allen a tract of 122 acres on both sides of Clear Creek with Uriah Weatherford and Gideon Freeman as witnesses. In 1792 Freeman sold the 122 acre and 40 acre tracts to Paul Furr for a nice profit.[3]

Allen Freeman received Revolutionary Pay Voucher #451 for a public Claim for £7.15 His son Gideon received a voucher #4306 in the amount of £8.16.6 for service in the Militia.

Allen appears on the 1790 census of Mecklenburg Co., NC. His sons Allen, Jr., Gideon and William were heads of separate households. The 1800 census shows Allin [sic] and the female in his household, both over 45 years old, and seven slaves.

Allen may have been the man of the same name who had previously resided in Mecklenburg County, Virginia. The names Gideon, Allen, Isham and Anderson Freeman appear together also in Granville Co., North Carolina. A strong probablility exists that these families share common roots in Virginia.

Allen Freeman wrote his will on 24 January 1807, probated in April of that year. He names his wife Barbara, leaving her a

---

[2]Herman W. Ferguson, *Genealogical Deed Abstracts, Mecklenburg County, North Carolina, Books 10-14* (Rocky Mount, NC: Herman W. Ferguson, 1990):21.

[3]*Ibid*:198-199.

negro Grace and a life estate in a third of the land on which he then lived. He appears to have already made settlement to his older children and left only 40 shillings each to: his son Gideon Freeman, daughter Nancy Wagstaff, son William Freeman, son Allen Freeman, daughter Sarah Freeman, son Charles Freeman (to whom he also left a negro "Wood") and daughter Susannah Garmon.

To Jemima, daughter of "my present wife," he left a negro, bed and furniture, to son Isham a negro, bed and furniture and all the land he now possessed, including the third reserved to his wife. To daughter Peggy a negro, bed and furniture. The balance of his estate was to be sold and divided among his twelve legatees.[4]

Issue of Allen Freeman by m(1) _____

i.	Gideon Freeman, m. Deborah Polk d/o Charles Polk.[5] Resided Anson Co., 1800 Census.
ii.	Nancy Freeman, m. ____ Wagstaff
iii.	William Freeman, m. Margaret "Peggy" Polk d/o Charles Polk
iv.	Allen Freeman, may be one who m. Rody Garmon 22 Jul 1817, Cabarrus Co.
v.	Sarah Freeman
vi.	Charles Freeman, m. 17 Jul 1795 Cabarrus Co., to Delilah Stewert,

---

[4]Ralph B. & Herman W. Ferguson, *Mecklenburg County, North Carolina Will Abstracts, 1791-1868 Books A-J; Tax Lists 1797, 1798, 1799, 1806 & 1807* (Rocky Mount, NC: Herman W. Ferguson, 1993):47. This abstract omits the name of son Anderson Freeman who appears in the cross index to Mecklenburg County wills.

[5]*Ibid*:123. Will of Charles Polk, Sr. written 1820, proved May Crt. 1821.

Gideon and Allen Freeman bondsmen.[6]

vii.   Anderson Freeman

viii.   Susannah Freeman, m. _____
Garmon

Issue of Allen Freeman by m(2) Barbara _____
ix.   Jemima Freeman

Issue of Allen Freeman by unspecified marriage.

x.   Isham Freeman

xi.   Peggy Freeman

---

[6]NC Marriage Bonds, NC State Archives.

WILLIAM FREEMAN OF GRANVILLE COUNTY
and
His Descendants of Bute and Warren Counties

William Freeman and his wife Elizabeth (Bridges) Freeman, daughter of William Bridges.[7] apparently moved into Granville County about 1757, since William first appears on the tax lists of that year. In 1760 he paid tax for one poll only, for his negro Jeffrey but not for himself, indicating that he was probably over 60 or released from the levy due to ill health. Appearing on the same list were William Freeman, Jr., and John Freeman.[8] Judging from the fact that William, Sr., had adult sons, and was levy free, he must have been born about 1700 or shortly thereafter. The family appears to be originally from Surry County, Virginia.

On 24 October 1701 a John Freeman and his wife Mary patented 300 acres on the South side of the Nottoway River in what was at first believed to be Charles City County for the transportation of six, including themselves.[9] In 1707 he petitioned the Council stating that the survey had proved the land to be in Surry County and asked that he be allowed to have the surveyor of Surry lay out the same.[10] In 1719 John Freeman, Jr. and Mary deeded 200 acres to George Cane. William Freeman, who signed with a mark, was one of the witnesses.

In May of 1725 John Freeman of Southwarke Parish deeded to his son, William, for love and affection a tract of 300

---

[7]Zae Hargett Gwynn, *Abstracts of Wills and Estate Records of Granville County, North Carolina, 1746-1808* (Rockey Mount, NC: 1973):5 Elizabeth was the daughter of William Bridges whose will was written 1 August 1756 and proved in Granville in May Court 1762.

[8]Granville Co., NC. Tax Lists. NC State Archives, C.R. 044.701.19.

[9] Nell Marion Nugent, *Cavaliers and Pioneer, Abstracts of Virginia land Patents and Grants, Vol. III, 1695-1732* (Richmond: Virginia State Library, 1979):52. This man was sometimes referred to in Surry County records as John Freeman, Jr. Another John Freeman (Sr.,), of Surry County, died testate in 1725.

[10]H.R. McIlwaine, ed., *Executive Journals of the Council of Colonial Virginia, Vol. III* (Richmond: Superintendent of Public Printing, 1928):157.

acres on South side of the Nottoway River on Coronesus Swamp. Living adjacent to the Freeman family of Surry County was William Bridges who in 1731 deeded land to his son Joseph Bridges.[11] In 1734 William Bridges patented another tract in Surry County crossing Flatt Swamp, Peter Poythress's line and adjacent to William Freeman's line.[12] Apparently, William Freeman married the daughter of his neighbor, William Bridges.

On 16 May 1760 William Freeman purchased 640 acres on Crooked Creek in Granville County, North Carolina, from Joseph Bridges. On 11 February 1761, William Freeman, Jr., gave to his brother Henry Freeman, 100 acres on South side of Crooked Creek part of 640 acres granted Joseph Bridges, **excepting that father and mother, William Freeman, Sr., and his wife Elizabeth, shall enjoy the 100 acres for their lifetime.** The deed from Bridges does not specify whether the grantee is William Sr., or William, Jr., but the second deed, from William Freeman, Junior, to his brother, indicates that William Freeman, Senior, was still alive and makes it certain that the man who purchased from Bridges was the younger William.[13]

A few months later, in November 1761, William Freeman purchased another 640 acre tract, this one from Richard Arrandall on both sides of Crooked Creek at John Wright's line.[14] The tax lists for 1761 show William Freman and John Freman on Pope's list and William Freeman charged for Samuel White, a total of two tithables.[15]

William Freeman, Sr., must have died late in 1761 or early

---

[11]William Lindsay Hopkins, *Surry County, Virginia, Deeds 1664-1733 and Other Court Papers* (Richmond, VA: Gen-n-dex, 1991):132, 158.

[12]William Lindsay Hopkins, "Virginia Land Patent Book 15," in *Magazine of Virginia Genealogy*, v. 24 #1 (Feb. 1986):15.

[13]Zae Hargett Gwynn, *Abstracts of The Early Deeds of Granville County, North Carolina, 1746-1765* (Rocky Mount, NC: Joseph W. Watson, 1974):138, 144; Margaret M. Hofmann, *The Granville District of North Carolina, 1748-1763* vol. 2 (Weldon, NC: Weldon News Press, 1987):10 Joseph Bridges received a grant for 640 acres on S side of Crooked Creek on 30 April 1754, surveyed 29 May 1751.

[14]*Ibid*:138.

[15]N. 8. *Supra.*

1762, Since Pope's lists for 1762 tax shows, side by side, Bridges Freeman, 1 tithe, Joseph Bridges, 1 tithe, Elizabeth Freeman, 3 tithes (Henry Freeman, negros Jeffrey & Babb, and a few names later, William Freeman.[16]

Bute County was formed from the eastern portion of Granville in 1764 and in that year James Arrendell and Richard Arrendell, his son, sold to William Freeman 100 acres on Jumping run on the South side of Crooked Creek. witnesses were David Doad, Bridges Freeman, and Benj. X Arrendell. In 1765 William Freeman deeded to John Freeman 90 acres, witnesses were David Doad, John Freeman and Henry Freeman.[17]

William Freeman, Jr, and Henry Freeman are identified from the deed records as children of William and Elizabeth. No such direct evidence is available for Bridges Freeman, but he was contemporary with William, Junior, lived in close proximity to him, witnessed documents signed by him and would be named after his maternal grandfather. The tax list of 1771 shows Elizabeth Freeman with sons Henry, John and Joseph (and one slave).[18]

Issue of William[2] and Elizabeth ( ) Freeman:

+	2	i.	William[3] Freeman, Jr.
+	3	iii.	Bridges[3] Freeman. In Johnston Co., 1784, in Limestone Co., AL, 1820.
	4	iv.	Henry[3] Freeman.
	5	v.	John[3] Freeman.
+	6	v.	Joseph[3] Freeman, b.c. 1755; m. Bute Co., 11 Nov. 1776 to Aggy Freeman, d. Wake Co., 1828.

[16]*Ibid.*

[17]Bute Co., NC. DB A:435, 352.

[18]William Perry Johnston, *Journal of North Carolina Genealogy* (Fall 1965) p. 1500. Tax lists in Archives Thomas M. Pittman Collection (Foile No 123.15).

2. William³ Freeman, Jr. (William,² John¹ Freeman) shown by tax lists of Bute and Warren as having the following family.

7.	i.	Robert⁴ Freeman, b.c. 1750 m. Mary ___, d. 1775, Bute Co.¹⁹
8.	ii.	William⁴ Freeman, b.c. 1750; prob. the one who d.t. 1824, naming children: Dilley m. 1810 John R. Richards, Mary m. 1809 William Richards, Robert Freeman, William Freeman and Eaton Freeman.²⁰

Probably others.

3. Bridges³ Freeman (William,² John¹ Freeman) was undoubtedly named for his grandfather, William Bridges, not for the Bridges Freeman who was in Virginia as early as 1623 and, like his namesake son, became prominent in the early affairs of the colony.²¹ The Bridges Freeman of Granville County purchased land on the fork of Andrew Branch in Bute County in 1762 from John Moony and in 1777 sold it to John Cooley.²²

In 1780 Bridges, as a resident of Franklin County sold 188 acre tract to Jacob Hartsfield part of a grant to him made 20 Sept 1779. By 1784 he listed his residence as Johnston Co., NC when he sold to Howell Freeman, also of Johnston Co., a 125 acre tract on Andrews Creek, Colly path and Jakes path adjacent to Hartsfield, Mullins and Henry Freeman. Witnesses were Henry

---

¹⁹Mary Hinton Kerr, *Warren County, North Carolina Records, vol. 1, Abstracted Records of Colonial Bute County, N.C., 1764-1779 and Bute County Marriages*(n.p.: National Society Colonial Dames of America, NC, n.d.):46.

²⁰Franklin Co., NC., Original Wills, NC State Archives. This could not have been William #2 who would have been over a hundred years old at this time.

²¹Virginia M Meyer and John Frederick Dorman, F.A.S.G. *Adventurers of Purse and Person, Virginia, 1607-1624/5*, third ed. (Richmond: Order of First Families of Virginia, 1607-1624/5, rev. 1987):271n, 294-296. Although many researchers have made undocumented claims to descent from this family for the Freeman families of Southside Virginia, Meyer and Dorman list no proven issue, stating only that George Freeman appeared to live on land previously owned by Bridges Freeman.

²²Warren Co. NC. DB 7:161.

and Chuby Freeman (a female).[23]

A Bridges Freeman with wife Elizabeth sold land in Brunswick County Virginia in 1764 and in Franklin County, NC, in 1780 Bridges and Elizabeth Freeman were witnesses to a deed from John to Henry Freeman.[24] Although no direct evidence has been found, it is possible that Howell was a son of Bridges.

6. Joseph[3] Freeman (William,[2] John[1] Freeman) died in Wake County in 1828. His obituary gives his age as 70, but his appearance as a tithable with brothers Henry and John of his mother Elizabeth in 1771 would make his birthdate closer to 1755 and his age at death as 73. He had served as a soldier of the Revolutionary War.[25] He was listed on the 1790 and 1800 Censuses as a resident of Franklin County. He married Aggy Freeman, probably a cousin, in Bute County on 11 Nov. 1778.[26]

Although his obituary identifies him as a Revolutionary soldier, no record has been found to support that report. He may have moved north across the border and served in a Virginia unit.

Joseph Freeman died before 1 May 1728. In the November session of the Court of Pleas and Quarter Sessions, his heirs requested division of the estate.

Issue of Joseph and Aggy (Freeman) Freeman.

9.	i.	Allen[4] Freeman
10.	ii.	Wilie[4] Freeman
11.	iii.	William[4] Freeman

---

[23]Watson, *Abstracts of the Early Deeds of Franklin County, North Carolina, 1779-1797*,(Rocky Mount, NC: By the Author, 1984):18,92.

[24]Watson, *Franklin Deeds, 1779-97*:15.

[25]Lois Smathers Neal, *Abstracts of Vital Records from Raleigh, North Carolina, Newspapers, 1820-1829*. v.2 (Spartanburg: The Reprint Company, Pub., 1980):236. Obituary of Joseph Freeman; Johnston, *J of NC Genealogy*:1500.

[26]LDS, *IGI*, 1992 edition.

12.	iv.	Robert[4] Freeman
13.	v.	Tempy[4] Freeman m. Timberlake
14.	vi.	Edward[4] Freeman
15.	vii.	Lucy[4] Freeman m. William Murray
16.	viii.	Biddy[4] Freeman, d. bef. Nov. 1824; m. William Roles. Children: James, Robert, Livea, Mary Ann, W.H.
17.	ix.	Kinchen[4] Freeman, m. Telitha ___; d. 23 Jul 1828. Children: James, Emily Ann, Kinchen, Sarah Ann, William, John, Jane.

A few others who appear to be connected to this family and were possibly third generation members or cousins include Howell Freeman, who witnessed the will of Wm Reeves of which Henry Freeman was executor.[27] Howell Freeman received a Revolutionary War Pension which states that he was born in Virginia, in 1760. Bute County was discontinued in 1779 and the southern part, which contained Crooked Creek, became Franklin County. Howell owned land in Chatham County. Howell Freeman's pension states that he enlisted at Franklin County, North Carolina and served three months under Capt Brittain Harrison 1779, 3 months in 1781 under Capt Robertson and one and a half months under Sharp, Brevard & Bush in 1781.[28] Edward Freeman does not appear as a minor tithable on any extant list, appearing only as an adult in 1766, responsible for his own poll tax. Edward died in 1811 leaving children: William, Robert of Wilson Co., TN, Joseph, Henry, Daniel of Wilson Co., TN, Rebeccah m. Wm Reaves, Sarah m. Wm Massey and had a

---

[27] *Ibid*:58.

[28] National Archives, Revolutionary War Pension File of Howell Freeman, W 19296.

daughter Temperance, Patience m. David Jones.[29]

Howell and a Robert Freeman appear on the 1790 census of Chatham County. In 1800 Howell alone appears there. His pension statement says he married on March 4 1830 in Dickson Co., Tennessee to Hannah Doty and died there on 4 May 1836. The widow received a pension on his service in 1856 while a resident of Humphrey Co., Tennessee. She was 80 years old in 1867.[30]

[29]Joseph W. Watson, *Kinfolks of Franklin County, North Carolina, 1793-1844* (Rocky Mount, NC: By the author, 1985):91; Dr. Stephen E. Bradley, Jr., *Will Book C, Franklin County, North Carolina, 1804-1812* (South Boston, VA: By the author, 1988):49.

[30]Rev. Pension file, Howell Freeman.

JOHN FREEMAN OF BEAUFORT
&
JOHN FREEMAN OF BLADEN

In May of 1737, William Daniel of Bath Town and Frances his wife sold to John Freeman a tract of 164 acres on the Eastern Branch of Town Creek in Beaufort Precinct adjacent to James Adams and a tract in the possession of Mr. Josiah Jones. On 14 June 1737, John Freeman of Bath Town, Merchant purchased from Roger Jones of Beaufort County, Gent, Lot 24 (½ acre in the town of Bath). A few months later Jones sold John Freeman of Bath, Merchant town lot # 25.[31] Freeman established an ordinary in the town of Bath.[32]

Two years later, in March of 1739 John Freeman, of Bath Town, Esq., with consent of Mary his wife, sold to Michael Coutanch of Boston, New England, mariner, the two town lots for £336. A few months later John "of Beaufort" Esq and Mary his wife sold the Old Town Creek plantation to John Jewel.[33] John and Mary purchased another plantation north of Bath and several more town lots. Freeman was serving as Sheriff of the county by 15 July 1746.[34] In 1740 he received a Patent for 100 acres in Beaufort "on the N. side of the old town creek, joining John Russell, the line of Bath town commons, the sd Creek, and the Eastermost branch of the sd creek."[35]

On 17 December 1752, John Freeman of Beaufort County, Gent., wrote his will, leaving his wife Mary his lots in the Town of Bath and several negroes and the time left on the service of his indentured servant William Hamilton. To his son John he left 5 negros and authorized his executors to dispose of nineteen hundred acres of land on Core Creek in Craven County and

---

[31]Beaufort Co, NC. DB 2:224, 251, 261.

[32]Ibid. 3:544.

[33]Ibid:331, 352.

[34]Ibid:396, 497-498, 500.

[35]Margaret M. Hoffmann, Colony of North Carolina, Abstracts of Land Patents, Volume I: 1735-1764:146.

thirteen hundred acres near the Tarr River in Beaufort County, the proceeds to be used to pay his debts, the remainder to his executors, Mary Freeman and son John, to divide the balance when his son John came of age. Witnesses were James Calef, James Pilkington and Wy: Ormond. The will was proved at the courthouse in the town of Bath on 13 March 1753.[36]

On 11 March 1754 John Devis of the Town of Newbern in Craven County, wrote a will leaving £14 to John Freeman of Bath, son of John Freeman of same. Mary, the well to do widow, soon remarried. On 20 Jan 1754 a prenuptual agreement was signed between Samuel Taylor of Beaufort County, Gent, and Mary Freeman of Bath Town, widow, allowing Mary to retain title of the lots left her by her late husband, John Freeman.[37]

In 1760 Samuel Taylor and Mary were required to give possession of the lots left to Mary to pay a judgement of £93.5.0 and £24 costs to the Sheriff to satisfy a judgement owed by John Freeman decd.[38] Young John continued to live in Beaufort County, described as a mariner, he was involved in land transactions through at least 1769.[39]

Another, apparently contemporaneous, John Freeman appeared in Bladen County, receiving a patent of 400 acres on 9 September 1735 on the North East side of the North West River, joining William Mason and the River.[40] Little is known of his life. He died intestate and Ruth his wife was apparently appointed administratrix since she filed an inventory of John's estate, taken on 30 April 1753 by Thomas Talley and Neile Bond or Beard.[41]

No indication is given of any issue of this couple.

---

[36]Secretary of State Wills, North Carolina State Archives.

[37]Beaufort Co., NC. DB 2:192.

[38]Beaufort Co., NC. DB 3:544.

[39]Beaufort Co., NC. DB 4:51, 166, 359.

[40]Hoffman, *North Carolina Patents*. v.1:96.

[41]Bladen Co., NC. North Carolina State Archives, Estate Papers.

HENRY FREEMAN OF NASH COUNTY

Henry Freeman married Massey Wall at some date prior to 10 January 1781.[42] On that date Henry with his wife Massey of Nash County sold to Thomas Denton of Edgecombe County, for the sum of 50,000 £ current money, two tracts in Edgecombe Co. on Griffin's Swamp adjoining Hardy Wall containing 259 acres. These were part of two tracts granted by Granville to Garrot Wall.[43]

There was no relinquishment of dower with that deed, so, on 7 November 1788, a commission was appointed by Edgecombe County Court to take the said relinquishment.[44]

Henry Freeman died testate in Nash County prior to 31 December 1796 for on that date Massee Freeman, executrix, took an inventory of his estate.[45] The will is not found in the archives or county record books. The widow, Massee Freeman, soon married Jethro Denson who died in 1801. Massee Denson died in Nash County in 1818. In her estate file dated 1829 is found a petition which reads in part as follows:

> To the Honourable the Judge of the court of Equity for the county of Nash/
> Humbly Complaining sheweth unto your Honour your Orator Joseph Arrington (Capt) of the County aforesaid. Executor of the last will and testament of Massy Denson late of said County and Administrator of Henry Freeman also formerly of said County, dec'd - That Massy Wall was seised in fee simple of a Tract of land situate in said County and Containing by estimation one Hundred & fifty

---

[42]Evidence of the marriage is found in a petition in her Nash County estate file dated 1818 which will be discussed later in greater detail.

[43]Joseph W. Watson, *Abstracts of the Early Deeds of Edgecombe Co., North Carolina, 1772-1788*, v. 2 (New Bern: Owen G. Dunn Co., 1967):303.

[44]Marvin K. Dorman, Jr., *Edgecombe County, North Carolina, Abstracts of court Minutes, 1744-46, 1757-94* (Winston-Salem: Hutchinson-Allgood Printing Co., Inc., 1968):76.

[45]Joseph W. Watson, *Abstracts of Early Records of Nash County, North Carolina, 1777-1859*, (Rocky Mount, NC: Dixie Letter Service, 1963):189.

acres adjoining the lands of Edward Cooper, Elisabeth Tayler and Mill Whitley, and afterwards intermarried with one Henry Freeman by whom she had issue John who died an infant intestate and without issue, Mathew a Merchant of the state of Tennessee, Henry, Martha who intermarried with Mills Whitley, Sally who intermarried with James Screws, Rebecca who intermarried with Lazarus Turner, Massey who intermarried with Jennings Hackney, and Mary who intermarried with Ben Cooper and died leaving issue Rebecca, Betsy, and Mathew Cooper who are her heirs at law & infants under the age of 21 years all residents of the County of Nash. The said Henry Freeman died in the year (blank) and his widow intermarried with one Jethro Denson by whom She had issue Isbel, now the wife of James Cooper of the county of Nash, and departed this life in the month of (blank_ 1818 having first duly made and published her last will & testament in writing, properly execute to pass real estate ....[46]

The petition continues, explaining that the will of Henry Freeman could not be found only an unsigned document in the papers of Massey Denson endorsed "a Copy of the Will of Henry Freeman" which is not certified. Massey was possessed during her life of some property consisting of a negro and other chattels which are said to have belonged to her first husband and to have been bequeathed to her for the Term of her life and at her death to his children. But if the will did not dispose of the property in such manner and it was acquired by Massey before her marriage to Denson, it vested in Denson by the marriage and will go to his daughter, Isbell Cooper, or if acquired by the said Massey after the death of Denson it will be distributed among all her children and grandchildren.

The suit must have been traumatic to the heirs, but is a bonanza to present day researchers, making clear what would otherwise be a very confusing family.

Issue of Henry and Massee (Wall) Freeman.

---

[46]Nash Co., NC. Estate File of Henry Freeman dated 1829. NC State Archives, C.R. 069.508.33.

2	i.	John Freeman, d. leaving nuncupative will 20 Nov. 1804, proved May 1805, Nash Co.[47]
3	ii.	Henry Freeman who was a resident of Robertson Co., TN the year 1819 and is probably the Henry who died in Robertson Co. 1845.[48]
4	iii.	Mathew Freeman, a merchant of Tennessee, probably the one who died in Robertson Co., 1861.[49]
5	iv.	Martha Freeman, m. Mills Whitley.
6	v.	Sally Freeman m. James Screws.
7	vi.	Rebecca Freeman m. Lazarus Turner.
8	vii.	Massee Freeman m. Jennings Hackney.
9	viii.	Mary Freeman died before petition m. Benjamin Cooper.

issue:

i.	Rebecca COOPER.
ii.	Massee COOPER.
iii.	Mathew COOPER.
iv.	Betsy COOPER (named in petition, not Massey Denson's will. May be same as Massee Cooper above.)

---

[47]Ruth Smith Williams and Margarette Glenn Griffin, *Abstracts of Will Book 1, Nash County, North carolina, 1778-1868* (Rocky Mount, NC: Joseph W. Watson):48. Although the Equity petition states that he died intestate and a minor, the above nuncupative will is surely his since he names his mother Massey Denson and brother Mathew Freeman.

[48]Joseph W. Watson, *Kinfolks of Nash County, North Carolina, 1778-1854* (1979):99, 100 (Nash Co., DB 10:200, 206). Henry Freman of Robertson Co., Tenn, sold his part of the plantation whereon his father, Henry Freman, and Massee Freman, his wife, formerly lived; Byron & Barbara Sistler, *Index to Early Tennessee Wills & Administrations* (Nashville: Byron Sistler & Assoc., Inc., 1990):128.

[49]Sistler, *Tennessee Wills*:128.

AARON FREEMAN
of
ROWAN, BURKE, IREDELL AND BUNCOMBE COUNTIES

On 17 December 1769 in Rowan County, Aaron Freeman married Mary Bently, daughter of Thomas Bently whose son Benjamin gave permission for the marriage.[50] To have married by this date he must have been born 1748 or earlier. At that time Rowan County covered all of northwestern North Carolina. In 1774 Aaron Freeman received a license for a Tavern in the Forks of the Yadkin.[51] Aaron and his growing family appear to have moved at about that time to Lambeth's Fork of Lower Little River, at that time in Burke County, later in Wilkes, Iredell and now in Alexander County. The obituary of Aaron's son, Rev. Moses Freeman, states that Moses was born 14 September 1774 in Wilkes County.[52]

Naming patterns in this family so closely parallel those in the families of Chowan and Bertie that many have believed this Aaron Freeman was a member of the Chowan and Bertie Freeman families, the subject of the main portion of this work. He has been confused with Aaron #56, son of John Freeman #11 (d. 1785 Bertie County), and with Aaron #45, son of Samuel Freeman #10 of Surry County. Neither identification can be correct. Aaron, son of John Freeman of Bertie, served in the Revolution then moved to Kentucky, where his wife applied for a pension stating that Aaron was born 1758 in Bertie County and gives names of his parents as John and Ann (?) Freeman. Aaron #45, son of Samuel of Surry County, appears on the 1800 census of Surry while this man and his son Aaron both appear in Iredell County.

---

[50]NC State Archives, Rowan Co., NC, Marriage Bond # 0124905.

[51]Jo White Linn, *Abstracts of Court of Pleas and Quarter Sessions, Rowan Co., North carolina, 1763-1774* (Salisbury, NC: By the author, 1979):150.

[52]*Newfound Baptist Association Minutes, 1860*: reprinted in *Rees Genealogy*, v. 13:6-7 (Jan-Feb 1980).

Aaron of Rowan's relatively early birth date around 1748 or earlier means that his father must have been born before 1725. For Aaron to be a member of the Chowan, Bertie family, he would have to be a member of the 4th generation. All members of that generation are accounted for, except that list of the children of Thomas Freeman #7 is probably incomplete. Since the name Thomas appears in one of the older sons in this family, it is possible that evidence will someday be found to connect the family of Aaron to Thomas. The possibility must be considered, however, that there is no connection to that family.

By 1790 Aaron was purchasing land on the Main head branch of the South Yadkin River. One tract was adjacent to that of his wife's brother Benjamin Bentley. In 1796 Aaron sold a 50 acre piece of his Lambeth Fork tract to his son Joshua Freeman. The same year, his son Moses received a grant on the east side of Little River.[53]

Starting after 1800 the family began to dispose of its lands in that area and moved west across the Blue Ridge to the eastern edge of the Great Smokey Mountains, purchasing land on the South side of the French Broad River, between Turkey Creek and Sandy Mush Creek. The land was then in Buncombe County. Aaron and his sons continued to engage in numerous land transaction, eventually purchasing tracts in Buncombe and what is now Madison County on Pyborn's branch of Big Ivy Creek, Flat Creek, Big Pine.[54]

On 18 August 1814, Aaron gave his son James the tract where Aaron then lived adjacent to land of Joshua and Aaron, Jr., Samuel Low, Joseph Willson, "but that James Freeman shall not persess the Land now belonging to the said Aaron Freeman Senr untill the death of the sd A. Freeman."[55] No will or probate record survives for Aaron. Unfortunately courthouse fires in 1830

[53]Shirley Counter, Edie Purdy and Lois Schneider, *Iredell County, North Carolina, Deed Abstracts, v. 1, 1788-1797: Abstracts of Books A&B* (Statesville, NC: Abstract Publishers, n.d.)p.12 (DB A:164-166), 80 (DB B:429-30), 83 (DB B:470-1); State to Moses Freeman, Iredell DB D:146.

[54]Buncombe Co., NC DB C:136,214; D:101; F:152; G:123, 145; 3:410; 7:350, 600; 8:92; 9:48; 11:134.

[55]Buncombe Co., NC DB F:152.

and 1865 destroyed many records. Only James is named as a son in a deed. Evidence of the relationship of his other sons must be assumed by the close association, many land records in Burke, Iredell and Buncombe Counties, and relative ages on census records.

Issue of Aaron and Mary (Bently) Freeman:[56]

	2	i.	Joshua[2] Freeman, b.c. 1770; m. trad. Patsy Caldwell.
+	3	ii.	Moses[2] Freeman, Rev., b. 14 Sep 1774, Rowan Co.; d. 18 Jan 1859; m. trad. Fanny Ball.
+	4	iii.	Thomas[2] Freeman, b.c. 1777, Rowan Co., d.c. 1864/5; m.trad. Mary Elizabeth Ball.
	5	iv.	Jesse[2] Freeman, b.c. 1772; m. trad. Fanny Price.
	6	v.	Isaac[2] Freeman, b.c. 1780; m. trad. Elizabeth Harper.
	7	vi.	Aaron[2] Freeman, b.c. 1782
	8	vii.	James[2] Freeman, b.c. 1785; m. trad. c. 1812 Jane Patterson.

Possible other children:

viii. John Freeman

several daughters.[57]

---

[56]Destruction of Buncombe Co., marriage records makes identification of daughters, and of spouses of the sons very difficult. Names of spouses of the sons are undocumented reports from descendants. Neva Bolton of Cortez, NM has submitted much data on this family to the Latter Day Saints International Genealogical Index.

[57]1800 Census, Iredell Co., NC p.630. Shows several young females in the household.

161

3. MOSES² FREEMAN (Aaron¹ Freeman). His obituary gives detail of his life and posting:

> Elder M. Freeman was born in Wilkes County, N.C., September 14th A.D. 1774, and died January 18th 1859. He joined the Baptist Church at Little River, Burke County, N.C., and was baptized by Wm. Dodson. He also then commenced exercising a public gift. He moved to Buncombe County in the year 1806, and joined the arm of Caney River Church that sat on Flat Creek....Then he moved his membership to Little ivy, A.D. 1812, and was ordained to the office of the ministry August 8th 1812, by Elders Thomas Snelson and Stephen Morgan; and in 1818 he joined at Bull Creek and in 1834 at the Newfound Church, and in 1848 he joined the Walnut Creek Church, and in 1852 he moved his membership to Bear Creek Church, and there remained until his death...[58]

The Reverend Moses Freeman died intestate. Minutes of the Madison County Court of Pleas & Quarter Sessions, January Term, 1859 contain the appointment of A.E. Baird as administrator of his estate.

His wife is identified as "Fanny" Ball by some researchers and "Elizabeth" Ball by others.[59] The 1850 Census lists the older woman in his household as "Elizabeth" aged 50.[60] Nancy Ball, age 22 and M___ Ball age 11 are members of the household. Records of earlier censuses indicate he had several sons and daughters. The large number of male issue of the progenitor, Aaron and the destruction of Buncombe probate records make it

---

[58]*Newfound Baptist Minutes* in *Rees Genealogy*, v.13:6-7.

[59]Neva Bolton gives his wife as Fanny Ball to the LDS International Genealogical Index, giving no source; *Rees Genealogy*, v. 13 Jan-Feb 1980 gives her name as Elizabeth Ball. However, the wife of his brother Thomas Freeman was Mary Elizabeth Ball.

[60]Buncombe County, NC, 1850 Census, p. 268. Household 987, family 987.

difficult to document names of children. Descendants disagree on names of his children.[61]

4. THOMAS[2] FREEMAN (Aaron[1] Freeman) appears in the 1850 census of Buncombe County aged 73, making his birth date about 1777. His wife on that census is "Mary" aged 66.[62] He died about 1864/5. His wife is traditionally given as Mary Elizabeth Ball.

His sons Seth, Hiram, Benjamin and Anderson are said to have moved to Pulaski County Kentucky.[63] Census records confirm the move of Seth, Hiram and Benjamin. Children named by descendants include Daniel Elihue, Aaron Pickney, Bailey, Seth, John P.(B?), William, Hiram, Alsey Beth, Tempe, Benjamin (m. Abigail Freeman) 5 Dec 1832, and Anderson.[64]

Further research on these families might eliminate some of the apparent contradictions. Since focus of this project has been Freeman families prior to 1800, no further research was undertaken.

---

[61] *Rees Genealogy* v. 13 Jan-Feb 1980:126 gives Moses' issue as: sons Green Hill Freeman, Moses Freeman, Daniel E. Freeman and Aaron P. Freeman; and daughters Lydia m. Joshua Roberts of Flat Creek and Mary Jane m. Rev. William Rees. Green Hill d. August 1867, Daniel E., b. 1802, d. Sept 1873. Aaron P. b. 1812, m. Tempa--and is buried at Freeman Gap Baptist Church, Madison Co. Bolton's submissions to the IGI give his children as: Green Hill 1794-1867, Moses 1796-1859, Tabitha 1797-, Alsey 1799-1852, m. Wm Blackwell, Lydia 1800-, m. Joshua Roberts; Mary Jane 1801-Feb 1863 m. William Rees, William, Elisha, Susan. Bolton gives Daniel E. and Aaron Pinkney as children of Thomas.

[62] Buncombe County, NC. 1850 Census p. 273. Household 1038, Family 1039.

[63] Letter. Miss Nell Freeman, Burgin, KY, Regent of Jane McAfee Chapter, D.A.R. to Mrs. Wm. S. Faulkner (via L.L.K. of the Boston Transcript), 7 Jan, 1926. Original in possession of the author.

[64] Bolton adds the following found as members of the household in 1850 as children: Andrew Jackson b.c. 1829, Hosea H. b.c. 1833 and Francis Kirby b.c. 1841. The approximate date of the marriage of Thomas to Mary Elizabeth Ball is given as 1794-5. Mary age 66 in 1850 would have been born circa 1784 and certainly could not have been married at age 10. It would be unrealistic to believe she was still bearing children in 1841. It seems likely that the children Jackson, Ailsey E, Hosea H.L. and Francis Kirby were grandchildren.

A QUAKER FREEMAN FAMILY
of
Orange County

1. JOHN FREEMAN and his wife Hannah of Chester County, Pennsylvania were parents of Nathan, Daniel, Robert and probably also Samuel and John, who were members of Cane Creek Meeting, Orange County,[65] Records of the meeting show that a John Freeman was received into membership on 4 August 1764. Whether this was John # 1 or his son is unknown. Nothing is known about the death of John and Hannah. Meeting records identify Daniel as the son of John and Hannah, and Revolutionary War Bounty Land Warrant files of Nathan identify Daniel and Robert as his brothers. Samuel and John are shown in the Cane Creek records as contemporary with Nathan, Daniel and Robert and are probably brothers.

Issue of John and Hannah ( ) Freeman:

+	2	i.	Nathan Freeman.
+	3	ii.	Daniel Freeman.
+	4	iii.	Robert Freeman.

Probable children.

+	5	iv.	Samuel Freeman.
+	6	v.	John Freeman.

2. Nathan, despite his Quaker background, enlisted in the North Carolina Continental Line. This may have been the reason that he was dismissed from Cane Creek in October of 1776.[66] He served

---

[65]William Wade Hinshaw, *Encyclopedia of American Quaker Genealogy*, v. 1. (Ann Arbor: Edwards Brothers, inc., 1936):352.

[66]*Ibid.*:389.

in Capt Veal's Company and died in service at either Boundary House, or Williamburg, Virginia, (statements in pension record disagree). A land warrant was issued in his name and on 30 August 1796, Nathan's brother Daniel relinquished any claim to Nathan's estate to another brother Robert Freeman, who pursued the claim. Robert, a resident of Surry County, appeared before Jesse Lester and Daniel Bills, Justices of the County of Surry, and applied to receive Nathan's pay and 100 acres of bounty land due him. Robert assigned his right to the land to Daniel Wheaton.[67]

3. Daniel[2] Freeman, was born 14 February 1749 in Chester Co., Pennsylvania. He married before 1777 to Jane Wood, daughter of John and Frances Wood. In 1786 he was dismissed from Cane Creek Monthly Meeting for misconduct. Daniel and Jane requested that their children, Frances, Hannah and Rebecca be received into meeting. Daniel purchased land in Orange County in 1788 and lived there until 1814 when he and his wife Jane sold their holdings to William Marshall, probably in preparation for a forthcoming move to Lick Creek Monthly Meeting to which they, with their family, got a certificate in April of 1815.[68]

Issue of Daniel and Jane (Wood) Freeman:

7.	i.	Frances Freeman, b. 24 Feb 1777, Orange Co., NC. m. Mr. Bradford. She was dismissed for marrying out of union.
8.	ii.	Hannah Freeman, b. 6 January 1782; d. 8 October 1798.
9.	iii.	Rebecca Freeman, b. 17 July 1783; dismissed 4 Jul 1801.
10.	iv.	John Freeman, b. 17 May 1784; m. 18 February 1805, Orange Co., to Charity Wells; dismissed 5 October 1805 for

---

[67]National Archives. File of Nathan Freeman. BLWt 121-100.

[68]Hinshaw, *Quaker Genealogy* v.1:389.

		marrying out of union. Charity was also dismissed.
11.	v.	Daniel Freeman, Jr., b. 14 Febraury 1788; dismissed 6 May 1809 for marrying out of union.
12.	vi.	Jane Freeman, b. 25 March 1791; d. 20 January 1803.
13.	vii.	Joshua Freeman, b. 19 May 1794. Dismissed 3 June 1815.

4. Robert, brother of Nathan and Daniel, moved to Surry County. There he married on 14 November 1805 to Susanah Gunston. Bondsman was Mos. Adams.

5. Samuel, probably a brother of Robert, Daniel and Nathan, died in Orange County, in 1796. Daniel Freeman was administrator of the estate. This is probably the Samuel who was mentioned in records of Cane Creek as having been dismissed from the Monthly Meeting in 1784 for marrying out of union. There is an Orange County marriage bond for a Samuel Freeman to a Rebecca Freeman on 24 Nov. 1783.

6. There was also a John Freeman who was dismissed from Cane Creek on 3 February 1781 for marrying out of union. He is also probably a member of this family.

GEORGE FREEMAN
of
Richmond Co., North Carolina

George Freeman resided in Richmond County which had been formed in 1779 from Anson County. He made his will in Richmond County on 8 April 1783. He did not live long after making the will which was proved in the June Court of that year by witnesses John Cole and Josias Freeman.[69] Josias was probably some kin to George Freeman, but evidence of relationship is not shown in the will.

George named his wife, Elisabeth Freeman, leaving her a horse, saddle, bed and furniture. He left to his granddaughters, Darky Alley and Ann Dicks Bownd, all his stock of Cattle and left the balance of his estate to his son-in-law George Bownd.

Issue of George and Elisabeth ( ) Freeman

    2   i.   (daughter) Freeman who married George Bownd and had three daughters.

          3   i.   Darky Bownd

          4   ii.   Alley Bownd

          5   iii.   Ann Dicks Bownd

---

[69] Richmond Co., NC. Wills C.R. 082.801.6

State of North Carolina
Rowan County } The worshipful Justices
of the County Court of Rowan:

The petition of Leonard Freeman, humbly sheweth to your worships. That some time about the latter end of the year of our Lord one thousand seven hundred eighty four, or beginning of the 1785. or there abouts, Isaac Freeman father of your petitioner died without executing Last Will and testament and seized and possessed of a tract or parcel of land lying and being in the County of Rowan on Swear creek. and leaving John Freeman, William Freeman and Leonard Freeman your petitioner his son and heirs at Law, your petitioner prays your worships to appoint five commissioners to devide and appropriate to your petitioner agreable to an act of Assembly in such case made and provided, one third part of the land aforesaid of his father aforesaid being the part to which your petitioner is entitled by the laws of inheritance. And your petitioner as in duty bound will ever pray.

Evan Alexander Att.
for plaintiff

Petition for Division of Isaac Freeman's land,
Rowan County, NC. C.R. 085.508.58.

170

ISAAC FREEMAN
FREE BLACK, OF ROWAN COUNTY

Isaac Freeman married Agnes Faggott in Rowan County. The marriage bond is dated 19 January 1762. Bondsmen were John Johnston and Henry Horah; and witnesses were Will Reed and John Frohock.[70]

Little is known of their lives. At the time of the 1778 Tax List, Isaac was taxed for 120 acres of land.[71] On 1786, Agness Freeman was appointed administratrix on the estate of "Isaac Freeman, a free Negroe."[72] Henry Giles was security for the £100 bond. No other mention has been found in county records identifying Isaac as negro, but later census records list the family as free blacks. Isaac is possibly the one of the name mentioned in the Secretary of State Military Papers as having died in service.[73] A petition filed by his sons was entered in November 1800:

> The petition of Leonard Freeman, humbly sheweth to your worships. That some time about the latter end of the year of our Lord one thousand seven hundred eighty four, or beginning of the [year] 1785 or there abouts Isaac Freeman

---

[70]NC State Archives, Marriage Index.

[71]Mrs. Stahle Linn, Jr., C.G., *Abstracts of Wills and Estates Records of Rowan County, North Carolina, 1753-1805 and Tax Lists of 1759 and 1778* (Salisbury: By the author, 1980):144.

[72]Jo White Linn, *The Minutes of the Court of Pleas and Quarter Sessions, Rowan County, North Carolina, 1775-1789, V. III* (Salisbury, NC: The author, 1982):147. This volume also mentions (p..81) a petition of Jenny Freeman a free Molatto Woman for return of a female free molatto child named Mary Ann, daughter of Abram Freeman and (p. 105) Samuel Cooper ordered to return a Mulatto child, born free, to Ruth Freeman, her mother. No relationship has been established between Isaac and these other free blacks of Rowan County.

[73]North Carolina State Archives, *Secretary of State Revolutionary Military Papers*, 1243.2; see also *North Carolina Revolutionary Army Accounts, Vol X* A List of Assembly Orders and others Vouchers, 1779(p. 67,p.17,fol.1)and *A list of Warrants Issued to the Officers and Soldiers in the Continental Line Raised in and Belonging to the State of North Carolina* #5236 Issac Freeman for 84 months of service, 640 acres, Dec 9, 1797 deliv. to R.D. Barry (No grant issued. Source: Sec. of State 756.2 Key to the Glasgow Land Frauds).

father of your petitioner died without executing a last will and testament and seized and possessed of a tract or parcel of land lying and being in the County of Rowan on Swans Creek and leaving John Freeman, William Freeman and Leonard Freeman your petitioners his sons and heirs at Law. Your petitioner prays your worships to appoint five commissioners to divide and appropriate to your petitioner agreeable to an act of Assembly in such case made and provided, one third part of the land aforesaid of his father aforesaid being the part to which your petitioner is entitled by the laws of inheritance. And your petitioner as is duty bound will ever pray.

Evans Alexander Att°
for plaintiff.[74]

The widow, Agga Freeman died testate. Her will is dated 28 June 1809 but no probate date is recorded.[75] She names the three sons mentioned above and a daughter, Mary Freeman who was named her executor.

Issue of Isaac and Agga (Faggott) Freeman:

2.	i.	John Freeman.
3.	ii.	William Freeman.
4.	iii.	Leonard Freeman, m. Love Birth, 17 Aug 1808, Rowan Co., John Freeman, bondsman, A.L. Osborne, witness.[76] Appears on 1810 census, Rowan Co., NC.
5.	iv.	Mary Freeman.

---

[74]Rowan Co., NC. Estate file of Isaac Freeman 1800. NC State Archives, C.R. 085.508.58.

[75]Jo White Linn, *Rowan County, North Carolina, Will Abstracts, Vol. II, 1805-1850* (Salisbury: By the Author, 1971):12 Agga Freeman, will G:133.

[76]NC Marriage Index.

JOHN FREEMAN OF WAKE COUNTY

John Freeman resided in what became Wake County at least by 1760 as his son gives that as his birthplace in his Revolutionary War Pension statement.[77] John married at uncertain date to Martha Linn whose father, James Lin, Sr., left her stock and household furniture in his 1797 Wake County will.[78]

He is probably the John Freeman who served as a chain bearer to surveyor Charles Young in Johnston County, one of the parent counties to Wake. One of the surveys, made 21 May 1762, for land of Joseph Lane, was on Linns branch of Swift Creek.[79]

He is probably the man who received vouchers for beef, pork and corn furnished during the Revolutionary War.[80]

At the time of the 1790 census he is one of the two men of the name resident there. Both have 2 white males over 16 and two white males under 16 but the elder John Freeman had 8 females in his household while the other had only 2. Neither household had any slaves. It is probable that the other John is the son. Also on that census is Needham Freeman, another son.

John Freeman wrote his will in Wake County on the 13th of September in 1797. The will was proved in December of 1800.[81] He names his wife Martha and 12 children. Martha appears as "Patsy" Freeman in Wake County on the 1800 Census.[82]

---

[77]National Archives, Revolutionary War Pension W.8832, John Freeman. Letter 26 May 1934 A.D. Hiller Asst to Administrator to Mrs. Lucile Freeman Jones, Ruby South Carolina.

[78]Wake County NC. WB 4:89.

[79]Margaret M. Hofmann, *The Granville District of North Carolina, 1748-1763,* v.2 (Weldon, NC: The Roanoke New Press, 1987):196,205.

[80]NC State Archives, *Revolutionary War Pay Vouchers and Certificates.* Wake Co., Certs #479, 324, 158.

[81]Wake Co., NC. WB 5:164.

[82]1800 Census, Wake County, NC, p.730. Shows m. 2 16/26; f. 1 und/10, 2 10/16; 1 16/26, 1 ov/45.

Issue of John and Martha (Linn/Lynn) Freeman in the order mentioned in John's will.

2   i.   Francis[2] Freeman, to receive ½ of 470 acre home plantation after death of Martha. Possibly the Francis in Dobbs Co., 1790; in Lenoir Co., 1800; and Wayne Co., 1810.

3   ii.   Alsey[2] Freeman, to receive other ½ of plantation after Martha's death. Probably the A in 1820 census of Pendleton Dist. SC, m. 2 und/16, 126/45; f. 4 und 10; 3 10/16; 1 26/45.[83]

+   4   iii.   Needham[2] Freeman, b.c. 1758; m. 29 Oct 1785, in Wake Co., to Martha Moore.[84] Moved to South Carolina, and later to Georgia.

+   5   iv.   John[2] Freeman, b.c. 1760, Wake Co., NC; d. 1825-36, Pickens Co., SC; m. 1780 or 1786 in Wake Co., to Francis Moore.[85]

6   v.   Jeptha[2] Freeman, b.c. 1755-74.[86]

7   vi.   Clary[2] Freeman, m. ___ Cooper.[87]

8   vii.   Irainey[2] (Irena) Freeman, m. 7 Mar 1795, Wake Co., Mark Moore.[88]

---

[83] 1820 Census Pendleton Dist., SC p. 223.

[84] J. Earle Freeman, *Mark Freeman and His Descendants* (n.p, 1918)10-13.

[85] Rev. War Pension W. 8832.

[86] 1820 Census of Pendleton Dist. SC, p. 175, shows m. 1/16/26, 1 16/18, 1 ov/45; f. 1 und/10, 1 26/45.

[87] Wake Co., NC WB 5:164.

[88] Liahona Research, Inc., Jordan R. Dodd, ed. *N. Carolina Marriages, Early to 1800* (Bountiful, UT: Precision Indexing Publishers, 1990):153.

9	viii.	Patsey² Freeman, m. 14 Dec 1799, Wake Co., Dempsey Massey.⁸⁹
10	ix.	Betsy² Freeman.
11	x.	Sally² Freeman.
12	xi.	Polley² Freeman.
13	xii.	Synthia² Freeman.

4. **NEEDHAM² FREEMAN**, (John¹ Freeman) was probably born about 1758 in Johnston Co., NC.⁹⁰ His brother, John, next in the order of children named in his father's will, served in the Revolutionary War. John's pension gives Wake County as his birthplace but Wake wasn't formed until 1770 from Cumberland, Johnston and Wake Counties).⁹¹

Needham married Martha Moore on 29 October 1785 in Wake County.⁹² Sometime between 1800 and 1810 he moved his family to Pendleton District, South Carolina. He is described by a descendant as a "large, tall, bony man of dark complexion. The Moores were of red complexion and the ruddy face of many of Needham's descendants comes from the Moores."⁹³ He lived some years in South Carolina and when about aged 50 moved to Georgia. He became a Baptist Minister. Date and location of his death are unknown.⁹⁴

---

⁸⁹*Ibid.*

⁹⁰Hofmann, *Granville Dist* v. 2

⁹¹Rev. War Pension W. 8832.

⁹²Liahona Research, *NC Marriages*:153.

⁹³Freeman, *Mark Freeman*:11. This 3½ by 6 inch, 38 page booklet gives a wealth of data on Needham and his descendants, focusing primarily on Needham's son Mark Freeman and his family to the time of World War I. All detail about Needham and his children, except that taken from the Federal Census is taken from this small publication.

⁹⁴*Ibid*:13.

Children of Needham and Martha (Moore) Freeman:[95]

14	i.	Benton[3] Freeman, buried foot of Langly Mountain, Pickens Co., SC m. Miss Ferguson, Had a son who lives (1918) on Cox Bridge Road in Greenville Co age 82.[96]
15	ii.	Jephtha,[3] Freeman, moved to Alabama but returned to SC after his wife's death. A shoemaker, One son David and perhaps others. David Marion Freeman who m. Martha Williams was a descendant through son David.[97]
16	iii.	Redden,[3] Freeman, settled Northwest of Pickens Court a house buried at Secona Baptist Church.[98]
17	iv.	Mark,[3] Freeman, b. 14 May 1795; d. 18 Sep 1865, b. present location of Cross Roads Church; m(1) Elizabeth Fowler, m(2) Jane Wimpie. Lived Pickens Co., SC. 9 chn by 1st marriage and 4 chn by 2nd marriage.
18	v.	Jake,[3] Freeman, moved to GA, Cherokee Co. Made a fortune.[99]
19	vi.	Barney[3] Freeman, moved to Habersham Co., GA and lived to age 90.[100]
20	vii.	daughter, m. Mr. Hunt, resided in GA.

---

[95] All data about Needham's children from Freeman, *Mark Freeman and His Descendants*. [see note

[96] 1850 Census Pickens Co., SC p. 522 shows him as age 62, b. NC.

[97] Accelerated Index Systems, 1850, Southern States, Microfiche ed., shows a Jephtha on p. 73, 1850 Census of Cherokee Co., AL.

[98] 1850 Census of Pickens Co., p. 524 shows Reden age 50 b. NC.

[99] AIS Census Index shows a Jacob Freeman on p. 523 of Cherokee Co., GA.

[100] AIS Census Index shows a Berny L. in Pendleton Dist., SC p. 212, in 1820; Barney L. Freeman on p. 278 of 1850 Habersham Co.

21	viii.	daughter, m. Mr. Cannon, resided in GA.
22	ix.	daughter, m. Mr. Henderson resided south of Easley in Anderson County, SC.

5. **JOHN² FREEMAN** (John¹ Freeman) was the only one of the family for whom there is a record of service in the Revolutionary War. He was probably born circa 1760, and gives his birth place as Wake County (not formed until 1770). He married Frances Moore, possibly a sister of Martha who married Needham. Date of the marriage is uncertain because dates of 1 Mar 1780 and 25 Mar 1786 are both given in the Pension papers.[101]

He enlisted in Wake County and served several tours as a private in Captain Lewis Blecher's of Blutcher's North Carolina Company. He was in the battles of Eutaw, Lindley's Mill, and at the surrender of Yorktown, serving in total, seventeen months.

In 1806 he moved to South Carolina settling in what became Pickens County. The Pension Papers give much confusing data, giving his death date as 1 Jan 1823, mid January 1825, 14 February 1835 or 36. The widow was allowed a pension in February, 1850 at which time her age was given as 80, but in 1855 as 90.

The pension states that the couple had fifteen children, the oldest a daughter, born about a year after the marriage, the next a son named "Noley, Urley or Uxley who was aged 64 in 1850." If this age is correct it would indicate that the marriage was probably in 1780 rather than 1786. The pension states that a David Freeman acted as a witness for the widow Frances in 1850 and an affidavit was made by a "nephew" Mark Freeman of Pickens County. Mark was son of Needham and had a son David.

Known Issue of John and Frances (Moore) Freeman:

---

[101]Rev. War Pension W.8832.

24	i.	Noley [Urley, Uxley] Freeman.[102]
25	ii.	Bennett Freeman "of Marrietta, Greenville Co., SC." [103]
26	iii.	Westly Freeman.[104] A man of the name is on 1850 census Greenville Co., SC.[105]

Twelve others.

---

[102]Letter to Lucille Freeman Jones in Pension file. Possibly this is the Westly shown below.

[103]Freeman, *Mark Freeman*:11. 1850 Census Greenville Co., SC p.322.

[104]*Ibid*.

[105]AIS Census Index, 1850.

WILLIAM FREEMAN
of
Norfolk, Virginia, and Bertie Co., North Carolina

Although this Freeman family followed the same migration path, from Norfolk, Virginia, to eastern North Carolina, as did two of the sons of the immigrant John Freeman, there seems to be no relationship between the families.

Mr. William Freeman was elected a Common Councilman of the Borough of Norfolk, Virginia, in the room of Mr. George Abyvon and took his oath of office on 24 January 1751. Records of his service to the town extend to Febraury 1774 when he was appointed Clerk of the Market of the Borough.[106] He seems to have taken a prominent part in community affairs and to have had considerable wealth.

William Freeman does not appear in records of the Borough nor on the tithable lists of Norfolk County until after his marriage on 7 Febraury 1749 to Tabitha Wilson. Tabitha's father, Solomon Wilson, gave consent for the marriage.[107] Solomon is probably the name of the man given as a son in the 1712 will of James Wilson.[108]

William was a large landowner with holdings in both Norfolk Borough and in the county.[109] In 1758, although remaining a resident of Virginia, William made his first land purchase in Bertie County, North Carolina. He is identified as a Norfolk Borough resident in the deed for 640 acres purchased from John Gray of Orange County.[110] Again in 1760 William of

---

[106]Brant Tarter, *The Order Book and Related Papers of the Common Hall of the Borough of Norfolk, Virginia, 1746-1709* (Richmond: Virginia State Library, 1979):80, 178.

[107]Elizabeth B. Wingo, *Marriages of Norfolk County, Virginia, 1706-1792* v. 1 (Norfolk: by the author, n.d.):25.

[108]Charles Fleming McIntosh, B.L., *Brief Abstracts of Norfolk County Wills, 1710-1753* (Easley, SC: Southern Historical Press, repr. 1982, Orig. pub. 1922):24-25.

[109]Norfolk Co., VA. Deed Index, and Norfolk Independent City Deed Index.

[110]Bertie Co., NC. DB I:114.

Norfolk Town bought a tract on Flagg Run from Needham Bryan, and in 1761, still "of Virginia," he bought a third tract, this time from Thomas Harrell.[111] A month later he sold 76 acres to David Harrell.[112] Other land transactions follow.

The political situation in Norfolk Borough deteriorated with the approach of the Revolutionary War. This may have influenced a temporary move by the family to Bertie. Although retaining property in Virginia, William apparently was residing in Bertie County in February of 1775 when he was appointed administrator with will attached of the estate of his father-in-law, Solomon Wilson.[113] The subsequent burning of the town of Norfolk by the British led by Lord Dunmore in January 1776, combined with further looting and burning by American soldiers, who believed the town a nest of Tories, may have influenced the family to remain in North Carolina.[114] In 1777 William, described as a resident of Bertie, spent £320 to purchase from Thomas Pugh 380 acres at the mouth of a small branch of Rocquisst.[115]

William Freeman died about December 1781.[116] His will was proved in Bertie County Court in February 1782. The will "loaned" to his wife Tabitha during her natural lifetime his whole estate of all kinds and after her decease to be disposed of as followeth. To daughter Mary Bark/Burk, a negro girl named Nell; to grandaughter, daughter of my daughter Frances McKerall, a negro, Polla; To mulatto woman Racher and all her children their freedom; daughter Frances McKerall has formerly been given her

---

[111]*Ibid*:415; DB K;39.

[112]Bertie Co., NC. DB K:87.

[113]Weynette Parks Haun, *Bertie County North Carolina County Court Minutes, 1772 thru 1780*: Bk 4 (Durham, NC: By the author, 1979):134.

[114]Virginius Dabney, *Virginia, The New Dominion* (Charlottesville: University Press of Virginia, 1971):132.

[115]Bertie Co., DB M:299.

[116]Orange Co., NC. Estate file of William and Tabitha Freeman. NC State Archives, C.R. 073.508.40. Petition of Francis Child, widow, and Mary Doherty, widow, daughters and Representateives of William Freeman May Term 1799.

part; To sons, John and Robert all his land in Virginia and in Bertie County to be divided between them, share and share alike. My son John is "now at sea and in case he should never return to my said son Robert."[117]

Tabitha and the children moved to Warren County where Tabitha's will was written 15 February 1794. It was probated in May 1797 in Warren County.[118] By this date the daughter Mary Burke had married a Mr. Daugherty. She was to receive £100 according to her mother's will. Granddaughter, Mary Burke, was to also receive £100 which was to revert to her mother if she died single and with out issue. Granddaughter Frances McKirol received £200. Tabitha specified that the money for the legacies was to be raised from the hire of the negroes in her husband's estate in the hands of her son Robert; also from the sale of a negro Moses belonging to her husband's estate to which she was entitled by his will, sold by Robert, for which she had received no payment and for £60 she had paid for taxes of property in Norfolk. The executors were to be Mary "Daugharty" and (granddaughter) Frances McKirol. Frances (Freeman) (McKirol) Child was the witness.

In 1800 Mary Daugherty sued her brother Robert Freeman in Orange County Court, charging that Robert sold property in Norfolk.[119] Another action was brought in 1798 against Robert Freeman by his sisters, "Frances Child, widow, and Mary Doherty, widow, daughters and Representatives of William Freeman late of Bertie, deceased."

> Humbly Sheweth - That William Freeman heretofore of Bertie County Departed this life some time in or about the Month of December that was in the year 1781- Having previous to his death made his last will and testament and thereof appointed Tabitha Freeman (his wife), Robert Freeman (his son), and Noah Hinton his Executors- That

---

[117]Bertie Co., NC. WB C:33.

[118]Will of Tabitha Freeman, Warren Co., WB 9:156A. as abstracted in Mary Hinter Kerr, *Warren County, North Carolina Records Vol III, Abstracts of Will Books, 1779-1814* (Warrenton, NC: by the author. Copy made 24 Oct 1812 which erroneously names Mary Burke, daughter of Mary Daugherty, as daughter instead of granddaughter.

[119]Orange Co., Estate Files, NC State Archives, C.R. 073.508.39.

Tabitha Freeman is since dead and Robert Freeman of Warren County is the only acting Executor of the said will - Your Petitioners further shew that a Mulatto woman named Racher formerly a Slave of the said William Freeman in his life time, had performed toward him Services highly meritorious during the period of the late war -more particularly at one time in saving for the said William and safely delivering to him thru' many perils and temptations a Box containing a large sum of Money the Property of the said William - which she had secured during the conflagration of the Town of Norfolk when set on fire by order of Lord Dunmore. - by means of the saving of which money the said William was enabled to purchase the Lands on which he afterwards lived in this State of North Carolina.- And your Petitioners shew that in grateful remembrance of Services so valuable the said William on his Death bed in his will aforesaid - bequeathed as follows - viz - "Item- I give and bequeath unto my Mulatto woman Racher and all her Children their freedoms to be free and clear from Bondage and Slavery for ever." -- and your Petitioners shew than a Mulatto man named Sam (otherwise Sam __[blank]__) now of this County is one of the Children of the said Racher - and is and ought to be free - But your Petitioners shew that the said Robert Freeman not performing his duty as Executor of his fathers Will in a faithful manner but neglecting and altogether failing so to do altho' he acknowledges the right of said Mulatto Sam to be free - refuses to let him enjoy his liberty which is contrary to equity & good conscience - And your Petitioners say that as the Representatives of their father the said William Freeman they feel it incumbent on them to demand that the meritorious Services of the said Racher may be compensated according to the wish and desire of their said Father - And that this worshipful Court by Virtue of the Power vested in them by the several Acts of the General Assembly in such case provided may adjudge the said Sam to be free and do such Acts as may be necessary to Establish him in his Rights. -

Norwood & Duffy for Pet[rs.][120]

A year later, in May 1799, a second petition was filed which repeated most of the above but stated that Rachel had three children: Sam who had been emancipated by the court and Billy,

---

[120]*Ibid*. C.R. 073.508.39-40. William and Tabitha Freeman 1818. A second copy of this petition dated May term 1799, gives the slave's name as Rachel.

a mulatto boy and Suckey, a mulatto girl, who, along with their mother Rachel, Robert Freeman refused to set free. An order of the court (undated) granted the petition, making Rachel and her children "Free Persons of Colour"and were to be known by the names of Rachel Joel, Billy Joel and Suckey Joel.[121]

These suits were followed by others. In September 1819 the Court made an order pursuant to a report of the Clerk and Master of the court granting to Mary W. Burke, $268.81; to Mary Doherty $268.81; and to Abner B. Bruce and his wife Frances, $537.62, for their legacies given by Tabitha's will.[122] Orange County estate records contain one full archives box and part of another containing records of these suits. Included are letters of Tabitha Freeman and many other documents. These records, too detailed to be discussed here, are a goldmine which should be consulted by descendants of this couple.[123]

Issue of William and Tabitha (Wilson) Freeman:

2   i.   **Mary Freeman**, a minor when m.(1) 28 Mar 1770 in Norfolk, VA to Thomas Burke or Bark.[124] She appears to have married a second time after 1781 to a Mr. Daugherty.[125] She had a daughter:

    7. i.   Mary Burke, named in Tabitha Freeman's will.

3   ii.   **Frances Freeman**, m.(1) with her father's consent, 13 April 1769, Norfolk Co., VA to John Mc Cariel[126] [variously Makerrel, McKerall, McKirol]. Frances, Sr. m(2) Francis Child who d. testate in

---

[121]*Ibid.*

[122]*Ibid.*

[123]*Ibid.* See also Warren County, NC. Estate Records.

[124]Wingo, *Norfolk Marriages*, v. 1.

[125]Orange Co., NC Estate file, William and Tabitha Freeman. NC State Archives C.R. 073.508.40.

[126]Wingo, *Marriages of Norfolk, 1706-1792*, v. 1.

May 1792. She witnessed Tabitha's will. She had a daughter:

> 8 i. Frances McKirol, named in Tabitha's will, who m. Abner Benton Bruce who qualified as co-executor of Tabitha's will (in right of his wife.)[127]

4 iii. **John Freeman,** named in the will of his father to equally share lands in Norfolk and Bertie with his brother Robert. The will states that John is at sea. No further record has been found of him and Robert is referred to as heir at law in later deeds. Apparently died young.

5 iv. **Robert Freeman,** named in will of his father as co-heir of land in Norfolk and in Bertie, and as sole heir, if John failed to return. Robert transacted much business in both Bertie and in Norfolk Co., Virginia, following his father's death. He is probably the Robert who m. 11 or 12 April 1793[128] to Sally Green, daughter of Capt. Green of Franklin County, resided in Warren Co., NC. She died in Warren County 21 Mar 1813.[129] Signatures on a the 1818 agreement to settle the suit of his sisters matches the signature on the will of Mr. Robert Freeman of Franklin County which was written 2 October 1821 and probated in January 1822.[130] It leaves land on Fox Swamp in Franklin County to his sons George W. and Robert; cuts his son William D. Freeman off with one cent " and the money which I have had to pay for him." His daughters received slaves. George W. Freeman was executor.

---

[127] Orange Co., NC Estate File, William and Tabitha Freeman.

[128] Orange Co., Estate File. Mary Doherty v. Robert Freeman 1818. Deposition of Jordan Hill, 15 July 1811.

[129] Lois Smathers Neal, *Abstracts of Vital Records from Raleigh, North Carolina Newspapers, 1799-1819* v. 1. (Spartanburg, SC: The Reprint Company, 1979): 171.

[130] Lois Smathers Neal, *Abstracts of Vital Records from Raleigh, North Carolina Newpapers, 1820-182,* v. 2.(Spartanburg, SC: The Reprint Company, Publishers, 1979):257.; v. 1: 171. lists his wife as Sarah Ge- -n [GETUN?], d. In Warren County on the 21st inst. [Mar 1813], and dau of Capt. GE- -N [GETUN?], of Franklin.

Issue as shown by will:

9 i. William D. Freeman, m. in Franklin Co. 26 January 1819, Harriet T. Green.

10 ii. Mary J. Freeman, m. ___ Lain.

11 iii. Mariah Freeman m. Warren co 30 Sep 1812 John Snow.[131]

12 iv. George W. Freeman, of Franklin Co. m. Miss Theresa T. Tartt, of Edgecombe, 13 Dec 1825.[132]

13 v. Robert Freeman. A minor 1821.

14 vi. Eliza N. Freeman. Unmarried 1821.

15 vii. Martha Freeman. Unm. 1821.

16 viii. Sally G. Freeman. Unm. 1821.

Possible child.

6 v. **William Freeman,** In the Norfolk County Court Order Book, p.257, 22 Jul 1768, is an order granting "William Freeman, Senr and William Freeman Jun: against Henry Rothery for fifty pounds tobacco Each for two days attendance each in his suit against Mathias Christian." Only one William Freeman appears in deeds and tithable lists of Norfolk prior to 1765. The 1771 list shows William of Norfolk with slaves but no son William.[133] It is

---

[131]International Genealogical Index, 1992 ed.

[132]Neal, *Vital Records from NC Newspapers* v. 2:236. Care must be taken to differentiate this man from the George W. Freeman, born Massachusetts, later of Wake County, who first taught at Oxford Academy and then became Rector of Christ Church in Raleigh and finally Bishop of the Episcopal Church for Arkansas and the SouthWest.

[133]Norfolk Co., VA, Tithable List. West Division Norfolk Borough, June 1771. William Freeman, negroes Arquil, Lewis, Bristol, Pleasant & Phillis- 6 tithes. From photocopies at Virginia State Archives as abstracted by Patricia J. Watson for the author.

possible that William Senior, had a son born about 1750 who was his fellow witness in this suit. If a son, he must have died before the 1771 tax list.

APPENDIX

FREEMAN REFERENCES IN
NORTH CAROLINA

REVOLUTIONARY WAR RECORDS

APPENDIX

FREEMAN REFERENCES IN NORTH CAROLINA REVOLUTIONARY WAR RECORDS

As an aid to future researchers, the following material is presented. It represents all references to Freeman family members found in the Revolutionary War Vouchers; Account Books; and Treasurer's and Comptoller's records at the North Carolina Department of Cultural Resources, Division of Archives and History.

These records were abstracted and compiled for the author by Harriette Riggs, of Raleigh, NC, with the able assistance of the Archives Staff.

The reader is cautioned that in many cases it is not possible to identify the person to whom the record makes reference. The majority of the following records must belong to Freeman males mentioned in the body of the text, however in a large number of cases it has been impossible to determine which of several men of the same name is the subject of the record. In the cases where only an initial is used, identification has been impossible.

North Carolina Revolutionary military records are complex. The reader is strongly advised to consult the following books and pamphlets to gain a better understanding of their history, origin, and use.

For a more complete understanding of North Carolina's Revolutionary War records contained in these volumes the reader should consult the following

Leary, Helen F. M. and Maurice R. Stirewalt, eds., *North Carolina Research: Genealogy and Local History* (Raleigh, NC: The North Carolina Genealogical Society, 1980)

Haun, Weynette Parks, *North Carolina Revolutionary Army Accounts Secretary of State Treasurer's & Comptroller's Papers,* v. I-III (Durham, NC: By the author, 1789-91)

Coker, Fred W. and Donald R. Lemon, "North Carolina's Revolutionary War Pay Records" *Archives Information Circular No. 1* (Raleigh, NC: North Carolina State Archives, 1976)

Stevenson, George, "North Carlina Revolutionary War Records of Primary Interest to Genealogists," *Archives Information Circular No. 13* (Raleigh NC: North Carolina State Arhives, 1980)

REVOLUTIONARY PAY VOUCHERS AND CERTIFICATES

The surviving original vouchers are housed at the North Carolina Archives. Photocopies of several appear as illustrations in the preceding text. With little hard cash available the colonies found it necessary to issue credit notes in lieu of cash. The system was used to pay soldiers and to pay for other goods and services purchased or confiscated by the army on the move. The holder often assigned the vouchers or paid taxed with them eventually the "paid" vouchers made their way back to the North Carolina State Treasurers office. Holes in the certificates were made to show that they were cancelled.

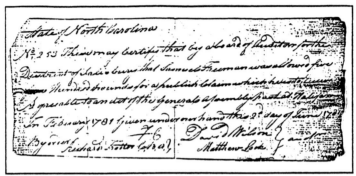

Example of Revolutionary Voucher.

FREEMAN Vouchers: Columns: County [if any], District, type [if shown], amount, voucher #, remarks.

AARON FREEMAN, Salisb. Dist, pub. clm, £90., 16 Nov 8-, voucher #610
AARON FREEMAN, Salisb. Dist, pub. clm, £6.10.6, 31 Aug 82, voucher #2297
AARON FREEMAN, Salisb. Dist, pub. clm, £3.16.0, 25 Sep 84, voucher #5201
AARON FREEMAN, Dobbs Co.,Newb. Dist, Cont.Ln, £32, 8 Mar 83, voucher #33
ALLEN FREEMAN, Salisb. Dist, pub. clm, £7.15, 2 Aug 82, voucher #451
ARCHIBALD FREEMAN, Hillsb. Dist, £9.2.0, 6 Oct 84, voucher #6928
BENJA FREEMAN, Wilmtn. Dist, Militia, £9, 22 Sep 83, voucher #4815
DANIEL FREEMAN, Hillsb. Dist, £9, 1 Oct 83, voucher #5700
DEMSEY FREEMAN, Edent. Dist, £2, 20 Nov 83, voucher #2504
GEORGE FREEMAN, Salisb. Dist, Militia, £9, 2 Jun 83, voucher #2985
GEORGE FREEMAN, Salisb. Dist, pub. clm, £16.0.6, 12 Sep 82, voucher #1791
GIDEON FREEMAN, Salisb. Dist, Militia, £8.15.6, 5 Sep 83, voucher #4306
HARDY FREEMAN, Edent. Dist, £10.14, 4 Nov 82, voucher #176
HENRY FREEMAN, Halif. Dist, £13.10, 27 May 82, voucher #6776
HENRY FREEMAN, Halif. Dist, £1.12.6, 14 Sep 81, voucher #1656, signd Edward Freeman.
HENRY FREEMAN, Halif. Dist, £4.4.8, 22 Jan 82,voucher #4427
HENRY FREEMAN, Salis. Dist, pub. clm, £5, 26 Aug 83, voucher #3958
HENRY FREEMAN, Franklin Co., Halif. Dist, £9, 14 Mar 84, voucher #9680
HENRY FREEMAN, Franklin Co., corn, 10 Feb 81, voucher #14
JAMES FREEMAN, Edent. Dist., £2, Dec 83, voucher #2801

JESSE FREEMAN, Cont Ln, £20.2.8, 1 May 92, voucher #611
JESSE FREEMAN, Cont Ln, £6.14.2, 1 May 92, voucher #795
JOEL FREEMAN, N Hampton, Halif. Dist, £5.10, 30 Aug 83, voucher #9037
JOHN FREEMAN, Edent. Dist, £16, 4 Nov 82, voucher #1065, Joshua Freeman recd ticket.
JOHN FREEMAN, Cont Ln, £46.13.2, Aug 83, voucher #195, sgn Wm Freeman
JOHN FREEMAN, ESQ, Edent. Dist, £8.10, 7 May 87, voucher #3871
JOHN FREEMAN, Edent. Dist, pub. clm, £11.10, 8 Jul 82, voucher #911
JOHN FREEMAN, Edent. Dist, £240, 19 Mar 81, voucher #102
JOHN FREEMAN, Dobbs Co., Newb. Dist, £1.4, 3 Aug 84, voucher #46
JOHN FREEMAN (Quiochison), Edent. Dist, £291, 24 Mar 81, voucher #196
JOHN FREEMAN, Lincoln Dist, Corn, 15 Nov 80, voucher #73
JOHN FREEMAN, Lincoln Dist, Corn, 18 Jan 82, voucher #169
JOHN FREEMAN, Wake Co., 250# beef, 12 Jul 81, voucher #479
JOHN FREEMAN, Wake Co., 167# Nett Pork, 15 Apr 82, voucher #324
JOHN FREEMAN, Wake Co., Corn, 5 Jan 81, voucher #158
JOSHUA FREEMAN, Edent. Dist, £19.5.8, 7 May 87, voucher #3864
JOSHUA FREEMAN, Edent. Dist, £1984.0.0, 19 Mar 81, voucher #92
JOSIAH FREEMAN, Salisb. Dist, pub. clm, £6.10.6, 3 Aug 82, voucher #2296
KING FREEMAN, Edent. Dist, £3.16, Sep 84, voucher #3413, Lewis Outlaw rec'd ticket
MICH: FREEMAN, Salisb.Dist, Militia, £7, 14 Jul 81, voucher #8149
MOSES FREEMAN, Edent. Dist, £3, 4 Nov 81, voucher #1087
NATHAN FREEMAN, Halif. Dist, £40.12, Mar 85,
RICHARD FREEMAN, Halif. Dist, £11.12.6, 14 Sep 81, voucher #1655
RUBIN FREEMAN, Wilm. Dist, £5.2.4, 26 Aug 83, voucher #2227
RUBIN FREEMAN, Dobbs Co., Newb. Dist, Militia, £1, 18 Sep 83, voucher #1378
SAMUEL FREEMAN, Cont Ln, £106.8.5, 1 May 92, voucher #117
SAMUEL FREEMAN, Salisb. Dist, pub. clm, £2.5.4, 13 Sep 82, voucher #1807
SAMUEL FREEMAN, Hillsb. Dist, £1519, 4 Apr 1781, voucher #131
SAMUEL FREEMAN, Rowan Co., Salisb. Dist, pub. clm, £500, 2 June 81, voucher #253
SOLOMON FREEMAN, Edent. Dist, £3.19.2, 7 May 87, voucher #3868
SOLOMON FREEMAN, Edent. Dist, £0.18.0, 2 Sep 84, voucher #3363
THOMAS FREEMAN, Ans/Mont/Rich, £2.9, 9 Jul 82, voucher #221
THOMAS FREEMAN, Dobbs Co., Newb. Dist, £0.12, 27 Mar 83, voucher #846
WILLIAM FREEMAN, Edent. Dist, £1800, 19 Mar 81, voucher #125, to Jacob Hinton
WILLIAM FREEMAN, Halif. Dist, £4.12, 4 Mar 82, voucher #6619
WILLIAM FREEMAN, Halif. Dist, £0.17, 28 Aug 81, voucher #119
WILLIAM FREEMAN, Salisb. Dist, pub. clm, £5, 26 Aug 83, voucher #3959

REVOLUTIONARY ARMY ACCOUNT BOOKS, CALL #S.115.57

These vouchers and volumes are found in the Search Room of the North Carolina State Archives & History, 109 East Jones Street, Raleigh, NC 27611.

The Index to Revolutionary Army Accounts, Vol. I-XII (Volumes 55-66) was used to locate references to records of all Freman/Freeman males who served in the Revolution from North Carolina.

EXPLANATION OF BOOK AND PAGE NUMBERS

Most of the volumes in the Revolutionary War Account Books have a page number in the upper right and left corners of the pages in the usual manner. However, there are several individually paginated books within a bound volume and the upper page numbers change as a new book begins. Most of these volumes show two pages on the one page. These pages have a different set of numbers with a folio number which is usually centered on the inside corners of the two inner pages. The numbers used in the printed indexes provided for the account books are the centered numbers (or 2nd number followed by the folio). The 2nd number is the one consistent number throughout the volumes.

Example: Two pages on one sheet

Pg. 56   pg. 78, folio 1   pg. 78, folio 2   Pg. 57

Pg. 58   pg. 78, folio 3   pg. 78, folio 4   Pg. 59
{Bracketed information was supplied by the Archival Staff}

REVOLUTIONARY ARMY ACCOUNT BOOKS, VOLUMES I-XII

These books are combinations of records from the Treasurer of the State, the Comptroller and his successor, the Auditor and are now collectively called TREASURER'S AND COMPTROLLER'S RECORDS.

VOLUME I

NORTH CAROLINA REVOLUTIONARY ARMY ACCOUNTS VOL I (OLD SERIES) VOL. 1 NOS. 1-5

Folio 1, pg 69, folio 2 & 3

AN ACCOUNT OF CERTIFICATES PAID INTO COMPTROLLER'S OFFICE BY JOHN ARMSTRONG ENTRY TAKER FOR LAND IN NORTH CAROLINA (VIZT)

(In Vol. I, the first number is listed as Folio--the 2nd number is still the consistent number)

COLUMN HEADINGS: No./ By whom granted/ To whom granted/ Date/ Sum/ Interest, To what time, Principal & Interest

BOOK 4

#1185   AULD & MILLER **HARTWELL FREEMAN** 20 Aug. 1783 13.10.0,
0.7.0   27 JAN 1784 13.17.0

#5700   MEBANE & NICHOLS **DANIEL FREEMAN** 10 N'R 1783 9.0.0,
0.4.7   MARCH 1784 9.4.7

#1655   GREEN & MACON **RICHARD FREEMAN** 13 sept. 1781 11.12.6,
1.14.3   8 MARCH 1784 13.6.9

BOOK 5

#3958   BRUCE & BRAGGE **HENRY FREEMAN** 26 Aug. 1783 5.0.0.,
0.4.3   10 MAY 1784 5.4.3 NO CHECK

#3959   BRUCE & BRAGGE **WILL FREEMAN** 26 Aug. 1783 5.0.0.,
0.4.3   10 MAY 1784 5.4.3 NO CHECK

#1791   WILSON & CATHEY **GEO. FREEMAN** 12 Sept. 82 15.0.0,
1.0.6   20 MAY 1784 16.0.6

#2985   WILSON & CATHEY **GEO. FREEMAN** 25 Jun. 83   9.0.0,
0.9.10   20 MAY 1784 9.9.10

VOLUME II

**NORTH CAROLINA REVOLUTIONARY ARMY ACCOUNTS, VOL II
(OLD SERIES) VOL 1, NO 6, VOL 2, NOS. 7-10**

HALIFAX SEPT'R 1, 1783
*JOURNAL OF THE PROCEEDINGS OF THE COMMISSIONERS
APPOINTED BY ACT OF ASSEMBLY PASSED IN MAY 1783 TO
LIQUIDATE AND FINALLY SETTLE THE ACCOUNTS OF THE
OFFICERS & SOLDIERS OF THE CONTINENTAL LINE OF THE
STATE OF NO.CAROLINA*

Ex'd the claim of **HOWELL FREEMAN,** A Common Soldier due him for pay
including interest to the 1st day of Aug. 1783 23.7.1

BOOK NO. 2

193

AN ACCOUNT OF ALLOWANCES MADE OFFICERS & SOLDIERS OF THE LATE CONTINENTAL LINE OF THIS STATE FOR PAY BY THE COMMISSIONERS OF ARMY ACCOUNTS AT HILLSBOROUGH MAY 1792

Pg. 100, pg. 71, folio 1
#611   Allowed **JESSE FREEMAN**, pvt. from 10 Nov. 1778 to 10 Aug. 1779
26.16.10

VOLUME III

NORTH CAROLINA REVOLUTIONARY ARMY ACCOUNTS, VOL III (OLD SERIES) VOL. III JOURNAL OF COMMISSIONERS

Pg. 1, pg. 1, folio 1
STATEMENT OF THE ACCOUNTS OF THE NON-COMMISSIONED OFFICERS AND PRIVATES OF THE NORTH CAROLINA LINE IN THE LATE ARMY OF THE UNITED STATES AS PASSED UPON BY THE COMMISSIONER OF ARMY ACCOUNTS.

JOURNAL OF COMMISSIONERS B

Pg.#-, pg. 1, folio 1
COLUMN HEADINGS: No., Names & Rank, Amount charged by each, Amount credited by each, Balance paid & charged by the state, Balance actually found, Difference between actual balance & what was pd. by state

Pg.#-, pg. 8, folio 2
#9   **HOWELL FREEMAN**, p   58.35, 0.0, 58.35, 53.30, 0.0

BOOK C
Pg.#-, pg. 56, folio 1

Pg.#-, pg. 67, folio 2
#754   **NATHAN FREEMAN**, p   464.22, 57.77, 406.35, 308.73, 0.0

Pg.#-, pg. 69, folio 1
#868   **RICHARD FREEMAN**, p   318.47, 57.77, 260.60, 0, 0, 0, 0

VOLUME IV

NORTH CAROLINA REVOLUTIONARY ARMY ACCOUNTS VOL. IV (OLD SERIES) VOL. 4, REMARKS OF COMMISSIONERS

THE UNITED STATES TO THE STATE OF NORTH CAROLINA DR.
FOR THE FOLLOWING DISBURSEMENTS MADE BY SAID STATE
FOR ARMY CONTINGENCIES

COLUMNS: Dates, To whom & what pd.

Pg.#-, pg. 103, folio 3
7 Dec. 1777 **SAMUEL FREEMAN**   Nov. 77   R.11,No.273.   No. of vouchers
1188., Old Emission drs. 90   45.0

VOLUME V

NORTH CAROLINA REVOLUTIONARY ARMY ACCOUNTS, VOL. V
(OLD SERIES) VOL. 5, L BOOK NO 11 & 175 TO 180

BOOK 175
AN ALPHABETICAL BOOK CONTAINING ALLOWANCES? (ILLEG.)
BY COMMITTEE OF CLAIMS FROM APRIL 1776 TO MAY 1779

COLUMN HEADINGS: Dates of report, No. of claim, Persons to whom granted, Amt. ea persons claim.

Pg. 17, pg. 5, folio 2
Novr. 1777   #273   **SAMUEL FREEMAN**   18.0.0

Jan. 26, 1779   #161   **WILLIAM FREEMAN**   15.15.0

BOOK NO. 178 [begins pg.#-, pg. 32, folio 1]

Pg. 1, pg. 32, folio 3
AN ACCOUNT OF CLOTHING CURRENCY AND SPECIE CERTIFICATES SENT TO COMMISSIONERS AT NEW YORK BY THE COMPTROLLER OF PUBLIC ACCOUNTS OF THE STATE OF NORTH CAROLINA MAY 1790

Pg. 10, pg. 34, folio 4
#420   **WM. FREEMAN**   5.13.0

BOOK NO. 11 [Begins pg. 1. pg.53, folio 1]
CLAIMS ALLOWED AND PASSED BY THE BOARD OF AUDITORS FOR THE DISTRICT OF WILMINGTON FROM THE 16TH OF JULY (INCLUDED) TO THE 19TH OF MARCH 1784 FOR WHICH CERTIFICATES ARE ISSUED FROM NO. 1459 TO NO. 3348 INCLUSIVE & RETURNED INTO THE COMPTROLLERS OFFICE

Pg. 22, pg. 58, folio 2   Militia
#2227   **RHUBEN FREEMAN**   5.2.4

NC REVOLUTIONARY ARMY ACCOUNTS, VOL. VI (OLD SERIES) VOL 6, BOOKS 21-25

BOOK NO. 21 [begins pg. 1, pg. 1, folio 1]
ACCOUNT OF CLAIMS EXHIBITED INTO COMPTROLLERS OFFICE AGREEABLE TO RESOLVE OF THE GENERAL ASSEMBLY OF NORTH CAROLINA PASSED DEC. 1787

Pg. 1, pg 20, folio 1

COLUMN HEADINGS: No., Persons name in whom issued, Principal, Interest, To whom the Certificates were delivered.

BOOK NO. 23
HILLSBORO TREASURY OFFICE

Pg. 44, pg. 30, folio 4   William Cherry, Sheriff of Bertie County
Pg. 47, pg. 31, folio 3

#63	**KING FREEMAN**	3.16.0	0.5.0
#76	**HARDY FREEMAN**	10.14.0	1.18.0

Pg. 147, pg. 56, folio 3   Richardson Fagan Sheriff Moore County

#16	**REUBEN FREEMAN**	5.2.4

Pg. 153, pg. 58, folio 1   Wm. Hunt Treas'r Granville County

#1	**John FREEMAN**	251.0.0

BOOK NO. 24 [Begins pg. 1, pg. 61, folio 1]
A LIST OF CERTIFICATES PAID INTO THE TREASURY FOR PAYMENT OF THE TAXES OF 1785 & 1786

Pg. 21, pg. 66, folio 1

#702	**J. FREEMAN**	8.10.0

Pg. 3, pg. 70, folio 1

#1217	**A. FREEMAN**	3.16.0	0.12.0

Pg. 44, pg. 71, folio 4

#1450	**A. FREEMAN**	3.18.0	0.1.5

Pg. 53, pg. 74, folio 1

#1760	**H. FREEMAN**	4.4.8	1.5.4

Pg. 59, pg. 75, folio 3
#2041 **A. FREEMAN**   32.0.0   3.12.8

BOOK #25 [Begins pg. 1, pg. 90, folio 1]
CERTIFICATES RECEIVED FOR THE YEAR 1786

Pg. 14, pg. 93, folio 2
#451 **A. FREEMAN**   7.15.0   2.3.0

Pg. 46, pg. 101, folio 2
#1514 **ARON FREEMAN**   6.10.6   1.16.6

Pg. 56, pg. 103, folio 4
#1805 **J. FREEMAN**   6.10.6   1.19.0

VOLUME VII

NORTH CAROLINA REVOLUTIONARY ARMY ACCOUNTS, VOLUME VII (OLD SERIES) VOL. 6 BOOKS 26-90, VOL. 7 BOOKS C13, C17, G16, G17

BOOK 26

Pg. 1, pg. 1, folio 1
A LIST OF CERTIFICATES TO BE PAID TO THE COMPT'S ACT.
FOR THE TAXES OF 1787 INCLUDING THOSE DUE FOR THE YEARS
1784, 1785 AND 1786

Pg. 33, pg. 9, folio 1
Numbers 759-849 appear to be W. Bryan, Shf of Bertie
#821 **J. FREEMAN**   19.5.8   1.5.8

#824 **D. FREEMAN**   2.0.0   0.10.5

Pg. 48, pg. 12, folio 4   Sharp and Rice of Gates
#1201 **D. FREEMAN**   18.0.0   5.5.1

Pg. 55-56, pg. 14, folio 3
Numbers 1392-1420 appear to be Thornton E. Tataker Surry
#1395 **A. FREEMAN**   13.10.0   3.4.0

Pg. 59, pg. 15, folio 3   Jos. Arrington Shff Nash
#1504 **E. FREEMAN**   2.6.6   0.9.10

Pg. 77, pg. 20, folio 1
#2053 **H. FREEMAN**   9.0.0   1.12.0

<u>Pg. 78, pg. 20, folio 2</u>   B. Sander, E. Taker Wake
<u>Pg. 80, pg. 20, folio 4</u>
#2133 **J. FREEMAN**   5.10.0   0.15.8

<u>Pg. 85, Pg. 22, folio 1</u>   Tho Parker Shff No'hampton

BOOK 26, NO. 90
Pg. 1, pg. 24, folio 1
*CERTIFICATES PAID THE COMPTROLLER BY JOHN HAYWOOD
PUBLIC
TREASURER IN THE FALL OF THE YEAR 1791*

<u>Pg. 18, pg. 27, folio 4</u>
#467 **SAMUEL FREEMAN**   10.2.6   5.8.0

<u>Page 23, pg. 29, folio 1</u>
DUE BILLS PAID BY M. HUNT LATE TREASURER

INDEX VOL. 1 BOOK C NO. 13, VOL 7 AD?
<u>Pg. 21, Pg. 34, folio 1</u>
#594 **NATHAN FREEMAN**   40.12.9
<u>Pg. 112, pg. 56, folio 4</u>
CONTINENTAL LOAN OFFICE CERTIFICATES

<u>Pg. 113, pg. 57, folio 1</u>
No#- **WILL FREEMAN**   880

<u>Pg. 115, pg. 57, folio 3</u>
*CERTIFICATES FOR CURRENCY REC'D FROM RICH'D COGDAL
FOR NEW BERN DISTRICT*

<u>Pg. 118, pg. 58, folio 2</u>
#99 **SAM'L FREEMAN**   862.8.0

*LIST OF SPECIE CERTIFICATES PAID BY GREEN HILL ESQR
TREASURER FOR THE DISTRICT OF HALIFAX 1783*

BOOK C No. 17
<u>Pg. 1, pg. 59, folio 1</u>

<u>Pg. 36, pg. 67, folio 3</u>
#678 **WILL FREEMAN**   18.5.0

BOOK G, NO. 16
<u>Pg. 1, pg. 82, folio 3</u>

*{CERTIFICATES   P}AID   BY   THE   TREASURER   TO   THE
COMPTROLLER JULY 1790*

Pg. 47 pg. 94, folio 1
#1328 **GIDEON FREEMAN**   8.15.6   2.19.6

Pg. 48, pg. 94, folio 2   Henry Deberry Shff Montgomery
Numbers 1308-1338)

Pg. 70, pg. 99, folio 4
Numbers 1978-2001   Hump. Brooks by J. Hogg
#1978 **G. FREEMAN**   15.12.0   8.16.10

BOOK G. No. 17 [Begins Pg#-, pg. 100, folio 1]

Pg#-, pg. 100, folio 3
*{STATEMENT} OF THE ACCOUNTS PAID THE {OFFICERS AND
SOLDIERS OF THE CONTIN}ENTAL LINE SINCE 1784*

Pg. 21, pg. 105, folio 3   AMOUNT   CASH   CERTIFICATES
       NATHAN FREEMAN   162.11.2 40.12.9 128.18.5

Pg. 25, pg. 106, folio 3
       RICHARD FREEMAN   104.5.4   26.1.4   73.(78?)4.0

VOLUME VIII

**NORTH CAROLINA REVOLUTIONARY ARMY ACCOUNTS VOLUME
VIII (OLD SERIES), VOL. 7, BOOK 18, VOL. 8, BOOKS E, F NO 1, F
NO 2, K**

BOOK G, No. 18
Pg. 1, pg. 1, folio 1

Pg. 16, pg. 4, folio 4
#1244 **S. FREEMAN**   3.19.2   0.9.7
Pg. 18, pg. 5, folio 2   Wm Bryan Shff Bertie

Pg. 50, pg. 13, folio 2
#1966 **J. FREEMAN**   5.10.9   2.12.8
Pg. 55, pg. 14, folio 3   J. Hinton Shff Wake Co.

Pg. 69, pg. 18, folio 1
#2403 **WM. FREEMAN**   4.12.0   1.18.6
Pg. 71, pg. 18, folio 3   Simon Jefferrs, Franklin

Pg. 1, pg. 21, folio 1
*THE UNITED STATES OF AMERICA TO THE STATE OF NORTH
CAROLINA FOR CASH PAID BY JACOB BLOUNT PAYMASTER TO*

THE OFFICERS AND SOLDIERS OF THE NORTH CAROLINA BRIGADE AS FOLLOWS, VIZ'T

BOOK E
<u>Pg. 55, pg. 34, folio 3</u>   Dec. 1778
                      CURRENCY   SPECIE
#1679 **LEWIS FREEMAN** 58   23.4.0   -

ARMY F, NO. 1, NO INDEX [Begins <u>Pg.#-, pg. 42, folio 1</u>]
THE UNITED STATES OF AMERICA TO THE STATE OF NORTH CAROLINA TO CASH PAID BY RICHARD BRADLEY TO THE OFFICERS AND SOLDIERS OF THE NORTH CAROLINA BRIGADE AS FOLLOWS

(The meaning of the numbers immediately following the name is unknown to the Archival Staff---when a certified typescript is prepared, they ignore them)

<u>Pg. 32, pg. 50, folio 2</u>   Aug. 1777
#903   **JESSE FREEMAN** 4.7   3.12.7

BOOK F, NO. 2 MILITIA LIST [Begins <u>Pg#-, pg. 56, folio 1</u>]

<u>Pg. 1, pg. 57, folio 1</u>
{TO CASH PAID SUNDRIES BY MATT LOCH PAYMASTER TO THE MECKLENBERG REGIMENT OF MILITIA FOR SERVICE DONE IN AN EXPEDITION AGAINST THE CHEROKEE INDIANS IN THE YEAR 1776 AS FOLLOWS}

<u>Pg. 76, pg. 75, folio 4</u>   January 1777
#2023   **JOSHUA FREEMAN**   SPECIE 11.10.0

BOOK K, MILITIA [Begins <u>Pg. 1, pg. 78, folio 1</u>]

<u>Pg. 47, pg. 89, folio 3</u>
TO SUNDRIES PAID BY WILLIAM SKINNER AS TREASURER OF THE DISTRICT OF EDENTON BY ORDER OF THE GENERAL ASSEMBLY FOR SUNDRIES FURNISHED THE MILITIA CONT'D FROM #629 OF THIS BOOK VIZ

<u>Pg. 49, pg. 90, folio 1</u>   Feb. 1779
877/#1169 **W'M FREEMAN**   SPECIE 15.15.0

<u>Pg. 57, pg. 92, folio 1</u>

TO SUNDRIES PAID BY WILLIAM CATHEY AS TREASURER BY ORDER OF THE GENERAL ASSEMBLY FOR SUNDRIES FURNISHED THE MILITIA, VIZ.

<u>Pg. 69, pg. 95, folio 1</u>   Dec. 1777
1188/#1668 **SAM'L FREEMAN**   18.0.0

VOLUME IX

NORTH CAROLINA REVOLUTIONARY WAR ACCOUNT BOOKS, VOLUME IX (OLD SERIES) VOL. 9, BOOKS L NOS. 1, 2, 3, P39, L26, VOL. 10 BOOKS 12, 14, 17

<u>Pg. 1, pg. 12, folio 1</u>
{AN ACCOUNT OF CE}RTIFICATES DELIVERED INTO THE TREASURERS OFFICE AND EXCHANGED PURSUANT TO ACT OF ASSEMBLY PASSED IN DECEMBER 1789 Book L, No 2

COLUMNS HEADINGS: To whom delivered, To whom originally issued, Amount of principal, Interest, To whom reissued

<u>Pg. 4, pg. 13, folio 3</u>   <u>PRINCIPAL INTEREST</u>
   REUBEN FREEMAN   1.0.0   0.9.8
   THOMAS FREEMAN   0.12.0   0.4.9

<u>Pg. 5, pg. 37, folio 1</u>
Certificates and delivered to **MOSES FREEMAN** 3.0.0 1.5.8,
William Reynolds

<u>Pg. 1, pg. 82, folio 1</u>
NO. 14
HILLSBOROUGH TREASURY OFFICE

A LIST OF SPECIE & CURRENCY CERTIFICATES RECEIVED FROM THE COUNTY TREASURERS ENTRY TAKERS, ETC.

HILLSBOROUGH TREASURY OFFICE SEPTT'ER 1785

<u>Pg. 89, pg. 104, folio 1</u>   <u>Isaac Hunter, Sheriff GATES CO.</u>
#10   **JAMES FREEMAN**   2.0.0

BOOK L, No. 26 [HEADING MISSING Pg. 1]

<u>Pg. 29, pg. 59, folio 1</u>

#780   **HENRY FREEMAN**   1.10.0 .0.14.4
Pg. 30, pg. 59, folio 2   Zachariah Harman Shff of Chatham County

No 14
Pg. 1, pg. 82, folio 1
HILLSBOROUGH TREASURY OFFICE

*A LIST OF SPECIE AND CURRENCY CERTIFICATES RECEIVED
FROM THE COUNTY TREASURER, ENTRY TAKER*

Pg. 7, pg. 83, folio 3
HILLSBOROUGH TREASURY OFFICE APRIL 1785

**COLUMN HEADINGS: By whom paid, No. on back of certificates,
Person in whom name issued, Principal, Interest, Amount**

No 5
     Nathaniel Jones, Esq. of Wake Co.
#1   **JOHN FREEMAN**   4.12.0 0.13.9 0.0.0

Pg. 87
HILLSBOROUGH TREASURY OFFICE SEPT. 26, 1785

No. 45
Pg.88, pg. 103, folio 4   Robert White Sheriff of Dobbs Co.
#25   **JOHN FREMAN**   1.4

Pg. 89, pg. 104, folio 1
HILLSBOROUGH TREASURY OFFICE SEPTE'R 27, 1784
No. 46 Isaac Hunter, Sheriff of Gates Co.
#10   **JAMES FREEMAN**   2.0.0.

Pg. 109, pg. 109, folio 1
No. 52   James Campbell Shff Bertie Co.
Pg. 111, pg. 109, folio 3
#68   **JOHN FREEMAN**   16.0.0

Pg.#-, pg. 123, folio 1
*A LIST OF DUE BILLS (TORN) OF THE N.CAR(TORN) Pg.#-, pg.
123, folio 3*
     THOMAS FREEMAN   15.10.4

VOLUME X

**NORTH CAROLINA ARMY ACCOUNTS, VOL X (OLD SERIES) Vol
10, Books 18, 19, Vol. 11 COMMISSIONER'S STATEMENTS A. B. C.**

Pg. 1, pg. 1, folio 1
BOOK NO. 18

Pg. 49, pg. 12, folio 3
CERTIFICATES ISSUED BY COOR & HAWKS & DELIVERED TO THE COMPTROLLERS BY MESSERS JONES MUNFORT & MCCULLOCH

Pg. 60, pg. 15, folio 2
A LIST OF ASSEMBLY ORDERS AND OTHERS VOUCHERS IN 1779
Pg. 67, pg. 17, folio 1
No#- **ISAAC FREEMAN**   12.0.0

VOL. 10, BOOK 19 [Begins Pg. 1, pg.20, folio 1]

EDENTON DISTRICT WILLIAM SKINNER TREASURER

COLUMN HEADINGS: By whom delivered to the comptroller, No of certificate, For whom issued, Amt. of principal on each certificate, Amt. of interest allowed on each certificate

Pg. 8, pg. 21, folio 4
| #322 | **JOHN FREEMAN** | _,291 |
| #335 | **JOHN FREEMAN** | _,240 |

Pg. 9, pg. 22, folio 1
| #366 | **JOSHUA FREEMAN** | 1,984 |

Pg. 15, pg. 23, folio 3
| #811 | **WILL FREEMAN** | 1,800 |

SPECIE CERTIFICATE BY WILLIAM SKINNER, TREASURER
Pg. 21, pg. 25, folio 1

| #155 | **JOHN FREEMAN** | 11.10.0 |

BOOK B-DUPLICATE
UNITED STATES TO STATE OF NO.CAROLINA FOR SETTLEMENT ARMY ACCOUNTS IN THE YEAR 1792, ETC.

Pg. 1, pg. 68, folio 1
THE UNITED STATES TO THE STATE OF NORTH CAROLINA FOR THE FOLLOWING PAYMENTS MADE BY SAID STATE TO THE OFFICERS AND SOLDIERS OF THE LATE CONTINENTAL LINE THEREOF FOR DEPRECIATION & ARREARAGE OF PAY FOR SERVICES PRIOR TO THE (?) DAY OF JAN. 1782, IN ADDITION TO & EXCLUSIVE OF THE SETTLEMENTS MADE AT HALIFAX IN THE

YEARS 1783, 4, 5, AS PER REPORT AT WARRENTON IN THE YEAR 1786

Pg. 8, pg. 71, folio 3
10 Nov. 1778 to 10 Aug 1779
#611   **JESSE FREEMAN**   26.16.10

Pg. 1, pg. 80, folio 1
AN ABSTRACT OF THE SETTLEMENTS OF ARMY ACCOUNTS AT HILLSBOROUGH IN 1792

COLUMN HEADINGS: Names of claimants, Allowed cash money?, The sums paid in due bills, The sums paid in certificates, By whom receipted

Pg. 7, pg. 82, folio 4   CASH   DUE BILLS   CERTIFICATES
    JESSE FREEMAN   26.16.10   6.14.2   20.2.8
Receipted by John Francks

{USED BY ARCHIVES STAFF IN CERTIFICATION OF TYPESCRIPT COPIES: "HEADING MISSING...OTHER INFORMATION:
THIS BOOK APPEARS TO COMPRISE AN ALPHABETICAL LIST OF VOUCHERS PAID BY THE STATE OF NORTH CAROLINA IN SUPPORT OF CONTINENTAL FORCES, OR AN INDEX TO A STATEMENT OF CONTINENTAL ACCOUNTS OR VOUCHERS PAID BY THE STATE."}

Pg.#-, pg. 97, folio 2
    HEZEKAIH FREEMAN   CASEYS DETACHMENT VA LINE 2158

VOLUME XI

NORTH CAROLINA REVOLUTIONARY WAR ACCOUNT BOOKS, VOLUME XI (No information on old series)

Pg. 21, pg. 20, folio 1
COMPTROLLERS OFFICE KINSTON THE UNITED STATES OF AMERICA TO THE STATE OF NORTH CAROLINA FOR SUNDRIES ALLOWED BY A COMMITTEE OF CLAIMS AS PER REPORT DATED NOVEMBER 1777

To   **SAMUEL FREEMAN** for waggon hire Oc Oc(etc?) 273.18.0

Pg. 49, pg. 27, folio 1
THE UNITED STATES OF AMERICA TO THE STATE OF NORTH CAROLINA FOR SUNDRIES ALLOWED BY A COMMITTEE OF CLAIMS AS PER REPORT DATED JANUARY 1779

To **WILLIAM FREEMAN** for acting as adjud't   161.15.15

Pg. 55, pg. 94, folio 1
LIST OF CURRENCY CERTIFICATES PAID BY GREEN HILL TREASURER FOR HALIFAX DISTRICT

Pg. 57, pg. 94, folio 3
#52   **HENRY FREEMAN**   157.10.0

Pg. 72, pg. 98, folio 2
#12   **HOWARD FREEMAN**   3,180.0.0

VOLUME XII

NORTH CAROLINA REVOLUTIONARY ARMY ACCOUNTS VOL XII (OLD SERIES) VOL. 13, BOOKS AA & ZZ

BOOK NO. 7
Folio 1, pg. 24, folio 2
AN ACCOUNT OF SPECIE CERTIFICATES PAID INTO COMPTROLLER'S OFFICE BY JOHN ARMSTRONG ENTRY TAKER FOR LAND IN NORTH CAROLINA

COLUMN HEADINGS: No., By whom granted, To whom granted, Date, Sum, Interest, To what time, Total amt. principal & interest, Remarks (In this volume two pages on one page are numbered only once and called a folio--the consistent number is the middle number)

Folio 35, pg. 41, folio 2
#221   AULD & MILLER **GEO. FREEMAN** JULY 82   2.9.10, 0.5.8
21 MAY 1784 2.15.6

Folio 26, pg. 82, folio 4
#6928   MEBANE & NICHOLS **ARCH'D FREEMAN** Oct"r. 83   9.2.0, NO INTEREST   25TH MAY 1784   9.2.0

Folio 1, pg. 86, folio 1
No. 10, Major Doherty

Folio 11, pg. 91, folio 2
#416   MCCULLOCH & MONTFORD **R. FREEMAN** MAY 83   78.4.0, 3.17.4
23 MAY 1784   82.1.4

Folio 31, pg. 101, folio 2
#1807   WILLSON & CATHEY **SAM'L FREEMAN** Sept. 1782   24.0.0, 2.5.4
16 APRIL 1784   26.5.4

A LIST OF WARRANTS ISSUED TO THE OFFICERS AND SOLDIERS IN THE CONTINENTAL LINE RAISED IN AND BELONGING TO THE STATE OF NC

These bounty lands warrants were issued for land that was North Carolina at that time, but later became part of Tennessee. In the event the soldier died, his heirs applied for the warrants based on his time of service. They frequently assigned or sold these warrants to others.

Additional information from MARS (North Carolina Archives Search Room, Computer System). Preceded by *.

#4307 **FREEMAN, ABEL**, pvt. for 84 months of service, 640 acres, Dec. 14, 1796, delivered by Stockley Donelson. NO GRANT ISSUED.

#1880 **FREEMAN, DAVID**, pvt. for 84 months of service, 640 acres, Oct. 21, 1783 delivered by self.

*MARS. ID#12.14.19.721, FILE #036, MILITARY LAND WARRANT #1880, Issued to heirs of **DAVID FREEMAN** for his service as a private in the Continental Line. John Nelson, Assignee of heirs of David Freeman. Microfilm Reel # S.108.39, Location 165-170.
Land on South fork of Selian, Tennessee Co., TN.

#15 **FREEMAN, DANIEL**, pvt. for 30 months of service, 228 acres, Aug. 6, 1800 by whom drawn Jesse Olive. (GRANT WAS ISSUED TO JAMES MCGILL. SOURCE: Secretary of State 756.2 List of Grants Issued On Military Warrants--By Number, Key No. I)

#5236 **FREEMAN, ISAAC** for 84 months of service, 640 acres, Dec. 9, 1797 delivered to R. D. Barry. (**NO GRANT ISSUED**. SOURCE: Secretary of State 756.2 Key To The Glasgow Land Frauds.)

#64 **FREEMAN, NATHAN**, dec'd, pvt. for 84 months service, 640 acres, Oct. 21, 1783 delivered to his heir **DANIEL FREEMAN**.

*MARS ID #12.14.2.443, File #443, William Heighlet, Assignee of **NATHAN FREEMAN**, 640 acres land on South side Cumberland River.

#8 **FREEMAN, SAMUEL**, pvt. for {84} months of service, 640 acres, March 4, 1800 drawn by Lewis Green-Samuel Freeman By resolution of Assembly dated December 10, 1799.

*MARS ID #12.14.18.1341, FILE #1451 GRANT #3363. Issued to **SAMUEL FREEMAN** on Nov. 14, 1800. Microfilm Reel S.108.387. Location: #301-305, Warrant #8 issued to Samuel Freeman a soldier in the Continental Line, by resolve of the General Assembly dated Dec. 20, 1799. Entry #8 was issued for 640 acres of land on the barren fork of Drakes Creek in Mero District,

#1254 **RICHARD FREEMAN,** pvt., dec'd--The heirs of were entitled to 640 acres of bounty land due to his service of 84 months. The Warrant issued Oct. 20, 1784 and was delivered to Cap. Bush.

*MARS ID #12.14.19.91--FILE #92, WARRANT #1254, Issued to **RICHARD FREEMAN.** Microfilm Reel S.108.388, Location: 189-193. Warrant originally issued to heirs of Richard Freeman for his service as a private in the Continental Line. Frederick Hargett, Assignee of Richard Freeman, 640 acres land on North side of Cumberland River in Tennessee County, TN.

#2847 **WILLIAM FREEMAN,** The heirs of were entitled to 640 acres of bounty land due to his service of 84 months. Warrant was issued Sept. 30, 1785 and was delivered to Capt. McNeese.

*MARS ID #12.14.2.2190--FILE #2195, WARRANT #2847, Issued to **WILLIAM FREEMAN.** Microfilm Reel S.108.360, Location: 151-155. Military Warrant #2847, originally issued to heirs of William Freeman for his service as a private in the Continental Line. John Donelson, Assignee of heirs of William Freeman for 640 acres of land on a small fork west side of Big Harpeth River in Davidson County, TN.

No#- *MARS ID #12.14.2.964--FILE #966, GRANT #983, Issued to **JOHN FREEMAN.** Microfilm Reel S.108.354, Location: 936-937. John Donelson, Assignee of John Freeman, 640 acres land on both sides of Big Harpeth River in Davidson County, TN.

TREASURERS AND COMPTROLLERS RECORDS, MILITARY PAPERS, VOLUMES 40-66 ARE AVAILABLE ON MICROFILM ONLY.

The information below is from the following Microfilm Reels: S.115.45, S.115.46, S.115.47 & S.115.48. There is one exception! The Receipt Book which is indexed as being on microfilm is found only in the original volume at Search Room Desk.

REVOLUTIONARY ARMY ACCOUNT BOOKS: K, W.1, W.2, 1-6, 19, VOLUME 28

BOOK K

Pg. 104 **COMPTROLLERS OFFICE KINGSTON:** *THE STATE OF NC TO GREEN HILL TREASURER OF HALIFAX DISTICT AMT. BROUGHT FORWORD*

678 **WILLIAM FREEMAN** claim SPECIE 0.16.0

DECEMBER 1790 TO A WARRANT ON THE TREASURERS OF NEW BERN DISTRICT

To distress on **JESSE FREEMAN** Currency 100.0.0

BOOK OF SETTLEMENTS FOR MILITARY SERVICE, NO. 28
ABSTRACT OF THE ARMY ACCOUNTS OF THE NORTH CAROLINA LINE SETTLED BY THE COMMISSIONERS AT HALIFAX FROM THE 1ST SEPTEMBER 1784 TO THE 1ST FEBY 1785 AT WARRENTON IN THE YEAR 1786, DESIGNATING BY WHOSE THE CLAIMS WERE RECEIPTED FOR RESPECTIVELY.

COLUMN HEADINGS: #, Name & Rank, Amount, By Whom Received, Remarks

Note at bottom of page above: "blank left in the receipt column opposite the name denotes that it was delivered by himself."

Pg. 37 #754	**NATHAN FREEMAN**	162.11.2	Robt Fenner	No remarks
#868	**RICHARD FREEMAN**	104.5.4	F. Harget	" "
Pg. 39 #2477	**SAMUEL FREEMAN**	155.4.6	T. Dixon	" "

TREASURER, STATE REVOLUTIONARY ARMY ACCOUNTS 1776-1792, BOOKS D, E-G

BOOK D, PG. 285 *THE MILITIA OF NORTH CAROLINA TO THE STATE OF NORTH CAROLINA SUNDRIES DELIVERED BY GEN'S THOMAS POLK COMMISS'R OF PURCHASES, VIZ*

COMPTROLLERS OFFICE KINGSTON, CURRENCY, SPECIE
57--137 lb flour del'd **CAP'T FREEMAN** 36/   0.0.0 2.9.3

4076 lb flour issued in rations as per Acc't Marks S 0.0.0.
73.7.4

6184 1/2 lbs beef issued in ditto as ditto 44/? 0.0.0 136.1.1

3956 gills equal to 123 5/8 gallons of spirits issued in ditto as ditto 0.0.0 61.16.3

BOOKS E-G, NO. 30 BOOK OF SETTLEMENTS

Pg. 25 The US of A in Acc' Current with the State of NC
7 To Cash **HOWELL FREEMAN**   Do   774.

Pg. 47 *THE UNITED STATES OF AMERICA IN ACCO'T WITH THE STATE OF NORTH CAROLINA THE EXPEDITION TO MOORES CREEK UNDER COLONEL CASWELL*

Pg. 60 Bundle No. 3
#50   **SAMUEL FREEMAN**   18.0.0 Specie

BOOKS 1-6 (Vol. 50) PUBLIC ACCOUNTS

Pg. 387 *COL. RICHARD CASWELL FOR THE SERVICES OF THE NEW BERN BATTALION OF MINUTE MEN AS PER AN EXPEDITION TO MOORS CREEK, WILMINGTON, ETC. AGAINST THE INSURGENTS.*

Pg. 397 **REUBEN FREEMAN**--one of 37 men for 36 days each @ 22 3/4, 22 Mar. 1776, Col. Richard Caswell

REVOLUTIONARY ARMY ACCOUNTS RECEIPT BOOK, TREASURERS & COMPTROLLERS MILITARY PAPERS, 54

Receipt Book commencing September 1st 1784--This is indexed as being on microfilm, but cannot be found there. Information is from the original--ask at Search Room Desk.

Pg. 87 #679   **NATHAN FREEMAN** amount 161.11.2, cash 40.12.9, certificate #1007-121.18.5, Re'c 10 March 1785 one hundred and twenty two pounds 12/2 cash and certificates. Receipts Robert Fannor

Pg. 100 #792   **RICHARD FREEMAN** amount 104.5.4, cash 26.1.4, certificate #416-78.42. Rec'd Halifax 24 January 1784 of Montfort & McCulloch for nine accounts (includes Richard Freeman)

Pg. 207 #1087   **SAMUEL FREEMAN** amount 155.4.6, due bills 38.16.1, certificate 116.8.5, Rec'd Warren 5 May 1786 of Macon McCulloch and Montfort for 21 accounts (includes Samuel Freeman)

Pg. 240 No#-   **NATHANIEL FREEMAN**   amount 40.12.9--no other information

Pg. 104 NO 19 (VOL. 51) SETTLEMENT OF ARMY ACCOUNTS
     HOWELL FREEMAN To what time paid by State-January 82, amt. paid by State 63.67/p?

Pg. 106 **NATHAN FREEMAN** To what time paid by State-January 82, amt. paid by State 400.35/?

RICHARD FREEMAN To what time paid by State-January 82, amt. paid 260.60

Pg. 110 **SAMUEL FREEMAN**, Walkers Company, 29 Mar. 77 3 yrs?, amt. paid 388.57

TREASURER, STATE.   REVOLUTIONARY ARMY ACCOUNTS 1776-1792 BOOKS A, B, C

ACCOUNTS OF THE UNITED STATES WITH NORTH CAROLINA WAR OF THE REVOLUTION, BOOK A

Pg. 12 *FOR SUNDRIES & CASH PAID THE MILITIA OF NC, VA, & SC AS ALLOWED BY A COMMITTEE OF CLAIMS AT HALIFAX OCTOBER 1779 R23*
#2976 To **WILLIAM FREEMAN** for 2 Fifes furnished p ditto 373.4.0

Pg. 68 *THE UNITED STATES OF AMERICA FOR SUNDRIES FURNISHED THE MILITIA OF NORTH CAROLINA VIRGINIA AND SOUTH CAROLINA AS ALLOWED BY ROCHESTER AND RAMSEY AUDITORS AT HARRISBURG IN NOVEMBER 1780 AS PER REPORTS NO 30*

Pg. 69
#1980 To **SAMUEL FREEMAN** for forage & etc per ditto 131 (Column heading looks like No Vo (# of Voucher) 1519.0.0

Pg. 90 *FOR SUNDRIES FURNISHED THE MILITIA OF NC, VA, & SC AS ALLOWED BY DAVID WILSON AUDITOR NOVEMBER 1781 AS PER REPORT NO 31.*

Pg. 91
#2706 To **ALLEN FREEMAN** for corn as per voucher 332 Specie 2.16.0

Pg. 100 *FOR SUNDRIES FURNISHED THE MILITIA OF NC VA & SC AS ALLOWED BY DAVID WILSON AUDITOR AS PER REPORT NO. 34*

Pg. 101
#3053 _To **ALLEN FREEMAN** for corn as per ditto Voucher No 1127 Specie 2.7.0

Pg. 122 *FOR SUNDRIES FURNISHED THE MILITIA OF NC, VA & SC AS ALLOWED BY WILSON AND CATHEY AND HARRIS, AUDITORS SALISBURY DISTRICT IN MAY 1781 AS [ER RE[PRT NO. 32*

#3713 To **GEORGE FREEMAN** for mutton as per ditto Vocher 98 Currency 362.0.0

Pg. 126 *THE UNITED STATES OF AMERICA FOR SUNDRIES FURNISHED THE MILITIA OF NORTH CAROLINA, VIRGINIA AND SOUTH CAROLINA AS ALLOWED BY WILSON CATHEY & HARGIS AUDITORS SALISBURY DISTRICT IN JUNE 1781 AS PER REPORT NO 32*

#3848 To **SAMUEL FREEMAN** for Rye & etc per ditto 253 Specie, 500.0.0 Currency 0.0.0 Specie

Pg. 136 *FOR SUNDRIES FURNISHED THE MILITIA OF NC, VA, & SC AS ALLOWED BY WILSON AND CATHEY AUDITORS, SALISBURY DISTRICT AS PER THEIR REPORT NO. 36*

#4175 To **GEORGE FREEMAN** for Ferriages as per ditto Voucher 3446 Specie .0.0.6

Pg. 190 *THE UNITED STATES OF AMERICA FOR SUNDRIES FURNISHED THE MILITIA OF NORTH CAROLINA VIRGINIA AND SOUTH CAROLINA AS ALLOWED BY BROWN MCKISSICK AND MILLER AUDITORS OF SALISBURY DISTRICT IN NOVEMBER 1781 AS PER REPORT NO 40.*

(Index says **AARON FREEMAN**)
#5886 __ __**ON FREEMAN** for __bus corn per ditto 618 Specie 90.0.0 Currency

Pg. 234 *FOR SUNDRIES FURNISHED THE MILITIA OF NC, VA & SC AS A;;PWED BY THE AUDITORS OF MORGAN DISTRICT AS PER THEIR REPORT NO. 43*

Pg. 235
#7344 To **JAMES FREEMAN** Voucher 4173 Specie 1.4.0 (no reason given for pay)

Pg. 250 *7880 CAPTAIN HENRY HIGHLAND FOR SERVICES OF HIMSELF AND COMPANY AS PER PAY ROLL FOR SUNDRIES FURNISHED THE MILITIA AS ALLOWED BY BRUCE AND BRAGGE AUDITORS OF THE UPPER BROAD OF SALISBURY DISTRICT AS PER REPORT NO. 45*

Pg. 251
#7923 To **WILLIAM FREEMAN** Voucher 61 Specie 6.12.0

ACCOUNTS OF THE UNITED STATES WITH NORTH CAROLINA WAR OF THE REVOLUTION, BOOK B

Pg. 88 *THE UNITED STATES OF AMERICA TO THE STATE OF NORTH CAROLINA FOR SUNDRIES ALLOWED BY A COMMITTEE OF CLAIMS AS PER REPORT DATED NOVEMBER 1777*

#273 To **SAMUEL FREEMAN** for waggon hire & etc 18.0.0

Pg. 121 *COMPTROLLERS OFFICE, KINSTON. THE USA TO THE STATE OF NC FOR SUNDRIED ALLOWED BY A COMMITTEE OR CLAIMS AS PER REPORT DATED JANUARY 1779*

#161 To **WILLIAM FREEMAN** for Acting as Adjutant Currency 15.15.0

Pg. 163 *SAME HEADING AS PG. 121 EXCEPT DATE IS OCTOBER 1779*

#373 To **WILLIAM FREEMAN** for two fifes Currency 4.0.0

Pg. 266 *THE UNITED STATES OF AMERICA TO THE STATE OF NORTH CAROLINA FOR SUNDRIES ALLOWED BY THE STATE BOARD OF AUDITORS FOR CLAIMS EXHIBITED AS PER REPORT DATED NOVEMBER 1780.*

#125 To **SAMUEL FREEMAN** for forage & etc 1519.0.0

ACCOUNTS OF THE UNITED STATES WITH NORTH CAROLINA WAR OF THE REVOLUTION, BOOK C

Pg. 4 *THE UNITED STATES OF AMERICA FOR SUNDRIES FURNISHED AND CASH PAID THE MILITIA OF NORTH CAROLINA VIRGINIA AND SOUTH CAROLINA AS ALLOWED BY THE AUDITORS OF EDENTON DISTRICT MARCH 1781 AS PER REPORT MARKED A NO 63*

There are no headings for the following:

#92 To **JOSHUA FREEMAN** for sundries 975.0.0

#102 To **JOHN FREEMAN** for a gun 240.0.0

#104 To **MOSES FREEMAN** for an ax 24.0.0

Pg. 5 #125 To **WILLIAM FREEMAN** for a horse 1,800.0.0

Pg. 6 *FOR SUNDRIES FURNISHED AND CASH PAID THE MILITIA OF NC, VA & SC AS ALLOWED BY THE AUDITORS OF EDENTON DISTRICT IN MARCH 1781 AS PER REPORT MARKED AS NO. 53*

Pg. 7 #196 To **JOHN FREEMAN** for a pair of wheels 196 (Voucher?) 291.0.0

Pg. 18 *[SAME HEADING AS PG 6 EXCEPT DATED OCTOBER 1781 AND REPORT NO. 65]*

#579 To **JOHN FREEMAN** for horse hire Voucher 911 SPECIE 11.10.0

Pg. 19 #611 To **JOHN FREEMAN** for a horse Voucher 1063 SPECIE 16.0.0

#631 To **MOSES FREEMAN** for a gun Voucher 1087 Specie 3.0.0

Pg. 26 *[SAME HEADING AS PG. 6 EXCEPT DATE IS MARCH 1783 AND REPORT NO. 69]*

Pg. 27 #850 To **DEMSEY FREEMAN** for a gun Voucher 2504 SPECIE 2.0.0

#851 To **WILLIAM FREEMAN** for ditto Voucher 2505 SPECIE 2.5.8

#872 To **JOHN FREEMAN JUN'R** for gun Voucher 2551 SPECIE 0.6.8

Pg. 29 #946 To **JAMES FREEMAN** for Sundries Voucher 2801 SPECIE 2.0.0

Pg. 22 *THE UNITED STATES OF AMERICA FOR SUNDRIES FURNISHED AND CASH PAID THE MILITIA OF NORTH CAROLINA VIRGINIA AND SOUTH CAROLINA AS ALLOWED BY THE AUDITORS OF EDENTON DISTRICT IN MARCH 1783 AS PER REPORT NO 69*

#693 To **KING FREEMAN** for sundries 1881 (NoVos) 4.6.11 Specie

Pg. 32 *FOR SUNDRIES FURNISHED AND CASH PAID THE MILITIA OF NC, VA AND SC AS ALLOWED BY THE AUDITORS OF EDENTON DIST. IN APRIL 1784 AS PER REPORT NO. 70*

#1022 To **SOLOMON FREEMAN** for cloathing Voucher 3363 SPECIE 0.18.0

Pg. 40 *[SAME HEADING AS PG. 32 EXCEPT DATED APRIL 1781]*

#1241 To **SOLOMON FREEMAN** Voucher 3868 SPECIE 2.13.8

Pg. 86 *FOR SUNDRIES FURNISHED AND CASH PAID THE MILITIA OF NC, VA & SC IN JULY 1783 AS ALLOWED BY THE AUDITORS OF HILLSBOROUGH DISTRICT AS PER REPORT 83*

Pg. 87 #2802 To **JOHN FREEMAN** Voucher 1422 SPECIE 2.10.0

Pg. 104 #3443 To **DANIEL FREEMAN** Voucher 3645 SPECIE 2.10.0

Pg. 158 *THE UNITED STATES OF AMERICA FOR SUNDRIES FURNISHED AND CASH PAID THE MILITIA OF NORTH CAROLINA VIRGINIA AND SOUTH CAROLINA AS ALLOWED BY THE AUDITORS OF HILLSBORO DISTRICT THE 11TH MAY 1784 AS PER REPORT NO 85*

#5387 **SAMUEL FREEMAN** 195 (NoVo) Specie 11.0.0

BOOK J (VOL.46)

Pg. 150 *FOR SUNDRIES PURCHASED AND CASH PAID THE MILITIA FOR NORTH CAROLINA VIRGINIA AND SOUTH CAROLINA AS ALLOWED BY THE AUDITORS OF SALISBURY DISTRICT 8TH JANUARY 1787 AS PER REPORT NO 89*

Pg. 151 #5196 To **SAMUEL FREEMAN**   126   9150

BOOK W-2

AMOUNTS OF CERTIFICATES FOR MILITIA PAY FROM THE 16TH JULY 1783 TO THE 19TH MARCH 1784, FOR THE DISTRICT OF WILMINGTON, THO ROUTLEDGE, W. DICKSON, THO SEWELL

Pg. 39 **BEN FREEMAN** 9.0.0 (This is payroll # 2740 Captain Thomas Ard)

214

INDEX

Generation numbers have been used to designate descendants of the principal Freeman Family, except when the individual also has a middle name. Entries pertaining to other Freeman families do not bear this designation.

217

FREEMAN (*continued*)
(Moore) 94, 94n; Druid[5] (Drued)
J.(I.) 101, 102; E. 197; Eaton
148; Edey[4] 56; Edie (Edey) 55,
57n; Edith[3] (ED, Edie, Edey) 23,
24, 26, 54, 55, 56, 57n; Edmund[5]
112; Edward 150, 190; Edward[6]
130; Edward B. 134; Elisabeth
[—?—] 169; Elisabeth (Canady)
134; Elisha 163n; Elisha[4] 50-52,
105, 107, 107n, 108, 108n, 134;
Elisha[5] 108; Elisha W. 134; Eliza[5]
101, 102; Eliza[6] 127; Eliza B. 135;
Eliza N. 185; Elizabeth 1, 108;
Elizabeth[3] 24, 26, 55, 57;
Elizabeth[4] 51, 61, 61n; Elizabeth[5]
71n, 72, 74, 95, 97, 111, 118;
Elizabeth[6] 121; Elizabeth A. 127;
Elizabeth D. (Miller) 127;
Elizabeth [—?—] 25, 44, 45, 47, 50,
50n, 52, 108, 149; Elizabeth
(Alexander) 19, 99; Elizabeth
(Ball) 162, 162n; Elizabeth
(Bridges) 145, 145n, 146, 147, 149;
Elizabeth (Fowler) 176; Elizabeth
(Haggard) 68, 121;Elizabeth
(Harper) 161; Elizabeth
(Haygood) 121; Elizabeth (Isbell)
68;Elizabeth (Martin) Waugh 129;
Elizabeth (Stoe) 68; Emily Ann
150; Family 44, 139, 179; Fanny
(Ball) 161, 162, 162n; Fanny
(Price) 161; Ferribar[5] 109; Foster[5]
98, 101, 102, 133; Frances 6, 166,
180, 181, 183; Frances[5] 119;
Frances[6] "Franky" 121; Frances
(Moore) 174, 177; Francis[5] 105,
106; Francis Asbury 133; Francis
Kirby 163n; Frederick 3n; G.
199; George (Geo.) 148n, 169,
185n, 190, 193, 205, 211; George[4]
63; George[5] 81, 82; George W.
184, 185; Gideon 141-143, 190,
199; Green Hill 163n; H. 196, 197;
H.L. 163n; Hannah 7n, 166;
Hannah[3] 10, 23-25, 54, 55;
Hannah[5] 109; Hannah [—?—] 8, 9,
11, 26, 165; Hannah (Doty) 151;

FREEMAN (*continued*)
Hannah (Hurdle) 80, 126, 127;
Hardy 190, 196; Hardy[5] 72, 73,
111, 113, 122; Harriet T. (Green)
185; Hartwell 193; Hawkins[6] 129;
Henry 146-150, 155-157, 157n, 190,
193, 202, 205; Henry[5] 111, 113;
Henry[6] 129; Hezekaih 204; Hiram
163; Hosea H. 163n; Howard 205;
Howell 148-151, 193, 194, 209;
Irainey (Irena) 174; Isaac 161,
171, 171n, 172, 203, 206; Isaac[5]
108; Isaac[6] 124; Isaac J. 134; Isaac
Pipkin 124; Isham 141-143; J.
196-199; Jackson 163n; Jacob 47n;
Jacob[4] 33-35, 65, 139; Jacob[5] 76,
124; Jacob[6] 74, 122; Jake 176;
James 7n, 100, 150, 160, 161, 190,
201, 202, 211, 213; James[3] 23, 25,
35, 51n, 52, 53, 109, 111, 115, 117,
135; James[4] 38, 47, 48, 70, 78, 79,
80n, 81, 97, 100-102, 105, 125, 126,
133; James[5] 36, 70, 75, 75n, 76,
76n, 95, 101, 102, 105-107, 107n,
109, 116, 118, 124n; James[6] 121,
134; James Trotman 79, 80, 80n,
125, 126, ; Jane 150, 167; Jane
(Patterson) 161; Jane (Wimpie)
176; Jane (Wood) 166; Jannett B.
135; Jarsey[5] 112; Jean [—?—]
Hayes 54, 116; Jemima 142, 143;
Jemimah[5] 116; Jenny 171n; Jeptha
(Jephtha) 174, 176; Jeremiah[5]
71n, 72, 73, 121, 122; Jesse 161,
191, 194, 200, 204, 208; Joel 191;
John 1, 2, 3, 3n, 4, 4n, 5, 5n, 6, 7n,
31, 33n, 45, 51n, 107n, 139, 145,
145n, 146-150, 153, 154, 156, 157,
161, 165-167, 172-175, 177, 179,
181, 184, 191, 196, 202, 203, 207,
212-214; John[1] (Jno) 1, 2, 3, 3n, 4,
5, 7, 7n, 8-11, 13, 14, 22, 26, 28, 31,
36, 39, 41, 43, 49, 52, 54, 55, 57, 59,
60, 62, 65, 68-71, 74, 76-78, 81-83,
87, 88, 90, 93, 95, 98, 100, 102, 105,
107, 109, 110, 115, 117, 121-128,
130, 132-135; John[2] (Jno) 1, 3,
9-11, 13, 15, 22-26, 49, 52, 54, 55,

FREEMAN (continued)
Nicholas 4, 4n, 5; Nicholas[5] 95;
Nicholas[6] 129; Noah[5] 67, 68;
Noley 177, 178; Patience[4] 63, 63n;
Patsey 175; Patsey[5] 113; Patsy
(Caldwell) 161; Patsy (Linn) 173;
Patsy (Wingate) 61; Peggy 142,
143; Penelope[5] 67, 68; Penniah[6]
135; Perthena (Bond) 80; Polley
175; Polly[5] (Polley) 38n, 68, 81, 95,
112; Polly[6] 135; Prisciller[4]
(Preciller, Presciller, Priciller) 34,
35, 69; R. 205; R. A. 94n; Rachel[4]
47, 48, 48n, 97n, 98, 99; Rachel[5]
72, 74, 95, 119, 122; Rachel[6] 127;
Rachel (Hurdle) 80, 126; Rachell
5; Rebecca (Rebeccah) 150, 156,
157, 166, 167; Rebecca[6] 129;
Rebecca (Ellis) 118; Rebecca
(Freeman) 167; Redden 176;
Reddick[5] 118; Reuben (Rhuben,
Rubin) 191, 195, 196, 201, 209;
Reuben[5] 116; Richard 70, 191,
193, 194, 199, 207-210; Richard[3]
17, 18, 18n, 32, 33, 33n, 39, 41, 42,
87, 88, 90; Richard[4] 33n, 34, 36,
70; Richard[5] 43, 67, 68, 81, 89, 90,
94, 121; Richard[6] 121, 124; Robert
4-6, 148, 150, 151, 165-167,
181-185; Robert[5] 101, 102; Robert
A. 94n; Robert King 133; Rody
(Garmon) 142; Ruth 42, 171n;
Ruth A. (Son) 113; Ruth [—?—]
42, 90, 154; Ruth (Hunter) 18; S.
199; Sally 156, 157, 175; Sally[5]
(Salley) 76, 82; Sally[6] (Saley) 74,
130; Sally G. 185; Sally (Green)
184; Sally (Mosely) 95, 128, 129;
Samuel (Sam'l) 43, 43n, 45, 47n,
165, 167, 191, 195, 198, 201, 204-
206, 208-212, 214; Samuel[3] (Saml)
17-19, 19n, 27-29, 33n, 35, 39, 40,
43-47, 48n, 60, 60n, 62, 63, 63n,
65n, 67, 75, 93, 93n, 95, 96, 98, 100,
101, 102, 128, 130, 132, 133, 159;
Samuel[4] (Saml) 27, 59, 60, 63, 65n;
Samuel Aaron 130; Sarah 142,
150; Sarah[4] (Sara) 34, 36, 38, 41,

FREEMAN (continued)
41n, 82, 83; Sarah[5] 70, 105-107,
107n, 116; Sarah[6] (Sary) 121, 122;
Sarah Ann 150; Sarah White
(Hearne) 127; Sarah [—?—] 11,
25, 26, 29, 34, 38, 43, 59, 60, 67, 81,
82, 88, 90; Sarah [—?—] Norfleet
121, 122; Sarah [—?—] Rice 78;
Sarah [—?—] White 5; Sarah
[—?—] Winborne Rascoe 25, 51,
51n, 111; Sarah (Bailey) 102;
Sarah (Getun) 184n; Sarah
(Gordon) Norfleet 38, 71, 71n,
72-74, 74n; Sarah (Hunter) 43, 88;
Sarah (Low) Wingate 11, 26-29;
Sarah (Moore) 74; Sarah (Perry)
Rice 38, 77, 77n, 78, 125; Sarah
(Pipkin) 76, 124; Selah [—?—]
78-80; Senith (Hunter) 73; Seth
163; Solomon 191, 213; Solomon[4]
50, 51, 52n, 53, 105-108, 110, 117;
Susan 163n; Susan G. (Garr) 127;
Susan J. 134; Susanah (Gunston)
167; Susane (Waugh) 130;
Susanna[4] 39; Susannah 142, 143;
Susannah [—?—] 109, 134; Sydney[6]
121; Synthia 175; Tabitha 163n;
Tabitha[3] 18n; Tabitha[4] 34, 35, 69;
Tabitha [—?—] 18, 31-34, 37, 37n,
39, 41; Tabitha (Hoter, Hoyter)
31n, 33n; Tabitha (Wilson) 6, 65n,
179-183; Telitha [—?—] 150;
Tempa (Tempe) [—?—] 163, 163n;
Temperance[4] 108n; Temperance[5]
96, 97, 130, 131; Tempy[4] 150;
Theresa T. (Tartt) 185; Thomas
160, 161, 162n, 163, 163n, 191, 201,
202; Thomas[2] 3, 9, 11, 13, 14, 23,
26-29, 41, 59, 60, 60n, 62; Thomas[3]
(Thos) 17, 17n, 18, 18n, 26-29, 32,
33, 39-41, 41n, 42, 59-61, 139, 160;
Thomas[4] 28, 40, 41, 60, 61;
Thomas[5] 78-80, 126, 127; Thomas
Paul 127; Timothy[5] 78, 78n, 80;
Tyre[5] 67, 68; Urley (Uxley) 177,
178; Virginia (Franklin) 129;
West(ly) M. 129; Westly 178;
Wilie 149; Will 193, 198, 203;

FREEMAN (*continued*)
William (W'm, Wm) 2, 3, 6, 6n, 37, 65n, 141, 142, 145-150, 163, 163n, 172, 179-183, 185, 185n, 191, 195,199, 200, 205, 207, 210-213; William[2] (W[m], Will[m]) 1, 3, 7n, 9, 9n, 10, 11, 13, 14, 14n, 15, 17, 17n, 18, 19, 19n, 22, 26, 28, 31, 31n, 32, 32n, 36, 39, 41, 43, 44, 59, 65, 68-71, 74, 76-78, 81-83, 87, 88, 90, 93, 95, 98, 100, 102, 121-128, 130, 132, 133; William[3] (Wm) 6, 17, 18, 18n, 32, 33, 36, 37, 37n, 38, 41, 42, 65, 65n, 71, 74, 74n, 76-78, 81-84, 87, 89, 121; William[4] (Wm) 34, 35n, 38, 38n, 47, 53, 54, 61, 61n, 65, 65n, 66, 67, 81, 82, 89, 93, 117, 121; William[5] 67, 75, 75n, 76n, 78-80, 80n, 81, 82, 105, 117, 124n, 125, 125n, 126; William D. 184, 185; William H. 127; William S. 121; Zilpah[4] 34, 35, 68
FROHOCK
John 171
FURR
Paul 141

GABON
John 5
GALLAHER
Callie 96n; George 133; Lucinda (King) 133; Mary "Polly" (King) 133; Sarah Jane 95n, 96n; William 133
GARMON
Mr. 143; Patricia 31n; Rody 142; Susannah (Freeman) 142, 143
GARR
Susan G. 127
GARRETT (Garret)
Bersheba (Perry) 85; Bethia [—?—] 14; Everard 34; Everet 65; John 35n, 66, 93; Thomas (Thos) 14, 33, 34, 41, 79;
GEORGE
Josiah Leith 133; Minerva E. (King) 133

GEORGIA 121, 174, 175
Baldwin Co. 101; Butts Co. 127; Cabiness-Burner Cemetery (Monroe Co.) 127; Cherokee Co. 176; Franklin Co. 68, 121; Freeman's District (Wilkes Co.) 127; Griffin (Pike Co.) 98, 102, 133; Griffin (Spalding Co.) 98, 102, 133; Habersham Co. 176; Harris Co. 102; Indian Springs 127; Jones Co. 127; Monroe Co. 80, 127; Oglethorpe Co. 68, 101, 121, 133; Pikes Co. 98; Randolph Co. 131, 132; Stewart Co. 131; Wilkes Co. 127
GETUN
Capt. 184n; Sarah 184n
GILES
Henry 171
GOODWIN
John 23; Mary [—?—] 23; Mr. 49
GORDON
John (Jn°) 49, 74n; Mary [—?—] 74n; Sarah 38, 71, 71n, 72-74, 74n
GORMON
Nancy (Horne) 104
GRAHAM
John 21
GRANT
"Polly"[6] 131, 131n; Ann (Diskin) 130; Elizabeth Caroline 131; Elizabeth Lefevre 132; Jacob[6] 132; James 130; James Freeman 97, 131n, 132; Joshua D. 131; Lucinda Ann 131, 131n; Matilda Dandridge 132; Nancy A. (Foree) 131; Reuben 96, 97, 108, 108n, 130, 131; Temperance (Freeman) 96, 97, 130, 131
GRAY
John 179; William 49
GREEN (Greene)
Capt. 184; Frederick 67; Harriet T. 185; Lewis 206; Sally 184
GREEN & MACON 193
GRESHAM
Edna J. 125

GRIFFIN
Hardy 65
GUNSTON
Susanah 167

HACKNEY
Jennings 156, 157; Massee
(Massey) (Freeman) 156, 157
HAINES (Hains)
Mr. 68; Penelope (Freeman) 67,
68; Sally 100;
HAMILTON
William 153
HARDIN (Harden)
Amanda E. 133; Robert W. 95n,
133; Tennie 48, 96n
HARDY
Humphrey 56; William 53
HARGETT (Harget)
F. 208; Frederick 207
HARMON (Harman)
Elizabeth (Freeman) 1; Robert 1;
Zachariah 202
HARPER
Elizabeth 161
HARRELL
Adam 53; David 180; Mary
"Polly" (Freeman) 75, 75n; Samuel
75, 75n; Thomas 180
HARRIS
Joseph 24; Susana 104
HARRISON
Brittain 150
HART
Col. 117
HARTLY
Mary 7, 7n
HARTSFIELD
Jacob 148
HARVEY
Albert 127; Eliza (Freeman) 127
HAWKINS
Nancy 47, 93, 94, 94n
HAYES (Haise)
Ann (Hayes) 83; Elizabeth 116;
Elizabeth[5] 83; Hardy 38, 82, 83;
Jean [—?—] 54, 116; Joshua[5] 83;

HAYES (continued)
Judah[5] 83; Penelope[5] 83; Sally[5]
83; Sarah (Freeman) 38, 82, 83;
Susannah[5] 83; Tempy[5] 83
HAYGOOD (Haggard)
Elizabeth 68, 121; Nancy (Hix)
121; Samuel 121
HAYWOOD
John 198
HEARNE
Sarah White 127
HEIGHLET
William 206
HENDERSON
[—?—] (Freeman) 177; Hannah
(Freeman) 109; Mr. 177; William
109
HEWETT (Huett) (Huitt)
Nancy 47, 47n
HICKS
Patrick 24, 49
HIGGS
Judah (Hayes) 83; Reuben 83
HIGHLAND
Henry 211
HILL
Green 198, 205, 207; Henry 33;
John 20; Thomas 101
HINCH
"Polly" (Grant) 131, 131n; M. H.
131, 131n
HINES
Chistopher 117
HINTON
[—?—] (Freeman) 39, 83;
Christian 36, 70; Elizabeth[5] 69; J.
199; Jacob 40, 191; John[5] 69;
Jonas 70; Kedar 70; Mary 41,
126; Mr. 39, 70, 83; Noah 181;
Preciller (Presciller, Presciller)
(Freeman) 34, 35, 69; Reuben 39;
Reuben[5] 83; Sally[5] 69; Sarah
(Freeman) 83; William 35;
William[5] 69
HIX
Nancy 121
HOBGOOD
Thos. 23; Wm 59

OLIVER
Andrew 55, 117
ORMOND
Wy: 154
OSBORNE
A.L. 172
OUTLAW
Ann (Rice) 68; Christian 18, 37,
38; Edward 22, 57, 71; Family 37;
George 37, 88, 89; Jacob 108;
James 69, 74, 122; James[5] 68, 69;
James[6] 122; John 71; Josiah 72;
Lewis 35, 68, 191; Lewis[6] 123;
Rachel (Freeman) 72, 74, 122;
Ralph 57, 71; Selah 90; Thomas
72; William 71; William[6] 123;
Zilpah (Freeman) 34, 35, 68

PAINTER
Frances (Freeman) 119; Jacob
119
PARKER
Jacob 109; Sarah 85; Thomas
(Tho.) 50, 53, 198
PATTERSON
Jane 161
PENNSYLVANIA
Chester Co. 165, 166
PERKINS
William 14, 22, 26
PERRY
Amellicent(Amelicent,Amellisent,
Amillicent) (Freeman) 39, 74n, 83,
84, 85. See also Melicant
(Freeman); Amellisant[5]
(Amillicent, Amillisant) 84, 85,
128. See also Mellisant[5];
Bersheba[5] 85; Celia[5] 85;
Christian[5] 85; Freeman[5] 85;
Frusanna[5] "Furzy" 85; James[5] 85;
John 77, 77n; John[5] 85; Josiah 39,
74n, 84; Josiah[5] 85; Mary[5] 85;
Melicant (Melicent, Mellicent)
(Freeman) 72, 74, 74n, 84, 127,
128; Millisant[5] 128; Mr. 74, 74n,
84; Nancy[5] 85; Penelope[5] 85, 127,
128; Salley[5] 85; Sarah 38, 77, 77n,

PERRY (continued)
78, 125; Sarah [—?—] 77, 77n;
Sarah (Parker) 85; William[5] 84,
85
PHELPS
David 42
PILKINGTON
James 154
PIPKIN
Mary 76, 124; Sarah 76, 124
POLK
Capt. 135; Charles 141, 142;
Deborah 142; John 141; Margaret
"Peggy" ; 142; Thomas 141, 208
POWELL
Charles 89; John 27
POWERS
Sampson (Samson) 22, 23
POYTHRESS
Peter 146
PRENCE
Mary 3; Mercy 1, 3, 3n; Patience
(Brewster) 1; Thomas 1, 3
PRICE
Fanny 161
PRYOR
Elizabeth (Badgett) Don Carlos
104; William 104
PUGH
Thomas 180
PULLEN
Mary 63
PUSHING
Jeremiah 32

QUAKER MEETING 4
Cane Creek 165-167; Lick Creek
166

RADFORD
John 19
RAINER
John 71
RASCOE
James 25, 51; Sarah [—?—]
Winborne 25, 51, 51n, 111

231

RAWLS
Richard 81
RAYNER
Celia (Perry) 85; Miles 85;
Richard 105
REAVES
Rebeccah (Freeman) 150; Wm
150
REDDICK
Daniel 81
REED
John 40; Will 171
REES
Mary Jane (Freeman) 163n;
William 163n
REEVES
Elizabeth (Early) 98-100, 100n;
Micajah 100; Wm 150
RENT ROLLS 8
REVOLUTIONARY WAR
Army Accounts (Edenton District)
75; Blutcher's North Carolina Co.
177; Boundary House, Battle of
166; Bounty Land Warrant 165;
Camden, Battle of 117; Cross
Creek Campaign 100; Eutaw,
Battle of 177; Ferguson's Defeat
(Battle) 46; Friday's Fort, Battle
of 135; Guilford, Battle of 117;
King's Mtn, Battle of 46; Lindley's
Mill, Battle of 177; Militia 77;
Orangeburgh Courthouse, Battle
of 135; Pay Voucher 77, 78;
Shubric's Plantation, Battle of
135; Voucher 66, 89, 105;
Williamburg, Battle of 166;
Yorktown, Surrender of 177
REYNOLDS
Rich. 7; William 201
RHODES (Rhoades, Roads)
Henry 17, 17n, 44; Thomas 55
RICE
Ann 68; James 77, 77n, 78; John
68, 78; Mary 77n; Sarah 77n;
Sarah [—?—] 78; Sarah (Perry)
38, 77, 78, 125; William (Willm) 38,
77, 77n, 78

RICHARDS
Dilley (Freeman) 148; John 44;
John R. 148; Mary (Freeman)
148; William 148
RIGGLESWORTH
Jane (Yates) 7n
RIGGS
Harriette 189
RIGHTON
Willm 72
RILEY
Elizabeth Lefevre 132
ROBERTS
Joshua 163n; Lydia (Freeman)
163n
ROBERTSON
Capt. 150
ROBINS
John 33; Mr. 33
ROCHESTER & RAMSEY 210
RODGERSON
Margrett 18
ROLES
Biddy (Freeman) 150; James 150;
Livea 150; Mary Ann 150; Robert
150; W.H. 150; William 150
ROTHERY
Henry 6, 185
ROUNTREE
Charles 38, 38n, 71; Christian 90;
Christian[5] 42, 91; Jethro 44; John
78-80, 80n, 125, 125n; Leah[5]
"Leach" 91; Levina[5] 91; Mary
(Freeman) 43, 90; Mary
(Trotman) 80, 125, 125n, 126;
Miles 125n; Miss 38, 73; Peniah[5]
91; Precilla[5] 91; Rachel[5] 91; Selah
(Outlaw) 90; Seth[5] 90; Thomas
(Thos) 33, 43, 44, 90
ROUTLEDGE
Tho. 214
RUDKINS
Henry 19
RUSSELL
John 153
RUTHERFORD
Col. 101

SPRAGUE
  Betsey (Baker) 125
SPRING
  Elizabeth 8; Moses 8; Robert 5n, 8
SPRUEL
  Mr. 39; Susanna (Freeman) 39
STALLINGS
  John 77
STEPHENS
  Mr. 85; Salley (Perry) 85
STEPHENSON
  Delilah (Freeman) 112; Jemimah (Freeman) 116; Mathew 112; Mr. 116
STEPTOE
  William 42
STEWERT
  Delilah 142
STOE
  Abraham 47n; Elizabeth 68
SUMNER
  James 49
SUTTON
  Sally (Freeman) Wood 76; Thomas 76

TAGGART (Tagert)
  J. 135; Joseph 116,
TAKER
  E. 198
TALLEY
  Thomas 154
TARTT
  Theresa T. 185
TARVER
  Samuel 44
TATAKER
  Thornton E. 197
TAX LIST
  Bertie Co., NC 105; Gates Co., NC 81; Norfolk Co., VA 61; Rowan Co., NC 45; Surry Co., NC 87
TAYLOR
  Andrew 10, 11; Betsy Ann (Freeman) 134; Capt. 117;

TAYLOR (continued)
  Christian (Hinton) Freeman 70; Elisabeth 156; Elizabeth (Freeman) 61, 61n; Isaac 134; James 61, 61n; Lemuel 37; Mary [—?—] Freeman 153, 154; Nathaniel 37; Robert 70; Samuel 154; Thomas 23
TENNESSEE 94, 107, 130, 157
  Big Harpeth River 207; Blount Co. 48, 101-104, 131; Concord (Knox Co.) 95n; Cumberland River, North Side 207; Davidson Co. 207; Dickson Co. 151; Drakes Creek (Metro Dist.) 206; Hawkins Co. 133; Humphrey Co. 151; Knox Co. 48, 97, 97n, 102-104, 131-133; Knoxville (Knox Co.) 96, 132; Lincoln Co. 94, 94n; Little River 97, 101; Maryville-Knoxville Pike Bridge 97; Monroe Co. 131, 132; Robertson Co. 157, 157n; Rockville (Monroe Co.) 131; Selian, South Fork of 206; Stock Creek 97; Sumner Co. 207; Tennessee Co. 206, 207; Wilson Co. 150
THOMAS
  Ann 43n
THOMPSON
  Betsy 102; Nancy W. 113
TIMBERLAKE
  Mr. 150; Tempy (Freeman) 150
TIPTON
  Abraham 97; Reuben 97, 97n
TROTMAN
  George[5] 38, 38n; Mary 80, 125, 125n, 126; Mary "Polley" (Freeman) 82; Noah 91; Peniah (Rountree) 91; Polly (Polley) (Freeman) 38n, 81n; Reddick 78; Thomas 38n, 82, 126
TURNER
  Lazarus 156, 157; Rebecca (Freeman) 156, 157
TUTTE
  Jno 7; Mr. 7n

234

UNDERWOOD
Miss 94

VALENTINE
Celah 80
VANHOUSER
Valentine 46
VEAL
Capt. 166
VIRGINIA 15, 180, 181
Borough of Norfolk 6, 179, 180;
Browne's Bay (Norfolk Co.) 19;
Brunswick Co. 149; Charles City
Co. 145; Chickahominy 7n; City
of Chesapeake 2; City of South
Norfolk 2; Commissioner (Lower
Norfolk Co.) 19, 20; Coronesus
Swamp (Surry Co.) 146; Elizabeth
City Co. 2, 4n; Elizabeth River
East Branch (Norfolk Co.) 19;
Elizabeth River Parish (Norfolk
Co.) 29, 62; Elizabeth River
Southern Branch (Norfolk Co.) 5;
Elizabeth River Western Branch
(Norfolk Co.) 5, 7, 8; Flatt Swamp
(Surry Co.) 146; Forgissons Run
(Norfolk Co.) 14; General Council
20; Governor 20; High Sheriff
(Lower Norfolk Co.) 19; Lancaster
Co. 21; Lower Norfolk Co. 1-4,
4n, 7, 8, 11, 19, 21; Lower Norfolk
Western Branch 8; Mecklenburg
Co. 141; Nansemond Co. 2, 4n, 7,
9, 10, 21, 81. See also Upper
Norfolk Co.; New Norfolk Co. 2,
4n; Norfolk (Norfolk Co.) 2n, 62,
179-183; Norfolk Co. 2, 3, 4n, 10,
11, 13, 14, 21-23, 26, 36, 37, 39,
65n, 139, 183-185; Northampton
Co. 34, 44; Northern Neck 21;
Nottoway River 145, 146; Parish
of Elizabeth (Norfolk Co.) 23;
Patentee 3; Poplar Neck Run
(Norfolk Co.) 8; Portsmouth 2;
Salem (Roanoke Co.) 132; Sheriff
(Lower Norfolk Co.) 20; Size of

VIRGINIA (continued)
Co. Courts 20; Southwarke Parish
145; Surry Co. 145, 146; Tithable
lists (Norfolk Co.) 28. See also
Tax List; Upper Norfolk Co. 2, 4n,
10. See also Nansemond Co.;
Vestryman Elizabeth River Parish
19; Westmoreland Co. 21; Wythe
Co. 100

WAGSTAFF
Mr. 142; Nancy (Freeman) 142
WAINWRIGHT
John 29
WALKER
Mary Elizabeth 127
WALL
Garrot 155; Hardy 155; Massee
(Massey, Massy) 155-157, 157n
WALLACE
Martha 28
WALLIS
Andrew 14; Children 11;
Elizabeth [—?—] 23; Hannah 10,
11; John (Jno) 4n, 10, 11, 22;
William (Wm) 10, 11, 13, 22, 23
WALTON
Christian (Perry) 85; John 32;
John B. 90; Mary 82; Mr. 85;
Thos 32, 44; Timothy 42, 72, 87
WARD
Deliah (Freeman) 72, 74; James
39n; Mary [—?—] 39n; Mary
(Freeman) 39; Michael 14, 41;
Mr. 39; Philip 39n; Thomas 71
WARRIN
Benjamin 71
WATFORD
Capt. 73
WATSON
Thomas 117
WAUGH
Elizabeth (Martin) 129; James
129; Susane 130
WEATHERFORD
Uriah 141

WEBB
Jas 72
WELLS
Charity 166
WESSON
Jno 59
WEST
Sarah (Smith) 55
WESTON
Malachi 124; Nancy (Freeman)
124
WHEATON
Daniel 166
WHITE
Elizabeth P. 3n; George 24; Luke
109; Robert 202; Samuel 146;
Sarah [—?—] 5; William 5
WHITEHALL
John 8
WHITLEY
Martha (Freeman) 156, 157; Mills
156, 157
WILDER
Edward 5; Joseph 4n; Mr. 5n
WILLIAMS (William)
Col. 101; Fanny 103; Jane 7;
Joseph 66, 100; Lavicy 118;
Martha 176; Mr. 7n
WILLIFORD
Mr. 107; Sarah (Freeman)
105-107, 107n
WILLOUGHTBY
Thomas 9
WILSON (Willson)
David 210; James 51, 106, 179;
Joseph 160; Solomon 6, 179, 180;
Tabitha 6, 65, 179-183
WILSON & CATHEY 193, 205,
211
WILSON & CATHEY & HARRIS
210
WILSON CATHEY & HARGIS
211
WIMPIE
Jane 176
WINBORNE
Henry 25, 51; Sarah [—?—] 25, 51,
51n, 111

WINGATE (Winget, Wingett,
Wingitt)
Edward 26, 28; John 28, 29, 61;
Martha 29; Martha "Patsy" 61,
61n, 62; Samuel 27, 61; Sarah 29;
Sarah (Low) 11, 26-29, 60, 61;
Willis 61n, 63
WISE
Matthew 109; Nancy (Freeman)
109
WOLFF
Betsy 112
WOOD
Celia[6] 123; Christian (Freeman)
75, 123; Cullen 76; Edward 23, 26,
60; Elizabeth[6] 123; Frances [—?—]
166; Freeman[6] 123; James 75, 123;
Jane 166; Jannett B. (Freeman)
135; John 60, 166; John[6] 123; John
Edwards 123; Margett [—?—] 60;
Mary[6] 123; Mary [—?—] 26, 60;
Mr. 135; Sally (Freeman) 76;
Sarah 123; Thomas 60; William
75
WOODEN
Richard 22; Thomas 9
WOODS
Edward 27, 28; John 26-28;
Margett [—?—] 26
WORMARLSDORFF
Ann (Freeman) 112; Daniel 112
WRIGHT
Elizabeth (Cording) 13; John 13,
146; Moses 96
WYNNE
John 36
WYNNS
John 55, 71

YARBROUGH
James 96; William 96
YATES
Family 7n; Jane 7n; John 14;
Mary 14
YOUNG
Charles 173; Elizabeth [—?—] 45;
William 45, 46

CPSIA information can be obtained at www.ICGtesting.com
Printed in the USA
BVOW061806230412

288412BV00006B/12/P